SERVICE SHEETS
A7 and A10
Pre-Unit
1947 to 1962

A Floyd Clymer Publication
Published in 2021 by VelocePress.com

INTRODUCTION

Welcome to the world of digital publishing ~ the book you now hold in your hand was printed using the latest state of the art digital technology. The advent of print-on-demand has forever changed the publishing process, never has information been so accessible and it is our hope that this book serves your informational needs for years to come. If this is your first exposure to digital publishing, we hope that you are pleased with the results. Many more titles of interest to the classic automobile and motorcycle enthusiast, collector and restorer are available via our website at www.VelocePress.com. We hope that you find this title as interesting as we do.

NOTE FROM THE PUBLISHER

The information presented is true and complete to the best of our knowledge. All recommendations are made without any guarantees on the part of the author or the publisher, who also disclaim all liability incurred with the use of this information.

TRADEMARKS

We recognize that some words, model names and designations, for example, mentioned herein are the property of the trademark holder. We use them for identification purposes only. This is not an official publication.

INFORMATION ON THE USE OF THIS PUBLICATION

This manual is an invaluable resource for those interested in performing their own maintenance. However, in today's information age we are constantly subject to changes in common practice, new technology, availability of improved materials and increased awareness of chemical toxicity. As such, it is advised that the user consult with an experienced professional prior to undertaking any procedure described herein. While every care has been taken to ensure correctness of information, it is obviously not possible to guarantee complete freedom from errors or omissions or to accept liability arising from such errors or omissions. Therefore, any individual that uses the information contained within, or elects to perform or participate in do-it-yourself repairs or modifications acknowledges that there is a risk factor involved and that the publisher or its associates cannot be held responsible for personal injury or property damage resulting from the use of the information or the outcome of such procedures.

WARNING!

One final word of advice, this publication is intended to be used as a reference guide, and when in doubt the reader should consult with a qualified technician.

BSA 'SERVICE SHEETS'

UNDERSTANDING AND INTERPRETING THE 1945 AND ONWARDS PUBLICATIONS

In 1945, after the war had ended, BSA resumed production of their civilian line of motorcycles. However, they continued their pre-war practice of publishing repair, overhaul and technical information in the form of individual 'Service Sheets'. It should be noted that BSA never intended that these service sheets would be distributed to the general public, they were 'dealer only' publications and, as such, the print quality was at times somewhat questionable. It was not until the early 1960's that BSA eventually started publishing model specific workshop manuals that were available to the general public. Consequently, these 'Service Sheets' were the only publications available for the maintenance and repair of BSA models that were manufactured through the early 1960's.

At some point in the 1930's, BSA adopted the practice of identifying their various model types by 'groups' and the models manufactured from 1945 through the early 1960's were in Groups A, B, C, D and M. The service sheets that were associated to a particular group were identified numerically and, while there were some exceptions due to overlapping data between models, in general terms the numbers relate to a particular model group. They are as follows: The 200 series of service sheets were applicable to Group A models, the 300 series to Group B, the 400 series to Group C, the 500 series to Group D and the 600 series to Group M. In addition, there were a 700 series applicable to mechanical maintenance and an 800 series for electronic service and wiring diagrams. Both the 700 and 800 series of service sheets contained information that was not model specific but was applicable across multiple model groups. Finally, there were a 900 series for the BSA Dandy and a 1000 series for the BSA Sunbeam and Triumph Tigress scooter.

Unfortunately, as these service sheets were issued individually and at random times, the numbering sequence within any group is not necessarily consecutive and, at times, illogical. Consequently, assembling those individual sheets into a publication that serves as a model specific workshop manual is a somewhat difficult task and owners of BSA motor cycles are subjected to considerable confusion surrounding the appropriate selection from the multitude of reprints that have recently flooded the on-line marketplace. Many of the reprints found on internet websites are from 'bedroom sellers' at enticingly low prices by individuals that really have no idea what they are selling. Many are nothing more than poor quality comb-bound photocopies that are scanned and printed complete with greasy pages and thumbprints and, as such, are deceptively described as 'pre-owned', 'used' or even 'refurbished'! In addition, they are often advertised for the incorrect series and/or model years of motorcycles.

The most complete compilation of the 1945 and onwards service sheets was issued by BSA in the form of a 'dealer only' ring binder that contained all of the individual service sheets totaling to almost 500 pages, it is extremely scarce and difficult to find. It is this ring bound publication that was used to create this 'Service Sheet' manual'.

'A' GROUP SERVICE SHEET MANUAL 1947-1962

This manual is a compilation of the service sheets that were collated and published by BSA in the late 1950's and early 1960's under part numbers 00-4017 (pre-swing arm) and 00-4047 (swing arm), which excluding duplicates, consisted of 44 service sheets in total. However, an additional 15 sheets from the ring bound 'dealer only' publication has been added to produce a single manual containing 59 service sheets (192 pages) that cover the entire range of pre-unit A7 and A10 models from 1947 to 1962. Please note that service sheets in the 300, 700 and 800 series that are included in this publication will also include data that is applicable to 'other' model groups, as that was the original intention. For additional information the reader is directed to **'The Book of the BSA Twins 650cc & 500cc 1948-1962'** (ISBN 9781588500977).

GENERAL INDEX

PAGE	SHEET	SUBJECT
3	201	Engine*
4	201A	Engine
5	201B	Gearbox
6	201C	Engine
7	202	Engine
9	203	Engine
13	204	Engine
17	205	Engine
19	206	Engine
23	207	Crankshaft
25	208	Engine
33	209	Gearbox
35	210	Clutch
37	211	Clutch
39	212	Brakes*
43	212A	Brakes
45	212B	Brakes
47	212C	Brakes
49	212D	Brakes
51	212E	Brakes
56	213	Rear Suspension
58	214	Engine
62	215	Engine
68	216	Technical Data
70	302A	Gearbox
71	302B	Gearbox*
73	308	Clutch
75	310	Primary Transmission
77	311	Gearbox
80	313	Rear Suspension

PAGE	SHEET	SUBJECT
82	612	Brakes*
84	701	Technical Data
86	702	Technical Data*
88	703	Technical Data*
90	704	Technical Data
92	705	General Maintenance*
93	706	Front Forks
97	708	Carburetter
105	708B	Carburetter
106	709	Fault Diagnosis
107	710	Chain
109	710X	Frame*
126	711	Special Tools*
134	711A	Special Tools*
138	711B	Special Tools*
145	712X	Flywheel*
147	713	Steering
148	714	Spokes*
152	801	Magneto
158	804	Regulator
162	804A	Control Box
166	805	Battery
170	806	Lights*
173	807	Horn*
175	808	Wiring Diagrams
177	808A	Wiring Diagrams
179	808F	Wiring Diagrams
181	809	Generator
189	813A	Alternator & Wiring Diagrams

*THESE SERVICE SHEETS ARE NOT INCLUDED IN EITHER OF THE B.S.A. COMPILATION PUBLICATIONS - Part No's 00-4017 or 00-4047

BSA SERVICE SHEET No. 201

Reprinted March, 1960

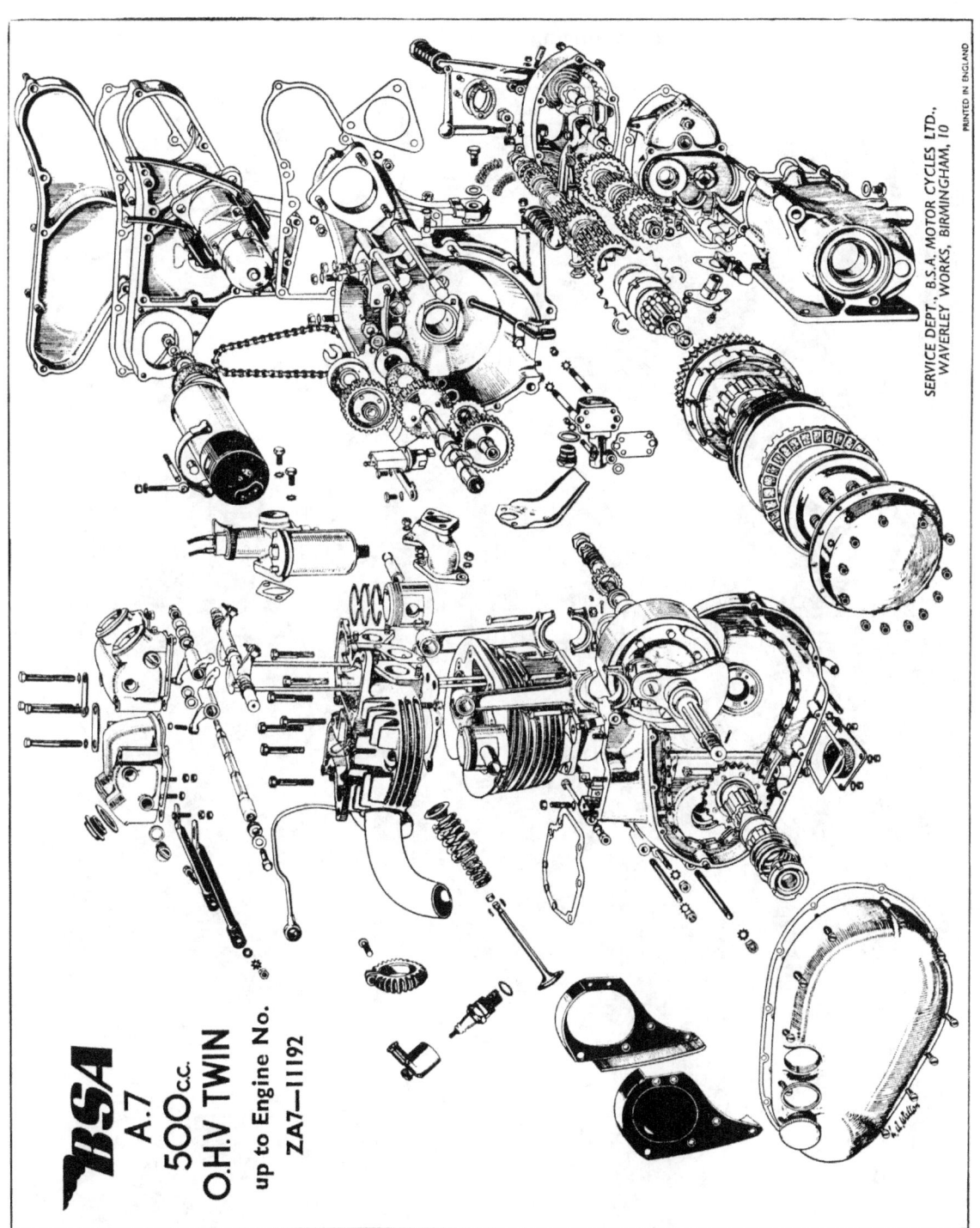

Fig. A1. The A7 Engine and Gearbox (Exploded View)

BSA SERVICE SHEET No. 201A

A GROUP
(Except Swinging Arm Type Frame)

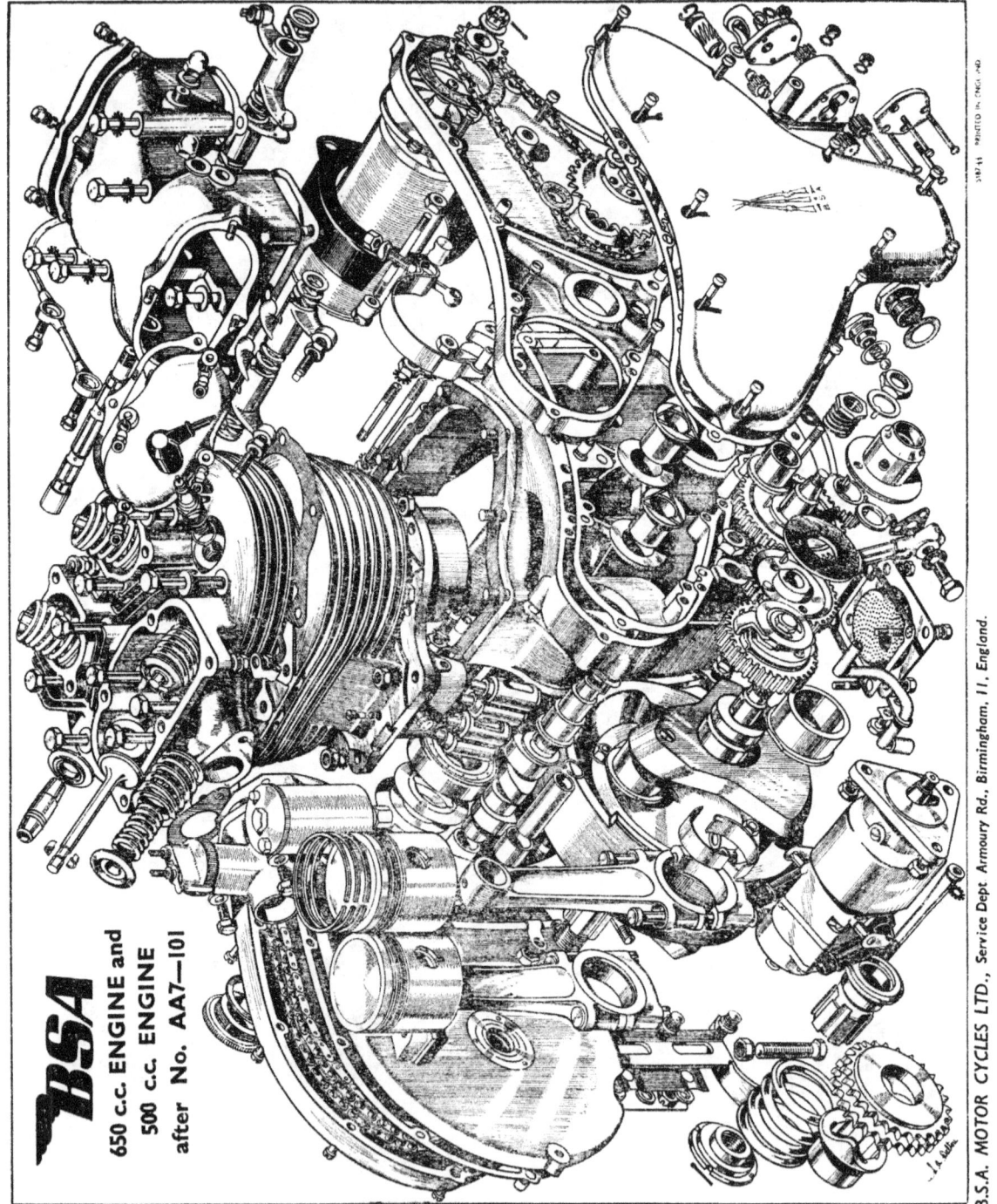

BSA 650 c.c. ENGINE and 500 c.c. ENGINE after No. AA7—101

BSA SERVICE SHEET No. 201B

Reprinted Oct. 1961.

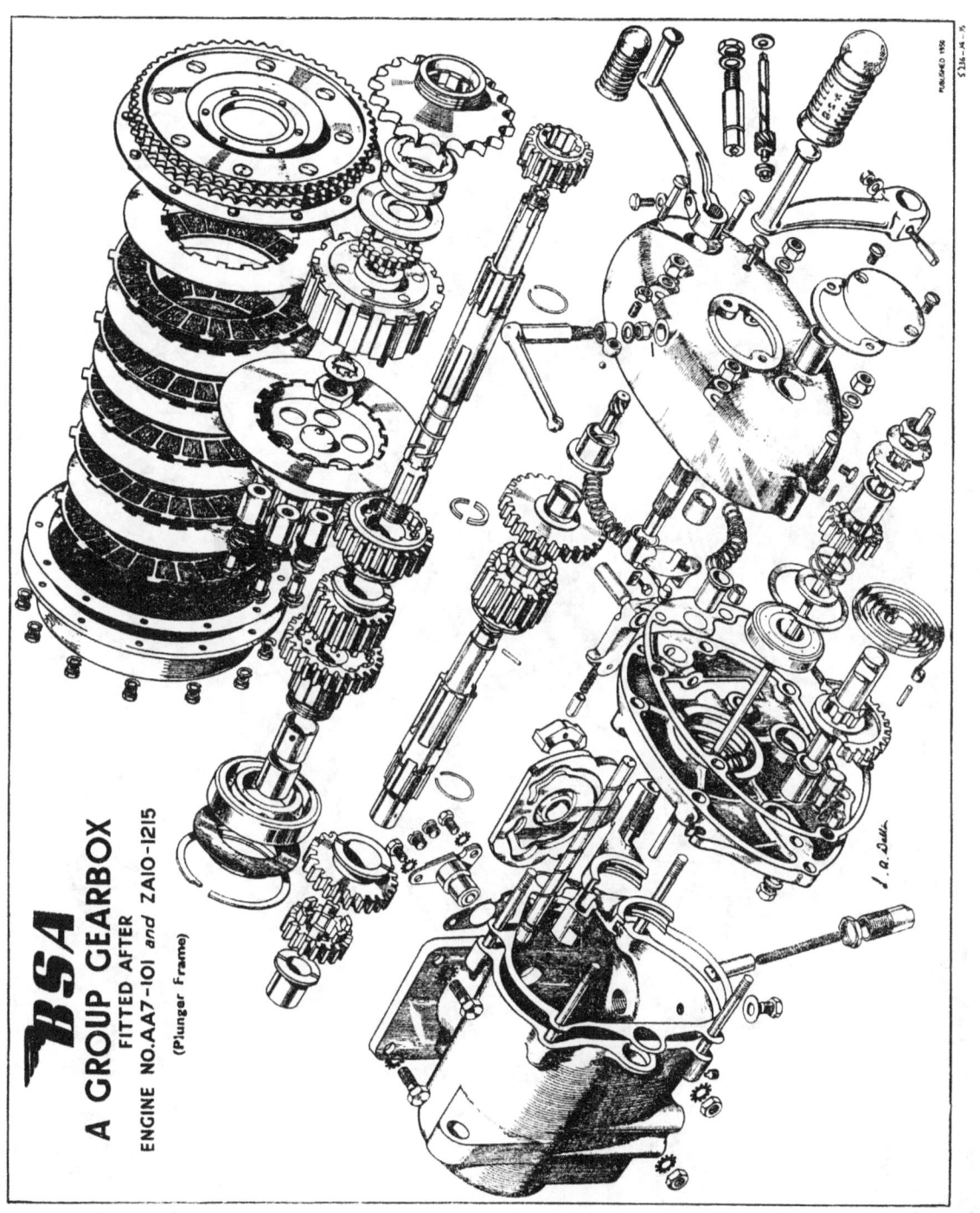

BSA A GROUP GEARBOX
FITTED AFTER
ENGINE NO. AA7-101 and ZA10-1215
(Plunger Frame)

B.S.A. MOTOR CYCLES LIMITED, Service Dept. Waverley Works, Birmingham, 10.

PRINTED IN ENGLAND

BSA SERVICE SHEET No. 201C

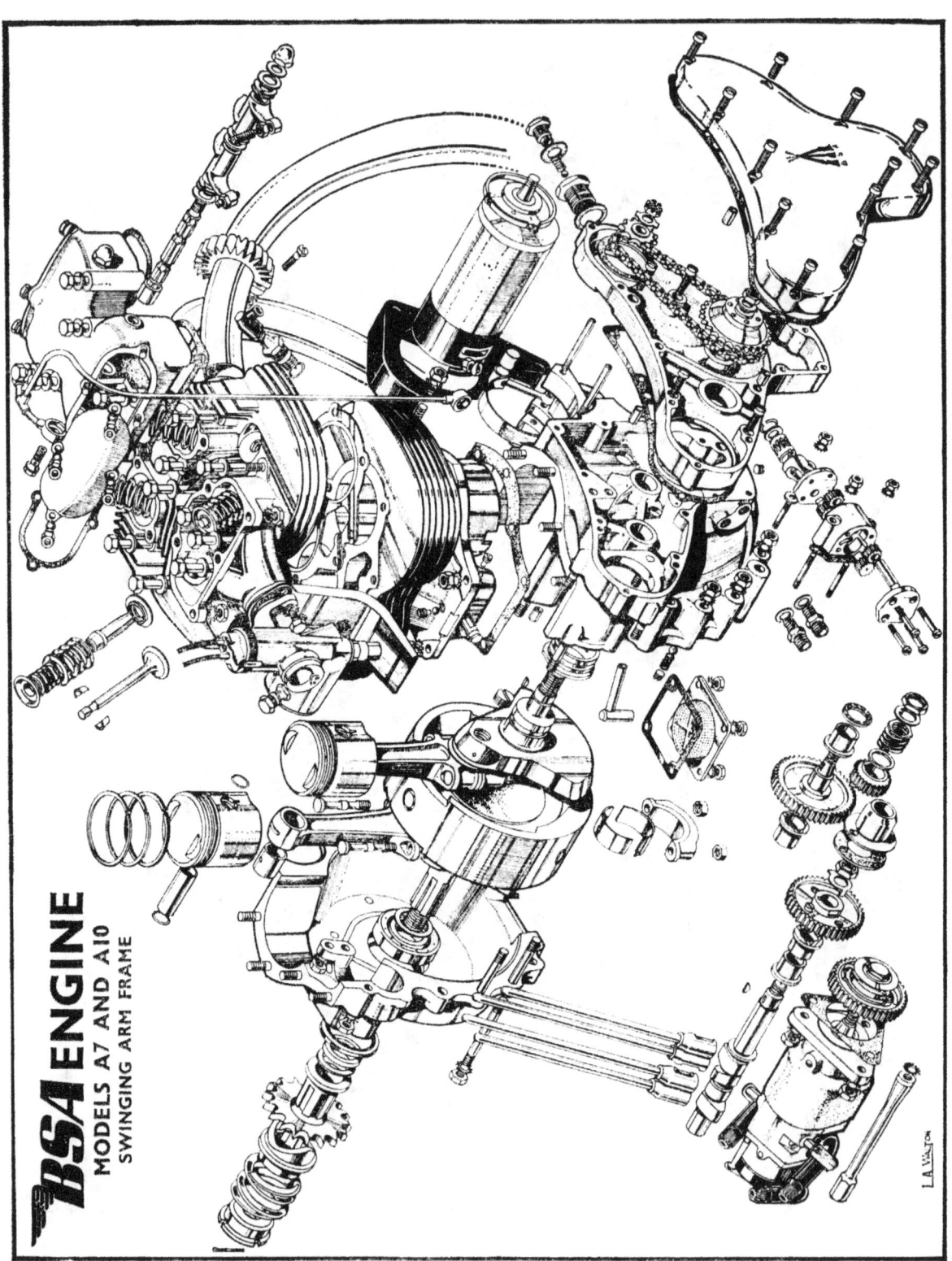

BSA SERVICE SHEET No. 202
"A" Group Models

THE LUBRICATION SYSTEM

The engine lubrication system is of the dry sump type operated by a double gear pump situated in the bottom of the timing case. All oilways are internal except for the supply and return pipes to the tank and the feed to the rocker spindles. The oil flows from the tank — through a filter in the tank — to the supply portion of the pump, which delivers it past an automatic valve to the timing side main bearing, and thence to the hollow crankshaft and the big-end bearings.

Oil pressure is maintained at the big-ends by the pressure release valve (A) Fig. A2. When the pressure in the system exceeds 50/60 lbs. per square inch, this valve opens and allows surplus oil to be passed into the bottom of the timing case.

On A10 machines after engine number ZA10-4712, and A7 machines after engine number AA7-101, the crankcase has been modified to provide an additional oil supply to the cylinders. The oil by-passed by the pressure release valve is now fed through drilled oilways to the camshaft trough, and is then directed on the cylinder walls (Fig. A2a). A small bleed hole also provides additional lubrication to the timing gear.

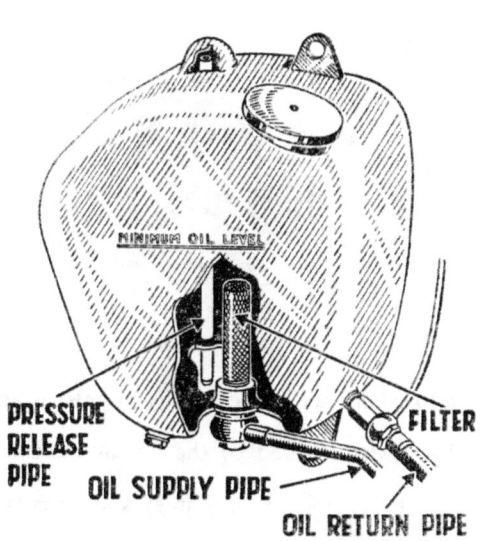

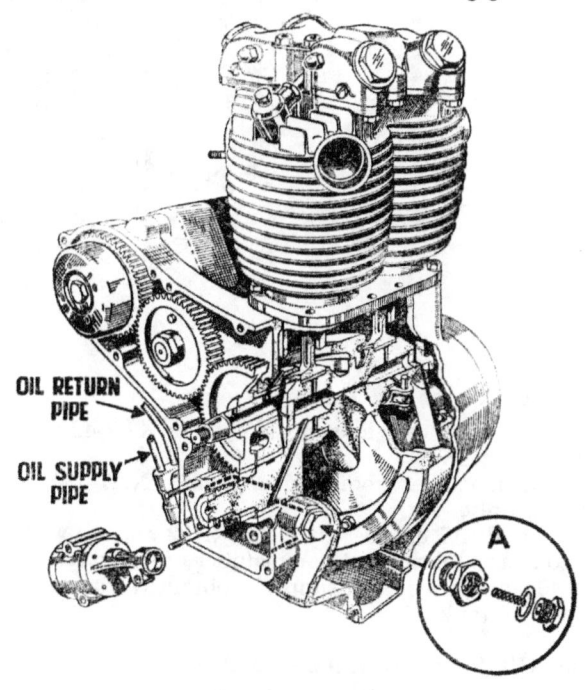

Fig. A2. Diagram showing how oil is circulated from the oil tank, throughout the engine, and returned to the tank.

After lubricating the big-ends and circulating through the engine in the form of mist, the oil drains down through a filter in the bottom of the crankcase.

From there it is drawn through a non-return valve by the return portion of the pump (large gear set) and delivered up the return pipe to the tank.

To check the flow of oil in the lubricating system, remove the tank filler cap while the engine is running. Oil should be seen issuing from the return pipe from the crankcase.

Any restriction in the pressure release pipe in the tank will cause an increase in pressure inside the oil tank, and will result in leakage of oil at the filler cap. This can be remedied by inserting a piece of flexible wire into the outer end of the pipe to clear any obstruction.

B.S.A. SERVICE SHEET No. 202 (contd.)

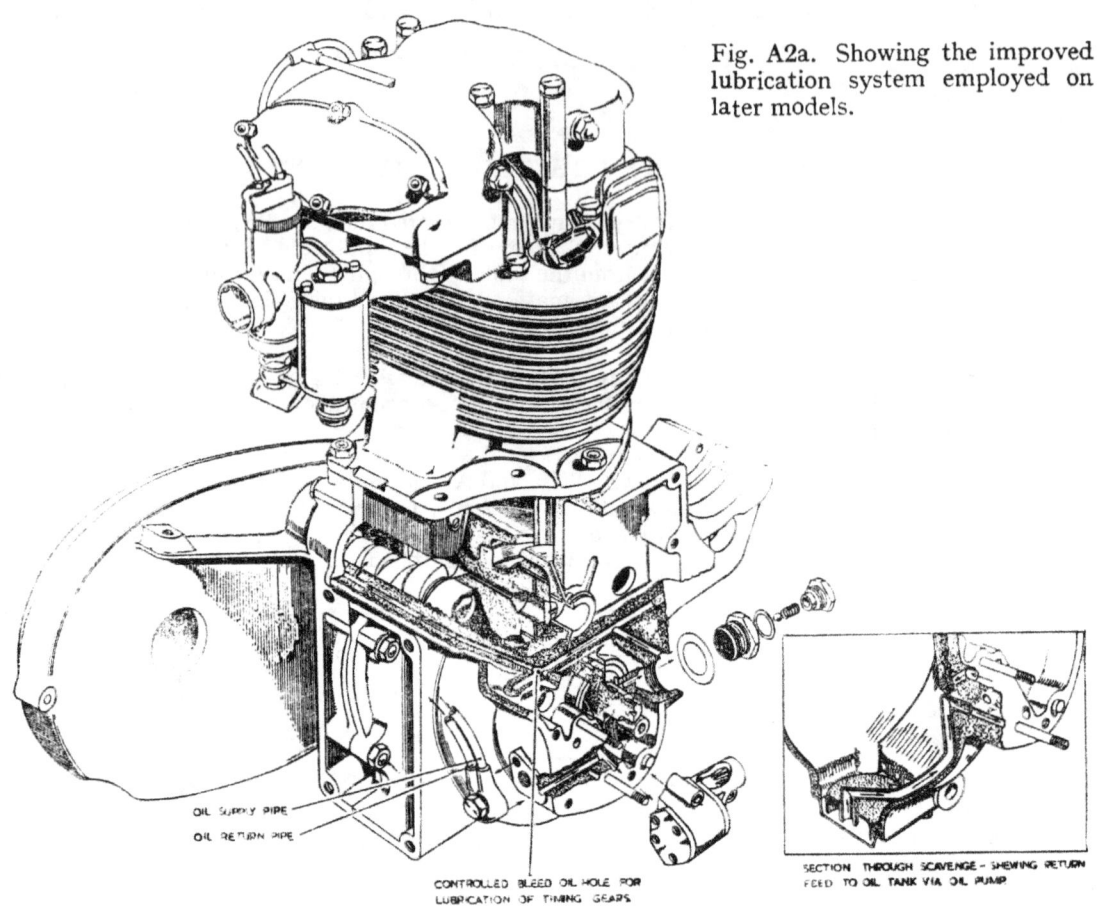

Fig. A2a. Showing the improved lubrication system employed on later models.

Lubrication of the Rockers.

On machines before engine number XA7-450, all the valves and rockers are lubricated by oil mist from the crankcase.

On machines from engine number XA7-450, and before YA7-3402 oil is fed to the exhaust rocker spindle only.

On all A7 engines after YA7-3402 and on all A10 machines oil is fed to both the inlet and exhaust rockers and lubricates the remainder of the valve gear in the form of oil mist.

The rocker box oil supply is obtained from a union to the point where the oil return pipe is attached to the oil tank.

The Oil Pressure Release Valve.

This valve should open when the pressure in the supply system reaches 50/60 lbs. per square inch. The valve ball is of 5/16-in. diameter. Remove the valve when oil changing, clean it and ensure that it is operating freely. See Service Sheet 203 for further details of dismantling.

Oil Change.

In case of new or reconditioned engines, the oil should be drained and renewed after the first 250 miles and again after 500 miles. Then periodically every 2,000 miles.

Drain the oil tank and the sump, preferably when the engine is hot, by removing the drain plug and the banjo with the filter at the bottom of the tank. Also the drain plug and the cover with the filter on the bottom of the crankcase. Clean by washing in petrol. Before replacing make sure that the parts are quite dry.

On swinging arm models the construction of the oil tank is slightly different, but the system of oil flow is the same. The oil filter is attached to the hexagon nut in the side of the tank and unscrewing it will provide access to the filter without disturbing the oil supply pipes.

B.S.A. Motor Cycles Ltd., Service Dept., Armoury Road, Birmingham 11.

Printed in England

B.S.A. Press.

BSA SERVICE SHEET No. 203

A Group Models

ENGINE ADJUSTMENTS WHICH CAN BE DONE WITHOUT DISMANTLING

Oil Pressure Release Valve

This valve (Fig. A3) is interposed between the delivery side of the pump and the big-end bearings. It is pre-set to control the pressure in the supply system and it should be examined periodically when changing the oil to ensure that it is operating freely and not impeded by the presence of even tiny particles of foreign matter. If the ball is prevented from seating properly there is a danger of oil starvation at the big-ends.

After dismantling all parts of the valve should be thoroughly rinsed in petrol and allowed to dry before reassembly. Note that both hexagons must be screwed right home and made really tight.

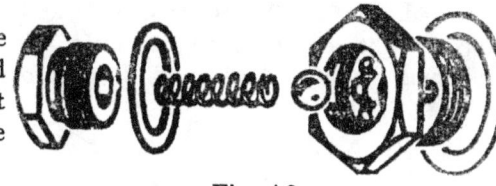

Fig. A3.
The Pressure Release Valve (exploded view).

Valve Clearances

Valve clearance checking or adjustment should only be carried out when the engine is quite cold. Remove the sparking plugs, and the rocker inspection covers (A) Figs. A4 or A4a. On the early models with separate rocker boxes, illustrated in Fig. A4, it is also necessary to remove the small plugs (D), to permit insertion of the feeler gauges and a special tool from the tool kit will assist in removing the caps (A).

On A10 and swinging arm models the petrol tank should be removed to provide access to the rocker box covers. Do not forget to disconnect the fuel pipes and the strap beneath the tank connecting the two halves

The cams are of special design. Because of this it is essential that when checking or adjusting the clearance of any valve it should be closed with its tappet on the base circle, or neutral portion of the cam. To obtain this position for the drive-side inlet valve turn the engine until the gear-side inlet valve is fully open. Similarly, to set the gear-side inlet valve in the correct position, turn the engine until the drive-side inlet valve is fully open. Follow the same procedure exactly for the two exhaust valves.

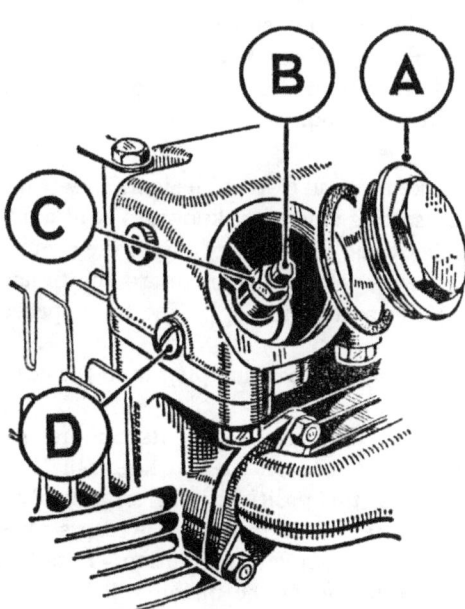

Fig. 4A. Tappet Adjustment

9

B.S.A. Service Sheet No. 203 (contd.)

Having turned the engine until the valve under consideration is in its correct position, insert a feeler gauge between the adjusting pin (B) and the valve stem or valve end cap. The clearances should be as follows:—

	Inlet	Exhaust
All A7 engines up to engine number XA7-601	.003 in.	.003 in.
All A7 engines from engine number XA7-601 to ZA7-11192	.015 in.	.015 in.
A10 engines and A7 engines after engine number AA7-101	.010 in.	.016 in.
A10 Super Flash	.008 in.	.008 in.
A7 Shooting Star	.008 in.	.012 in.
A10 Road Rocket	.008 in.	.008 in.
A10 and A10 S.R. with frame prefixed "GA"	.008 in.	.010 in.

To adjust the clearance; if it is found to be incorrect, hold the pin with one of the tappet spanners and with the other tappet spanner release the locknut (C). Then, holding nut (C), screw pin (B) up or down as required until the correct amount of play is obtained.

Hold the pin (B) with its spanner and tighten nut (C) very securely. When (C) is properly tightened, check the play again, to make certain that it has not been altered while tightening the nut. Check and adjust all four adjusters in the same manner, and do not forget that this must be done while the engine is quite cold. Finally, replace the rocker box covers, the caps (D) and the sparking plugs.

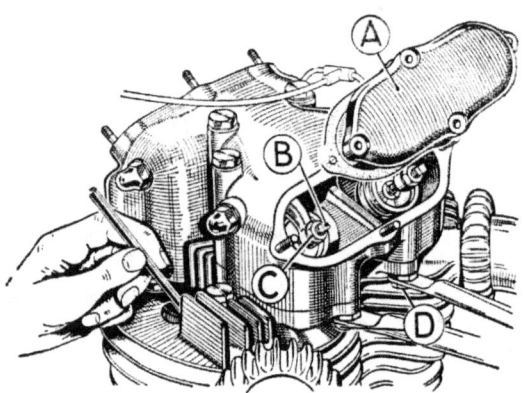

Fig. A4a. Valve Clearance Adjustment and Ignition Setting.

Clearances tend to increase slightly when the engine warms up to its working temperature, and if an attempt is made to adjust clearances while the engine is temperature, and if an attempt is made to adjust clearances while the engine is warm there may be insufficient clearance when the engine is cold. Running an engine without enough tappet clearance is harmful to the valve seats, and is one of the commonest sources of trouble in this direction.

Ignition Timing

It is a rare occurrence for the magneto pinion to slacken off and disturb the ignition setting. and it is not advisable to interfere with the standard setting unless it is known to be at fault,

Before checking the timing it is advisable to check and if necessary adjust the contact breaker points, as a slight variation of the points tends to advance or retard the timing (opening the points advances the timing, closing them retards timing). The fully opened gap at the points should be .010 — .012 in.

To check the timing remove the rocker box caps and the sparking plug from the gear-side cylinder.

Turn the engine forward until the gear-side piston is at the top of its compression stroke. This can be checked by means of a rod inserted through the sparking plug hole and resting on the piston head. If, when the piston is in this position, either of the valves is found to be partly open, this means that the piston is at the top of the wrong stroke, and the engine must accordingly be turned through one complete revolution. If tappet clearance can be felt at both valves (see Tappet Adjustment) the piston will be at its correct top dead centre for ignition timing

B.S.A. Service Sheet No. 203 (contd.)

The timing points for the different "A" Group models are as follows:—

A7 Standard	5/16-in. before T.D.C. fully advanced
A7 Star Twin, A7 Shooting Star ...	3/8-in. before T.D.C. fully advanced
A10 Golden Flash	11/32-in. before T.D.C. fully advanced
A10 Super Flash, A10 Road Rocket ...	3/8-in. before T.D.C. fully advanced
A10 and A10 S.R. with frame number prefixed "GA"	13/32-in. B.T.D.C.

Having satisfied yourself that the piston is at the correct top dead centre, turn the engine back until the piston has descended by the amount shown in the above table.

Leaving the engine set in this position, turn the contact breaker in its normal direction of rotation, until it is in the fully advanced position, the points should just be beginning to open, by not more than .002-in. on she bottom contact breaker cam (A) Fig. A5.

Fig. A5. The Contact Breaker Mechanism.

If the timing requires resetting, remove the timing cover and unscrew the bolt locking the magneto pinion and automatic advance mechanism on its shaft.

Note that the pinion is self-extracting, and as the bolt is unscrewed the pinion will be drawn from its taper.

Leaving the engine set in the position described for checking the ignition, turn the contact breaker in its normal direction of rotation, i.e. clockwise, until the points are just beginning to open, by the action of the arm on the bottom cam.

Wedge the automatic advance mechanism in the advanced position as shown at (B), Fig. A5, and holding the contact breaker in position tighten the magneto pinion bolt. Finally recheck the ignition setting.

It cannot be too strongly emphasised that the ignition timing must be correctly set for satisfactory engine performance, and also that any temptation to improve upon the maker's setting should be advoided, as this setting has been found best after careful trial and experiment. The fact that this engine is fitted with automatic ignition advance makes it all the more necessary that the above timing instructions should be faithfully carried out.

Sparking Plugs

The machine is supplied with Champion non-detachable type sparking plugs to suit the characteristics of the engine. If the best performance with regard to both power and economy is to be obtained then they must remain clean and properly gapped.

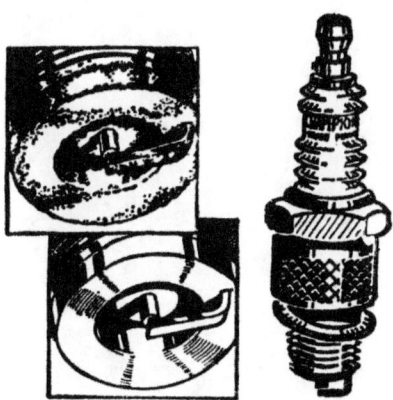

Fig. A6. The Sparking Plug.

The sparking plugs should be removed periodically for examination. If the carburation is correct and the engine is in good condition the plugs will remain clean for considerable periods. An over rich mixture will however cause the formation of a sooty deposit on the plug points and eventually on the plug body (see upper view of Fig. A6). Heavily leaded fuels may form a greyish deposit in a

B.S.A. Service Sheet No. 203 (contd.)

similar manner. If a heavy deposit is found, the plug should be cleaned, with the aid of the sand blast type of plug cleaner found at most garages, as otherwise the performance of the machine may be affected. If a heavy deposit is allowed to build up inside the plug it may prevent the engine from firing altogether. A weak mixture will cause burning of the plug points and give the plug a whitish appearance (see Service Sheet 708).

Check that the gap between the sparking plug points is correct and if necessary re-set to .018 — .020-in. (.45 — .50 mm.) by bending the side wire. In no circumstances attempt to move the central electrode as this may damage the insulation. If the points are badly burnt away or cleaning fails to restore the plug to its full efficiency, then it should be replaced by a new one.

When replacing the plug make sure that the copper washer is in good condition. Use a tubular spanner to prevent damage to the plug and keep the outside of the insulation free from oil and dirt by wiping with a clean rag.

B.S.A. MOTOR CYCLES LTD., Service Department, Armoury Road, Birmingham 11.

B.S.A. PRESS

Printed in England

BSA SERVICE SHEET No. 204

"A" GROUP MODELS
(Except Models A50 and A65)
ENGINE DISMANTLING FOR DECARBONISING

Decarbonising and "top overhaul" of an engine is extremely simple, but it should be carried out only when the engine really needs it. The usual symptoms are an increased tendency to "pink" (a metallic knocking when under heavy load) due to the building-up of carbon on the tops of the pistons and inside the cylinder heads, a general falling-off of power noticeable mainly on hills, and a tendency for the engine to run hotter than usual.

It is first necessary to remove the petrol tank. To do this turn off the petrol taps and detach the petrol pipes. If the speedometer is mounted in the tank, disconnect the drive by releasing the strainer bolt under the tank, raising the speedometer clear of the tank and unscrewing the knurled nut connecting the drive to the instrument. At the same time, disconnect the cable for the speedometer light. The tank is secured to the frame by a bolt through the steering head lug and another through the seat lug at the rear of the frame top tube. When these bolts are removed, the tank can be taken off. The tanks on certain models are quickly detachable and it is only necessary to slacken the nuts to enable the tank to be lifted at the rear end and withdrawn from the frame. On swinging arm models it is only necessary to remove the central retaining bolt beneath the rubber plug on top of the tank. On A10 and all swinging arm models a metal strap beneath the tank joins the two halves and this must be removed to allow the tank to be withdrawn.

Next detach the high-tension leads and remove the sparking plugs. Disconnect the steady-stays from the cylinder head to the frame, and then take off the carburetter by removing the flange bolts and sliding it off sideways after freeing it from the rubber sleeve which connects it to the air cleaner. By unscrewing the ring nut at the top of the carburetter, the slide can be pulled right out and tied up to the top tube out of the way, while the main body of the instrument can be completely removed. By unscrewing the exhaust pipe and silencer brackets to the frame, the pipes and silencers can be removed complete. Note that the silencer brackets are attached by means of the pillion footrest bolts on models with rigid frame.

A7 Models up to Engine No. ZA7-11192

Remove the rocker box connecting links and oil feed pipe. The rocker boxes are bolted to the head by bolts above and studs and nuts from underneath. Take off all nuts and bolts and lift the rocker boxes clear. Remove the hardened valve end caps (A7 standard models only).

The cylinder head holding-down bolts can now be removed. There are seven of these, including the central one which is inclined at an angle, and which should be removed first, and replaced last. The head unit is attached to the cylinder block at the rear by means of two inverted studs, and the nuts must be removed from these before the head can be lifted off. These nuts are situated between the fins, adjacent to the inlet manifold.

B.S.A. Service Sheet No. 204 (contd.)

A10 Models and A7 Models after Engine No. AA7-101

Remove the rocker box oil feed pipe. The rocker box is held in position by four bolts on the outside, one inside and one stud with nut and washer at each corner.

Remove the inspection covers, take out the bolts. Remove the nuts and washers. On 650 c.c. models it is necessary to remove the top stud for the rear inspection cover and flats are formed on the stud for this purpose. The box can now be lifted clear of the cylinder head.

When the rocker box is removed the nine cylinder head bolts will be exposed. Remove the bolts, carefully noting the position of the various lengths of bolt (Fig. A6a.)

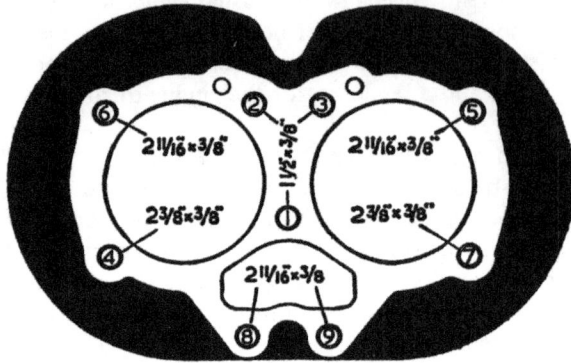

Fig. *A6a.*

All Models

The cylinder head unit can now be removed. If it shows a tendency to stick, a few light taps with a wooden mallet under the exhaust ports will loosen it. There is no necessity to remove the separate inlet manifold fitted to Shooting Star and Road Rocket models.

Rotate the engine by means of the kickstarter until the pistons are at the top of their stroke, and remove the carbon deposit with a suitable scraper, taking care not to damage the piston crowns.

All traces of carbon must be cleaned from the cylinder heads and valve ports. Where the head is an aluminium casting, particular care must be taken to ensure that the head is not scored or the joint faces damaged.

Grinding-in Valves

Using Service Tool 61-3340 compress the valve springs until the split collets can be removed When the collets are out, the valve springs and top collar can be lifted from the valve stem

Check the play of the valves in the guides. If it is excessive the valve guides should be replaced and it may be necessary to change the valves at the same time. The old guides may be driven out from the inside and the new ones may be driven in from the outside of the cylinder head by means of the valve guide fitting punch, Service Tool number 61–3265. When removing guides from the aluminium heads, the head should first be heated in a degreaser or hot water.

If new valve guides have been fitted or deep pit marks appear, the valve seats in the cylinder head should be re-cut. When pitting in the valve heads is deep, they should be re-faced. Then the valves can be ground-in with fine grinding compound, each valve to its own seat.

B.S.A. Service Sheet No. 204 (contd.)

Smear a small quantity of grinding compound (obtainable from any garage or accessory shop) over the face of the valve, and return the valve to its seat. Note that a light spring inserted under the valve head greatly facilitates the grinding-in operation, allowing the valve to lift and be rotated to a new position periodically. Hold the valve with the special tool provided in the tool kit, and rotate the valve backwards and forwards whilst maintaining a steady pressure. The valve should be raised and turned to a new position after every few strokes. Grinding should be continued until the valve seat and face show a uniformly smooth matt surface all round.

Valve grinding without re-facing should only be attempted if pitting is not deep.

Before replacing the valves and springs all traces of grinding compound must be removed from both face and seat, and the valve stems smeared with engine oil.

Valve Springs

After a period of several thousand miles it may be desirable to renew the valve springs as these tend ultimately to lose their efficiency due to heat. If the springs are renewed whilst decarbonising, it will save dismantling specially to replace them at a later date.

Valve Rockers

To remove the rockers from the rocker boxes, if this should be required for any reason it is only necessary to undo the acorn nuts on the rocker spindles, and also the banjo oil pipe unions on the rocker spindles, if fitted, and tap the spindles out, applying a small centre-punch to the threaded ends exposed when the nuts are removed, so as to avoid damaging the threads. Careful note should be kept of the rocker assembly for replacement, as the various washers must obviously be inserted in the correct order (see Fig. A7).

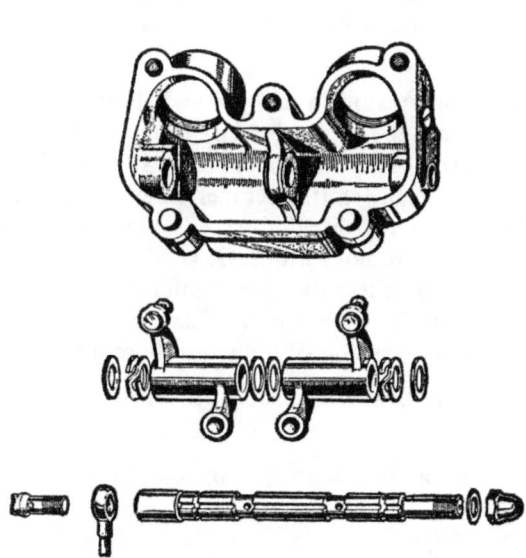

Fig. A7. *The Rocker Assembly Model A7.*

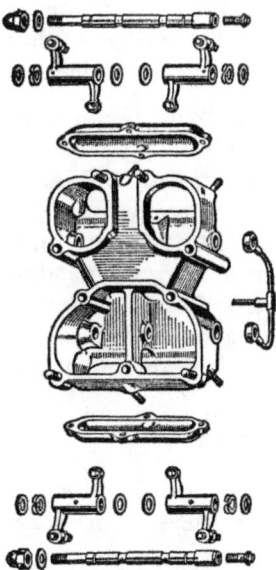

The Rocker Assembly Model A10 and Model A7 after AA7-101.

B.S.A. Service Sheet No. 204 (contd.)

Cylinder Block

In the ordinary course of events it should rarely be necessary to remove the cylinder block, since top overhaul, already described, usually suffices to keep the machine in first-class working condition. In any case, this operation is difficult to carry out without the help of an assistant, and unless the condition of the engine indicates that the pistons, rings or cylinder bores require attention, the cylinder block should not be disturbed.

Symptoms indicating faulty piston rings might include heavy oil consumption, poor compression (but only if the valves are in good order; otherwise they are much more likely to be the cause) and excessive piston slap when warm. This latter might be due to worn bores, which could be checked without removing the block, if the pistons were moved to bottom dead centre, thus exposing the bores for examination and measurement.

To remove the cylinder block, undo the cylinder base nuts, turn the engine until the pistons are at bottom dead centre, and then, preferably getting astride the machine, carefully lift the block up until the pistons are clear of the bores. While this is being done, get an assistant to steady the pistons as they emerge and to relieve you of the weight of the block, so that it may be lifted clear. When the block is removed, cover the mouth of the crankcase with rag to prevent dust and grit falling in. To remove a piston from its connecting rod it is first necessary to take out one of the gudgeon pin circlips. This is best accomplished with a pointed instrument such as the tang of a file suitably ground.

Before a gudgeon pin can be withdrawn it may be necessary to heat the piston with the aid of rags immersed in hot water, wrung out, and held round the piston. Then, supporting the piston, tap the gudgeon pin through, using a light hammer and a punch.

When the piston is free, mark the inside of the piston skirt at the back, so that it can be replaced the correct way round and on the same connecting rod.

If the rings are stuck in their grooves they will need to be carefully prised free and removed from the piston. All carbon deposit should be carefully scraped from the grooves and the inside edges of the rings. If any of the rings show brown patches on the surface, replace with a new ring.

Check the piston ring gaps by inserting each piston in its bore and sliding each ring independently up to the skirt of the piston. Check the gap with feeler gauges. This should not be less than .010 in. or more than .013 in. for the two upper rings, and .008 in. and .011 in. respectively for the bottom ring, which is the slotted scraper ring. These are the correct gaps for new rings. Fit new rings if the gap greatly exceeds the figure stated, although a few thousandths of an inch extra gap are not serious. It is advisable to check the gap of new rings before fitting, and if the gap is less than the minimum stated above the ends of the rings should be carefully filed to the correct limit. Ensure that when the piston ring gaps are measured the rings are in the position of minimum bore wear.

It should be noted that piston rings are very brittle, and unless handled carefully are easily broken.

The procedure for reassembly is in the reverse order to that for dismantling but for further details see Service Sheet 208 or 215.

B.S.A. MOTOR CYCLES LTD., Service Department, Armoury Road, Birmingham 11.

B.S.A. Press.

Printed in England

BSA SERVICE SHEET No. 205

October, 1948
Reprinted March, 1966

"A" GROUP MODELS (Rigid and Plunger Type Frames)
REMOVAL OF THE ENGINE GEAR UNIT FROM FRAME

It is first necessary to remove the petrol tank. To do this turn off the petrol taps and detach the petrol pipes. If the speedometer is mounted in the tank, disconnect the drive by releasing the strainer bolt under the tank, raising the speedometer clear of the tank and unscrewing the knurled nut connecting the drive to the instrument. At the same time, disconnect the cable for the speedometer light. The tank is secured to the frame by a bolt through the steering head lug and another through the seat lug at the rear of the frame top tube. The saddle nose bolt may also be taken out. When these bolts are removed, the tank can be taken off. The tanks on certain models are quickly detachable and it is only necessary to slacken the nuts to enable the tank to be lifted at the rear end and withdrawn from the frame. In some instances a metal strap beneath the tank joins the two halves and this must be removed to allow the tank to be withdrawn.

The left- and right-hand exhaust pipes and silencers should now be removed. These are secured to the frame by means of a long bolt passing through the front of the crankcase underneath the engine, and at the rear by the pillion footrest securing bolts, the nearside nut of which is inside the tower rear chain cover. (Rigid frame models only).

The exhaust pipes are a push fit into the cylinder head, and the finned collars, when fitted, need not be detached.

Remove the carburetter by releasing the two 5/16 in. Whitworth bolts from the manifold. The carburetter may then be tied to the rear of the frame out of the way of possible damage during the ensuing work.

Release the two 5/16 in. Whitworth nuts on the underside of the front rocker boxes and allow the two steady straps bo fall away from the engine.

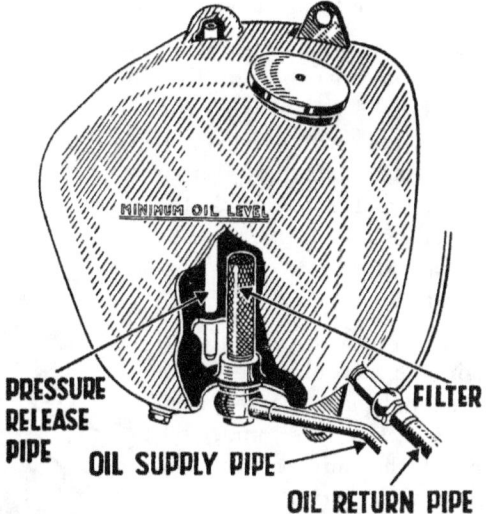

Fig. A8.

It is now necessary to drain the oil from the oil tank, this is accomplished by unscrewting the 5/16 in. Whitworth hexagon-headed plug at the rear corner of the tank, or by un screwing the supply pipe banjo union when no drain plug is fitted (Fig. A8).

When the oil tank is empty, remove the two oil pipe unions secured to the underside of the oil tank, using the B.S.A. combination spanner from the tool kit. Observe that the rear joint houses the oil filter unit, and take care to avoid damaging this component during removal.

The front pipe union also secures the O.H.V. rocker oil supply pipe, and this may be left attached to the engine.

Release the rear chain spring link and rotate the wheel to remove the chain from the gearbox sprocket.

B.S.A. Service Sheet No. 205 (contd.)

Now remove the remaining front engine securing bolt. This bolt passes through the dynamo cover, and the frame distance piece, which will fall away when the bolt is removed (A) Fig. A10.

The dynamo cover is secured to the engine by three bolts (B) Fig. A10, which must now be removed, noting that three plain washers are situated between the engine crankcase and the dynamo cover, left-hand side only, one on each bolt. These must be replaced on re-assembly.

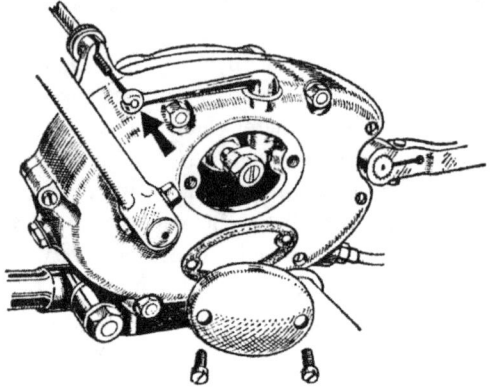

The rear of the power unit assembly is secured to the frame by three further bolts, two underneath the gearbox and one behind the magneto. A bolt at the rear of the primary chaincase casting, by the magneto, holds the front of the chainguard, which together with the bolt passing through a bracket on the lifting stay, must be released, and the chainguard drawn away towards the rear wheel.

The nut on the central rear cheese-headed primary chain cover screw should be released, allowing the bottom chainguard (rigid frame models) and the oil tank breather pipe clip to become free from the engine unit.

Fig. A9.

It will be observed that the engine unit is now entirely free from the frame except for the speedometer cable and the clutch cable on top of the gearbox. Push the clutch lever towards the centre of the machine, allowing the inner cable nipple to be removed from the arm, and screw back the cable adjuster on the gearbox to release the outer cable from the unit (Fig. A9).

It is now advisable to obtain the help of an assistant who should place a lever, such as a 12 in. tyre lever, under the front of the unit between the frame and crankcase. Depression of the lever will cause the engine unit to pass over the lower frame tubes to the offside, at which point the engine should be steadied, before removing to a substantial wooden box set on this side of the machine.

Now lift the power unit complete on to the wooden box, crankcase downwards, taking care that the unit does not fall over.

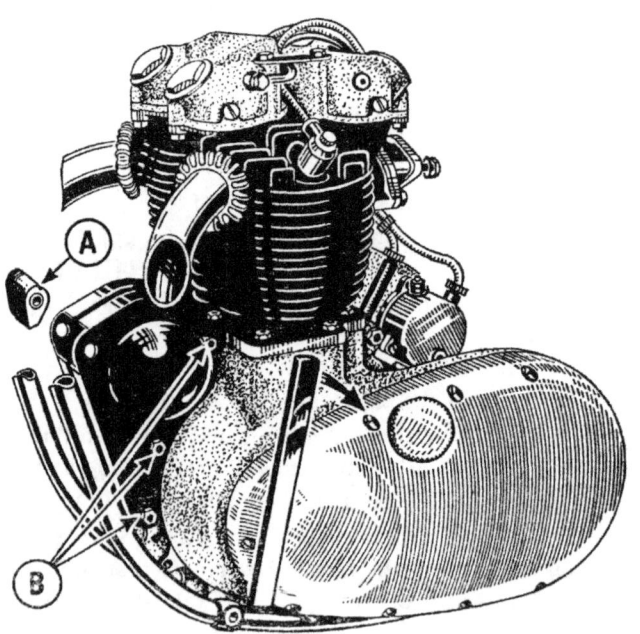

Fig. A10.

B.S.A. MOTOR CYCLES LTD., Service Department, Armoury Road, Birmingham **11.**

Printed in England

BSA SERVICE SHEET No. 206

October 1948
Revised November, 1951
Reprinted Feb., 1963

"A" Group Models
(Rigid and Plunger type frames)

COMPLETE DISMANTLING OF THE ENGINE

The procedure for the dismantling of the engine will be described from the point reached on Service Sheet No. 204, when the cylinder head and barrel have been removed.

NOTE:—The A10 instructions apply to all A7 models after engine No. AA7 101.

Before commencing to dismantle the engine it will be advantageous to construct a fixture and wooden block such as those illustrated in Figs. A11 and A15(a).

Detach the foot gear change lever from its spindle on the gearbox, and then withdraw the twelve cheese headed screws to allow the removal of the outer timing cover, noting that the lower five screws on the A7 and four on the A10 are the longest screws in the set, and the three at the dynamo end of the cover are the shortest.

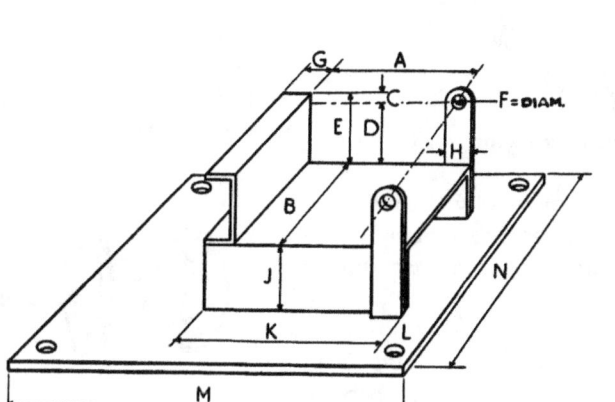

	Inches.	mm.
A	4¾–5	120–125
B	3½	85–90
C	⅜	9
D	1⅝	41
E	2	50
F	⁷⁄₁₆ dia.	11.5 ø
G	1	25
H	¾	20
J	2	50
K	6¼–6½	155–160
L	1	25
M	12	300
N	8	200

Fig. A11. Engine Bench Fixture.

A pan should be placed under the engine before the cover is finally removed to hold the waste oil which will fall from the inside of the cover.

Release the dynamo securing strap and turn the dynamo in its housing to allow the tension on the dynamo chain to be relaxed. Remove the large dynamo driving sprocket, that is secured on its taper seat, by a nut and locking washer. After the nut and washer have been removed, a light tap with a hammer on a soft drift placed against the side of the sprocket will loosen it. The sprocket can then be withdrawn together with the chain.

The inner cover is held in position by five screws on the A7 and four on the A10. Take out the screws, remove the cover, and expose the timing gears.

The camshaft gear carries the crankcase breather Part No. 67/130 and a ⅛in. thick cork washer between the gear and the breather.

The automatic ignition device may now be removed by releasing its central securing nut. The mechanism is self extracting and as the nut is unscrewed the gear will be pulled from its taper

B.S.A. Service Sheet No. 206 (cont.)

Remove the breather Part No. 67/130 if this was not removed at the withdrawal of the inner cover, followed by the circular cork washer in the centre of the pinion.

The camshaft pinion is keyed and screwed by means of a locknut and washer. Release this nut and washer, and the pinion may be drawn from its shaft in the same manner as the dynamo driving sprocket using Tool No. 61-3676.

Now follows the removal of the idler pinion and its shaft complete, by pulling away from the crankcase bush with the fingers.

Fig. A12. Timing Pinion Extractor No. 61-3676

The three securing nuts and washers holding the oil pump in position may now be removed. Undo the locknut and washers from the end of the crankshaft, as the pump is withdrawn, release the hexagon headed worm gear from the crankshaft. Note that both locknut and worm gear are left-hand threaded.

The timing pinion which is keyed to the crankshaft may now be extracted. On all engines after ZA7-1400, AA7-101 and all A10 engines by means of Service Tool 61-3676. Pinions on earlier engines should be removed by the insertion of a small lever behind the gear, care being taken not to damage the bearing or crankcase during the removal of the pinion.

Remove the oil pressure release valve from the crankcase to clean and check it, see Service Sheet No. 202.

Fig. A13 The Oil Pressure Release Valve.

If a composition washer has been inserted into the crankcase below the release valve, a new washer should be used when re-assembling.

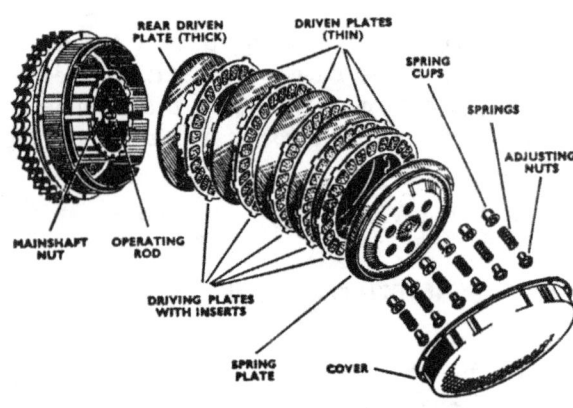

Fig. A14.

Three studs, the one underneath having a long nut, secure the magneto to the crankcase. After the nuts have been removed, the magneto can be pulled from its housing.

Remove the primary chain cover by releasing the twelve securing pins, observing that these are of varying lengths and must be replaced in their correct positions when re-assembling. Access to the clutch is gained by the removal of a cover held in position by twelve nuts and bolts. Take care not to damage the oil sealing washer between the cover and the clutch body, when the clutch cover is drawn off.

B.S.A. Service Sheet No. 206 (cont.)

Withdraw the six hexagon headed clutch spring adjusting nuts, together with the springs and cups. The spring plate should now be removed and the clutch mainshaft nut unscrewed after "punching up" the securing washer. Do not remove the clutch plate assembly until the cush drive assembly has been released and removed by taking out the split pin and unscrewing the circular slotted nut on the mainshaft. The two assemblies, with the duplex primary chain, can then be drawn together. Take care that the 18 clutch centre race rollers do not fall out during this operation.

Draw the ground faced clutch thrust plate, Part No. 67-3250, along the splined shaft and remove the two halves of the abutment ring, Part No. 67-3251, from the rear of this plate.

It is now necessary to remove the two securing nuts and the two bolts from the crankcase to release the gearbox. Early A7 models have four bolts.

Remove the sump plate and filter from the base of the engine, allowing the waste oil to drain into the pan. Do not withdraw the pump suction pipe from the crankcase.

The tappet guide fixing plate can now be removed (A7 only).

Remove the engine from the bench fixture, and place on a wooden block, drive side downwards. After all the crankcase securing bolts have been slackened, the crankcase

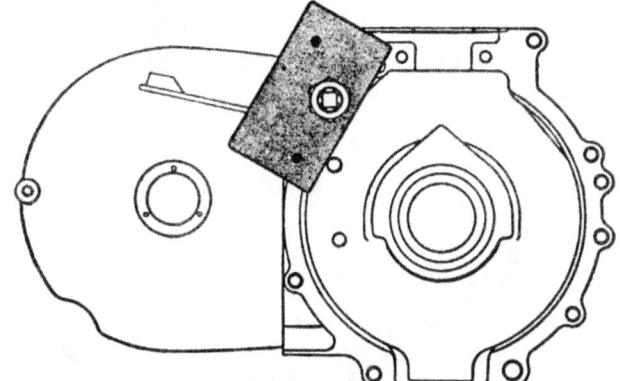

Fig. A15. Withdrawing blind camshaft bush (Service Tool No. 61-3159)

halves can be separated. On A7 models it is advisable to leave nuts and washers on one side of the studs between the gearbox flange, as these cannot be replaced after the crankcase has been reassembled.

Gently tap the front and rear of the cases with a soft mallet to part the halves.

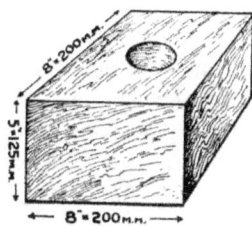

Fig. A15(a).

Note the number of shims, if any, on the mainshaft, between the mainshaft bearing and the crankshaft web.

The drive side ballrace on the A7, roller race on the A10 models, and the gear side white metal bearing, may now be pressed from their respective cases to the inside if in need of attention. It is advisable to warm the crankcase halves in a degreasing plant, or hot water, before attempting to remove the bearings.

Note that there is a steel washer between the drive side race and the case. This acts as an oil seal.

Service Tool No. 61-3159 will withdraw the blind camshaft bush from the drive side crankcase (see Fig. A15).

The tappet and tappet guides will not normally require attention. If they must be removed, they can be taken out as follows :—

B.S.A. Service Sheet No. 206 (cont.)

A7 Models. The tappets are carried in the crankcase. The exhaust centre double tappet block will fall away when the crankcase halves are separated. The inlet tappet guides may be removed using Service Tool No. 61-3069.

A10 Model & A7 after Engine AA7-101. The tappets are carried in the cylinder block. Remove the two setscrews "A" (Fig. A15b) and remove the inlet tappets "B." Remove the setscrew "C" taking care not to lose the 3/16in. ball. Push out the retaining pin from the inside of the barrel, and remove the exhaust tappets. Note that the exhaust and inlet tappets are not interchangeable.

Withdrawal of the two securing bolts attaching each of the big end bearing caps to the crankshaft allows the removal of the connecting rods and completes the dismantling of the A7 engine. No useful purpose will be served by attempting to split the actual flywheel assembly, if of the earlier built-up design, because crankshaft grinding can be done in the same way as the normal car engine crankshaft.

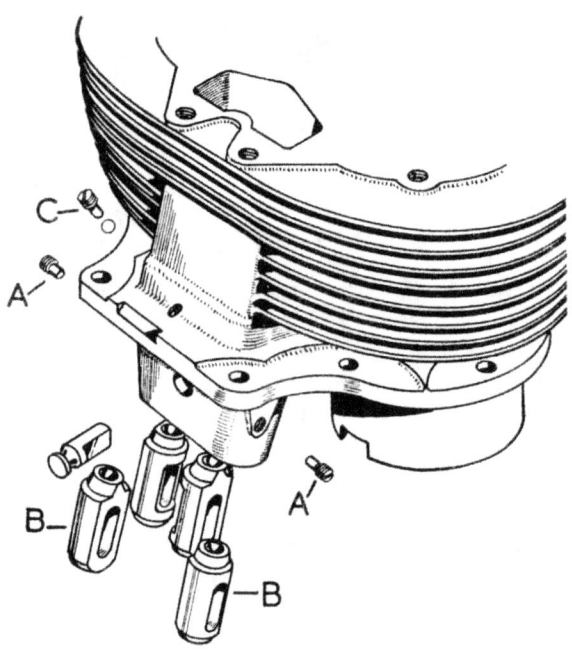

Fig. A15(b).

The big end bearing liners cannot be replaced in the caps otherwise than in the correct position because these are indented, and fit into their respective slots in the rods and caps.

Dimensions for the regrinding of the crankpins are given in Service Sheet No. 207 and must be strictly adhered to, because the bearing liners are manufactured for these dimensions.

The flywheel is bolted to the crankshaft, and should only be disturbed if a new crankshaft has to be fitted. The oilways in the crankshaft should be cleared of any sludge that may have formed. The plugs at each end of the crankshaft may be removed for this purpose.

Three steel rivets passing through the rear end of the drive side crankcase casting hold the gearbox oil seal in position between two steel plates, and their removal for replacement of the oil seal must be effected with due care, so as not to damage case. (*See Fig. A16, Sheet* 208).

The suction pipe from the sump to the pump on the gear side case must not be disturbed because this is cemented into the case before leaving the works, and a new pipe is supplied as a standard fitting with a new gear side crankcase. This also applies to the small grub screw by the mainshaft plain bearing behind which is situated a ball valve and this must not be disturbed.

There is no need to remove the chain tensioner or adjuster unless a new crankcase is being fitted. After Engine No. AA7-101 the A10 instructions will apply.

B.S.A. MOTOR CYCLES LIMITED, Service Dept.   Armoury Road
Birmingham, 11.
B.S.A. PRESS.

BSA SERVICE SHEET No. 207

"A" Group Models

CRANKSHAFT RE-GRINDING.

It will be necessary to regrind the bearing surfaces of the crankshaft when the overall wear of the crankpins or gear side journal exceeds .002", or if the surfaces have been damaged by bearing seizure.

Worn bearings will develop a distinct "knock" and the engine will become generally rough.

Suitable undersized big end bearing shells and gear side bushes can be supplied for crankshafts ground to the dimensions shown.

The crankshafts fitted to A7 models having engine numbers from XA7-101 to XA7-600 have crankpins of larger diameter than those fitted to later models. Provision is made for one regrind only on this earlier crankshaft, after which connecting rods 67-1200 and standard bearing shells 67-320 must be fitted. No subsequent regrinding is recommended.

Although only the left-hand connecting rod is drilled for lubrication purposes, all shells are now drilled for standardisation. The plain shell is no longer being supplied

The following tables give dimensions of reground bearings, for crankshafts, together with the part numbers of undersize shells and bushes. **These numbers must be quoted when ordering.**

Engine Nos. XA7-101 to XA7-600.
First Regrind.

Grind the crankpins to 1.4600"–1.4595" with a .090"/.085" face radius both sides. This is the standard dimension on machines Engine Nos. XA7-601 upwards.

Fit connecting rod assembly 67-1200(2) with standard bearing shell 67-320(4).

Mark webs as shown below:—

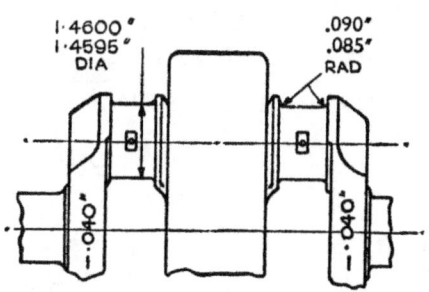

(P.T.O.)

B.S.A. Service Sheet No. 207—continued.

Engine Nos. XA7-601 upwards, A10, A50 and A65 Models.

CRANKSHAFT ASSEMBLIES
Part No. 67-384
Part No. 67-664

Grind the crankpins to 1.4500/1.4495" diameter with .090"/.085" face radius. Fit bearing shell 67-244 (4 off) marked .010" undersize.

FIRST REGRIND.

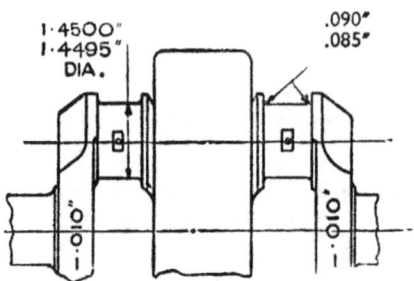

Mark crankshaft web face as shown.

CRANKSHAFT ASSEMBLIES
Part No. 67-1149
Part No. 67-1218
Part No. 68-175
Part No. 68-179

Grind the crankpins to 1.677"/1.6765" diameter with .085"/.090" face radius. Fit bearing shell 67-1431 (4 off) marked .010" undersize.

SECOND REGRIND.

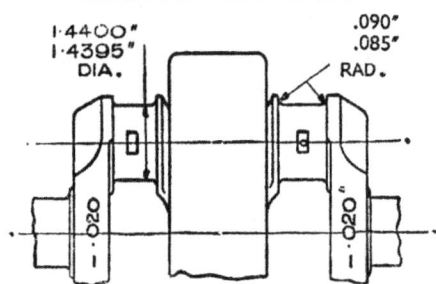

Mark crankshaft webs as shown.

Grind the crankpins to 1.4400"/1.4395" diameter with .090"/.085" face radius. Fit bearing shell 67-245 (4 off) marked .020" undersize.

Grind the crankpins to 1.667"/1.6665" diameter with .085"/.090" face radius. Fit bearing shell 67-1432 (4 off) marked .020" undersize.

THIRD REGRIND.

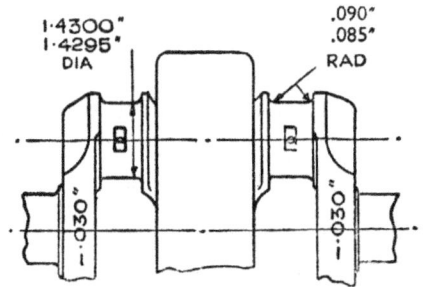

Mark crankshaft webs as shown.

Grind the crankpins to 1.4300"/1.4295" diameter with .090"/.085" face radius. Fit bearing shell 67-246 (4 off) marked .030" undersize.

Grind the crankpins to 1.657"/1.6565" diameter with .085"/.090" face radius. Fit bearing shell 67-1433 (4 off) marked .030" undersize.

GEAR SIDE JOURNAL.

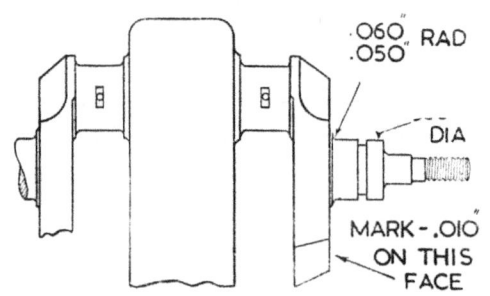

Mark crankshaft web face as shown.

Shafts, 67-384, 67-664, 67-1149, 67-1218. Grind the journal 1.3640"/1.3634" with .060"/.050" face radius.

Shafts 68-175. Grind journal to 1.4885"/1.489 with .050"/.060" face radius.

Fit .010" undersize bush 67-799 or .020" undersize 67-787 (use bush 67-652 for engines XA-7101 to XA7-600).

Use undersize bush No. 68-334-.010" or 68-332-.020" for 68-175 or 68-179 shafts (A50 and A65 models).*

—.010" or .020"

*1966 models onwards use undersize bushes No. 68-647 (—.010") or 68-648 (—.020")

B.S.A. MOTOR CYCLES LIMITED, Service Dept., Armoury Road- Birmingham, II.

Printed in England

B.S.A. PRESS

BSA SERVICE SHEET No. 208

October 1948
Reprinted June 1966

"A" GROUP MODELS
RE-ASSEMBLY OF THE ENGINE

The need for cleanliness cannot be over emphasised; all parts should be clean and free from dirt or rust.

The A10 instructions apply to all A7 models after engine number AA7-101.

Smear all bearing surfaces with engine oil.

If the crankshaft has been replaced, the original flywheel, if serviceable, may be retained, and fitted by passing it over the drive-side of the crankshaft and bolting to the flange by six high tensile steel bolts. After securely tightening the bolts, they should be peened over on to the nuts to lock them.

The flywheel is positioned with the counter-weight part at the opposite side to the big-ends of the cranks. See Service Sheet No. 712X for balancing.

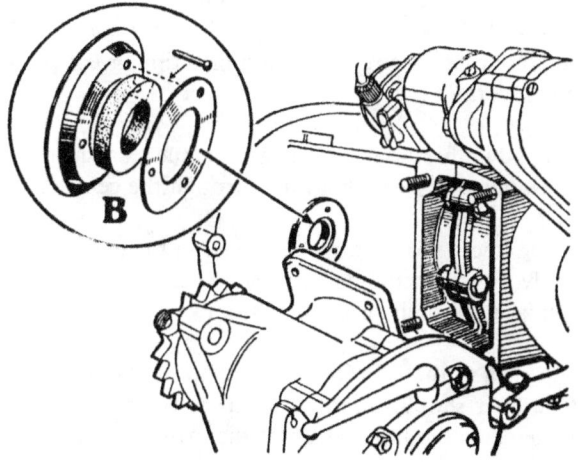

Fig. A16.

If the chaincase oil seal is to be renewed, this is effected by placing the actual composition seal part number 67-1242, round end outward, into the hole in the crankcase casting extension, and riveting two steel plates, the larger, part number 67-1241 inside, and part number 67-1243 outside, by three steel rivets, part number 67-1244, care being taken not to damage the aluminium case during the riveting operation (Fig. A16).

Having warmed the crankcase halves in a degreasing plant, or hot water, insert the steel oil seal washer into the race recess in the drive-side crankcase. Then, by means of an arbor press, insert the race and the blind camshaft phosphor bronze bush. Now press the plain main bearing into the gear-side crankcase. The cases must be suitably supported during these operations to prevent damage.

Press the two camshaft bushes into the case, one from inside and one from outside, and also the idler pinion spindle bush if these parts have been removed.

B.S.A. Service Sheet No. 208 (contd.)

A phosphor bronze bush is also inserted into the inner cover to carry the outer end of the idler pinion spindle.

If new camshaft and idler pinion bushes have been fitted it is now necessary to bolt the crankcase together and attach the inner cover, then with the aid of Service Tools number 61-3275 for A7 or 61-3281 for A10 and A7 after AA7-101 use reamer 61-3167 to ream the bushes to .7495—.7485 in. internal diameter (Fig. A17). These reaming jigs should also be used to locate the mainshaft reamer if a new mainshaft bush has been fitted. See Service Sheet No. 711 for details of reamer.

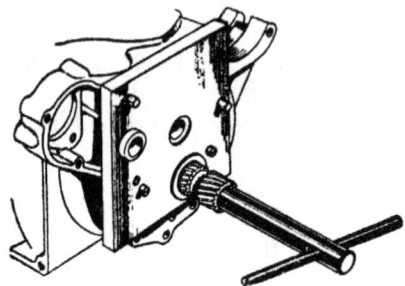

Fig. A17. *The Reaming Jig.*
(*Service Tool 61-3275 for A7, 61-3281 for A10 and A7 after engine AA7-101*)

Then unbolt the crankcase and remove the inner timing cover. Remove all trace of swarf after the reaming operation.

At this point it is advisable to obtain a fixture such as shown in Fig. A11 Service Sheet No. 206, and a wooden block with a hole through the centre as shown in Fig. A15a.

The big-end bearing liners should now be placed in the end caps and connecting rods, note that these can only be put in the correct way, because the liners are lipped, but they must, of course, be replaced in their original positions.

When fitting new liners to the A10 it should be noted that each set of four has a small central drill hole. One liner should be fitted in the left-hand con-rod to line up with the bleed hole which supplements the lubrication of the cylinder bore.

Connect each rod and cap to its crank journal, noting that their numbers correspond, and insert the big-end bolts and tighten them. On no account must the castellated nuts be slackened back to allow the insertion of the split pins. If the nut slot does not line up with the hole in the pin when the nut has been fully tightened, the latter must be removed and filed on its flat face until the hole in the pin and nut slot line up.

A torque spanner should be used for tightening these nuts to ensure that they are not over-tightened. Two types of big-end bolts have been employed. Early models use 22 t.p.i. B.S.F. bolts and for these the torque spanner should be set at 10 lb./ft. The later type bolt is 26 t.p.i. C.E.I. and a setting of $8\frac{1}{2}$ lb./ft. is correct. The later type bolts complete with nut can be used as replacements for the earlier type. From 1956 onwards the torque spanner setting is 22 lb./ft.

No scraping is necessary with these big-end liners, and it must not be attempted or damage will result.

B.S.A. Service Sheet No. 208 (contd.)

Crankshaft end play: on the A7 when the sprocket is tightened up, the float is taken up. Before tightening, the float should be .005—.010 in.

A10, on this engine the float is not taken up when tightening the sprocket. The maximum float should be .005 in. Any error should be corrected with additional packing shims.

Replace on the drive-shaft of the crankshaft assembly any packing shims which were removed in the dismantling of the engine.

Place this assembly on a thick wooden block through which a hole large enough to take the gear-side mainshaft has been bored. Then place the drive-side crankcase half over the drive-shaft and gently tap into position, making sure that the shaft enters the race squarely and goes right home.

Reverse the whole assembly on the block, and then, insert the camshaft into the blind phosphor bronze bush in the drive-side crankcase half. On the A7 place the large twin tappet block with tappets into the recess at the top of the case, so that the oil hole in the block faces towards the gearbox end of the engine, and the opposite side of the block, with slope for securing plate, faces the inside of the engine. On the A10 the tappets are in the cylinder block.

Smear the joint face of the crankcase with jointing compound, and after it has become tacky, place the gear-side crankcase in position and bolt the crankcases together, making sure that each nut has a shakeproof washer. The two top inside securing bolts have plain locking washers, one side of which is bent over to form a securing tab on the nut.

Insert the two tappet blocks with tappets (A7 only) and before finally tightening the two top inside crankcase securing bolts and the top rear outside bolt, the tappet blocks should be finally lined up by placing a 6 in. steel rule across the milled flats.

When the cases are bolted securely together, the camshaft must rotate freely; otherwise the case alignment is incorrect.

The crankcase breather pipe is a push-fit into a hole at the top of the drive-side case, immediately behind the primary chaincase casting and should be cemented, the lower end being secured by a clip.

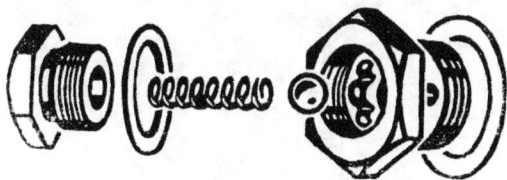

Fig. A19.

Attach the sump plate filter, with the pump suction pipe from the inside of the crankcase passing through the hole in the filter gauze, a paper washer being inserted between the case and plate.

Now bolt the twin oil tank pipes to the gear-side of the crankcase using jointing compound, and insert the oil release valve unit and rubber washer, if fitted, into its socket (Fig. A19).

B.S.A. Service Sheet No. 208 (contd.)

The dynamo securing straps and offside dynamo cover plate, if previously removed, should now be attached to the gear-side case. The nearside dynamo cover plate was removed when the engine was taken from the frame, and will be replaced when the engine is again inserted into the frame.

On A7 engines replace the tappet block securing plate at the top inside of the crankcase.

Attach the gearbox to the engine by the two securing studs and two bolts in the crankcase, making them really tight. On certain models a fibre or hallite separating washer is used between the two units and care should be taken that this is not omitted on reassembly.

The keyed timing pinion should be placed on the crankshaft, concave side to crankcase, followed by a mild steel plain washer. Before mounting the pump, replace the thick washer so that the holes match, and the round fibre washer. Slide the pump and the driving worm on together, turning the worm anti-clockwise. The driving worm is left-hand threaded and care must be taken to avoid damage to the worm gears during assembly.

The driving worm is secured by a keyed washer and a left-hand nut, the outside edge of the washer being subsequently turned over on to the nut to form a locking device.

Place a screwdriver inside the engine against one of the cams and the inside top crankcase lug, to prevent the camshaft from sliding inwards and so disturbing the key when putting the cam pinion on the shaft. Now, holding the screwdriver, the cam pinion may be inserted, with the breather actuating stud outwards, on to the keyed end of the camshaft, and secured by its locknut and special locking washer, the tabs of which must be turned down on to the nut after tightening.

Check to see that the camshaft key has not become dislodged from the pinion.

Fig. A20. *Valve Timing.*

Rotate the crankshaft until the dot on the timing or crankshaft **pinion** is upwards, and insert the idler pinion so that the dot on the crankshaft pinion meshes with **the dot** on the idler pinion and the dash mark on the camshaft pinion meshes with the corresponding dash mark on the idler pinion (Fig. A20).

B.S.A. Service Sheet No. 208 (contd.)

The magneto should now be bolted in position by its three securing bolts, the two short bolts on top and the long bolt underneath the magneto, with a paper washer between the magneto and crankcase.

Timing of the magneto is carried out at a later stage in the assembly, and the magneto drive pinion with its automatic ignition advance device should now be only loosely attached to the magneto spindle.

Place the dynamo in position in its securing carrier on the front of the engine without tightening up. Smear the inner joint face of the inner timing cover with jointing compound, and place the paper joint washer in position on the inner side of the inner cover.

The crankcase breather should now be inserted on to the cam pinion, with a cork washer between the pinion and breather. Smear the breather with engine oil, and place the inner cover in position, securing with the screws. Check end float on the breather and correct if necessary by fitting a thicker cork washer.

Now fit the pistons to the connecting rods, making sure by the marks previously scribed on the inside of each piston, if they are the original ones, that they are in the correct positions.

On the A10 replace the tappets in the reverse order to that for dismantling (see Sheet number 206).

Place the paper cylinder base washer in position on the top of the crankcase, and rotate engine to bring the connecting rods to top dead centre. Turn the piston rings so that the gaps, which should be .008—.012 in. are not in line with each other. Smear the pistons with engine oil.

Now lower the cylinder block over the pistons, compressing the rings, preferably by the use of Tool number 61-3061, on the A7 (Tool number 61-3334 after engine number AA7-101), or 61-3262 for the A10, which should be removed when the rings have fully entered the cylinders, and secure the block to the crankcase with the holding down nuts and shakeproof washers.

Replace the four push rods through the tunnel on to their tappets. The two long rods are the inner ones and the two short rods the outer ones.

The magneto should now be timed. To do this, see Sheet number 203.

Place the chain on the dynamo driven sprocket and the dynamo driving sprocket, which should now be inserted on to the shaft, the concave side of the sprocket inwards, a cork washer being placed between sprocket and case. Fit the nut and a plain washer, turning the edge of the washer on to the nut to lock it after securely tightening.

Adjust the dynamo chain by rotating the dynamo in its cradle to give approx. $\frac{1}{8}$ in. to 3/16 in. up and down play on the chain, but not sufficient to foul the inner case retaining screw boss in the centre of the cover, near which the chain passes. Then tighten up the dynamo in its cradle.

The aperture in which the dynamo chain drive runs should now have approx. $\frac{1}{4}$ lb. of light grease inserted, as no other means of lubrication is provided.

B.S.A. Service Sheet No. 208 (contd.)

Smear the inner side of the outer cover joint face with jointing compound, place a paper washer on the face when the compound is tacky. Place the cover on to its dowels, and secure with the twelve securing screws, the longest screws at the lower end of the case, and the three shortest screws at the dynamo end of the case.

Next replace the valves into their respective ports, place the springs over the stems and with the top collars in position, and using Service Tool 61-3340 as before, compress the springs until the split collets can be inserted. A dab of grease on the inside of the collets will serve to hold them in position, until the spring is released. Make quite sure that the collets are correctly located.

Check that the push rods are on their respective tappets, position the cylinder head gasket and then lift the cylinder head into position. Replace the cylinder head bolts, and on the A7 the nuts on the two inverted studs at the rear. Make them all really tight, working diagonally in order to secure even tightness, and leaving the central inclined bolt to the last. When they are all right down give them a final wrench to make certain that they really are tight.

Now replace the rocker box or boxes, making sure that the push rods are correctly inserted into the rocker ends, and thoroughly tighten the various nuts and bolts. A special push-rod locating tool part number 67-9114 is available which facilitates the location of the push rods while replacing the rocker box of A10 models and A7 after engine number AA7-101. The tool should be inserted between the cylinder head and the rocker box from the right-hand side, with the shaped edge to the rear and with the outside recesses located by the two rear rocker box holding-down bolts, as shown in Fig. A21. The rocker box should then be tightened down and the tool removed just before it is gripped between the rocker box and cylinder head.

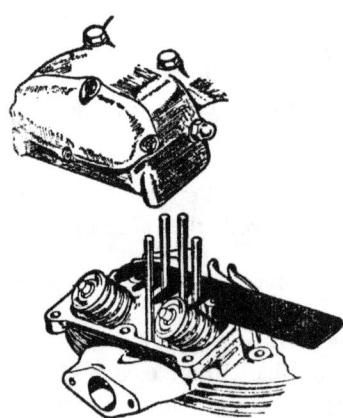

Fig. A21. *Push Rod Assembly Tool.*

Unless care is exercised when replacing the one-piece rocker box fitted to the later models it is possible to cause damage to the valve stems. To fit the rocker box, place in position over the valves, and gently ease the four holding-down studs through their locating holes in the cylinder head. Check that the rocker box is well clear of the valve spring collars and push it firmly down to its seating on the cylinder head. No force must be used in this operation. After ensuring that the box is firmly seated, fit and tighten the bolts.

B.S.A. Service Sheet No. 208 (contd.)

Failure to use this method may result in the valve stems being bent, by fouling the rocker box. Although not noticeable in the test run of the engine, this will result in sticking valves and loss of power at high speeds.

Before replacing the rocker box caps or covers, check the tappet clearances and adjust if necessary. For correct clearances, see Service Sheet No. 203.

Replace the rocker box connecting links on the A7 and rocker box oil supply pipe.

Replace the primary chain tensioner and adjuster, locking the securing nuts with a length of wire as in Fig. A22.

Place the two halves of the clutch thrust plate abutment ring, in position in the groove at the rear of the splined shaft, with a smear of grease to hold them in position.

Slide the clutch thrust washer along the splines over the abutment ring.

Place the clutch centre on a table, rear end upwards, put the clutch chainwheel over the clutch centre, chainwheel upwards, and insert a small quantity of grease into the space between the clutch centre and the chainwheel centre, to hold the eighteen $\frac{1}{4}$ in. $\times$ $\frac{1}{4}$ in. rollers in position.

Insert the rollers, bring the chain tensioner to its lowest point of adjustment downwards, and then place the duplex chain over the clutch and engine sprockets.

Taking the engine sprocket in the left hand and the clutch chainwheel, including the clutch centre with rollers in the right hand, slide the whole on to the engine and clutch splined shaft at one and the same operation, making sure that no rollers fall from the clutch centre race.

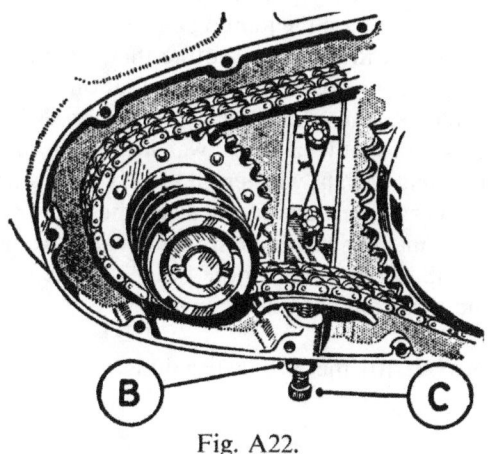

Fig. A22.

Insert the main shaft locking washer over the splined shaft, with a smear of grease to hold the washer in position. Screw the gearbox mainshaft nut on to the mainshaft, turning the edge of the locking washer over to lock the nut.

B.S.A. Service Sheet No. 208 (contd.)

Slide the clutch plates into the chainwheel housing, rear, driven plate first (see Fig. A23).

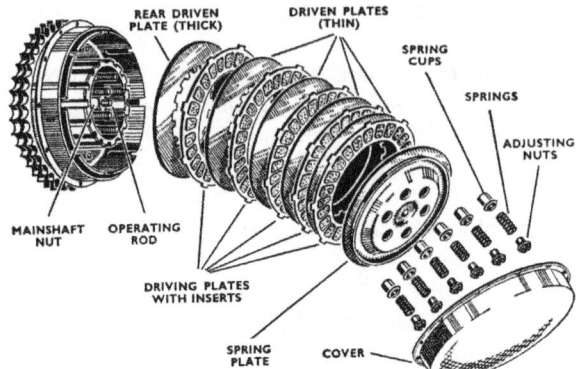

Fig. A23. *The Clutch (exploded view)*.

Fit the spring plate last, and then insert the spring cups and springs into the spring plate, and secure by the six adjusting nuts, screwing these into the spring plate until the collars on the adjusting nuts are flush with the face of the plate.

Place the cush-drive sleeve over the engine shaft, followed by the cush-drive spring over the sleeve, and screw the mainshaft nut on to the engine shaft with a "C" spanner, tightening the mainshaft nut up as securely as possible. Put a split cotter pin through the hole in the engine mainshaft, and spread open the split ends.

Adjust the chain by raising the chain tensioner by means of its adjusting screw (C) Fig. A22, in the lower part of the chaincase until there is $\frac{1}{2}$ in. total up and down movement at the tightest point. Tighten the locknut (B) and check the adjustment.

Smear the outer primary chaincase jointing edge with jointing compound, allow it to become tacky, place a paper washer on the jointing edge of the cover, and secure in position by means of the twelve cheese-headed screws, noting that these are of varying lengths and must be replaced in their correct positions. Note also that one of the screws is painted red. This serves as an oil level plug and should be located in the screw hole adjacent to the chain tensioner. On earlier models the oil level screw was located in the next hole forward, but the rearward position providing a slightly lower oil level is more suitable. The new position can be obtained on the earlier models by cutting away the rear screw hole on the inside of the outer cover in a similar manner to the existing cutaway. Remove the paint from the original screw and put a dab of red paint on the head of the new drain screw. The screws are of different length and therefore not interchangeable.

After engine number AA7-101 the A10 instructions will apply to the A7.

B.S.A. MOTOR CYCLES LTD., Service Department, Armoury Road, Birmingham 11.

B.S.A. PRESS

BSA SERVICE SHEET No. 209

"C" GROUP, 4-SPEED (1951-57) & "A" GROUP RIGID & PLUNGER

DISMANTLING AND RE-ASSEMBLY OF GEARBOX AND GEARCHANGE

Removal

In most cases it will be found convenient to dismantle the gearbox while it is in position in the frame. If it is necessary to remove the gearbox sprocket or sleeve pinion on a "A" Group machine, the engine/gearbox unit must be removed from the frame and the gearbox separated from the crankcase (see Service Sheet No. 206). To remove the gearbox from the frame of a "C" Group machine for attention to bearings see Service Sheets Nos. 308 and 411.

Dismantling the Gearbox

Move the gears to the neutral position between first and second. Next remove the gearbox outer cover which is held in position by three screws and four nuts. The cover will come away with the kickstarter, the gearchange and the clutch lever still in position, and these need not be disturbed unless obviously requiring attention. Note that as the cover is withdrawn, the spring pressure on the kickstarter pedal is released. The clutch operating lever should be pulled out to the fullest extent, allowing the kickstarter lever to come to rest against it, thus preventing the kickstarter return spring from being released.

Pull out the clutch operating rod which passes through the centre of the mainshaft, and then release the nut on the mainshaft which holds the kickstarter ratchet pinion and spring, laying the latter aside. The gearbox partition can then be removed together with the foot gearchange rocking lever (M) Fig. A24.

The rod (G) is pressed into the gearbox shell at the clutch end and secured by a grub screw which is accessible under the gearbox. Release this grub screw and then pull out the rod. It should then be possible to withdraw the entire gear cluster complete with shafts and the two sliding forks bodily from the gearbox, although, if preferred, the components may be withdrawn separately. This may call for a certain amount of manoeuvring, but the experienced mechanic will have no difficulty. Before removing the gear selector plate (H), note the notch in which the gear control plunger engages. This is the neutral position between first and second gear, and the plate must be rotated to this position before the box can be reassembled. Unscrew the selector plunger housing locknut and remove the plunger assembly from the gearbox shell. The gear selector plate will now slide from its pivot. The layshaft bushes are a press-fit in the gearbox and if necessary must be driven out with the aid of a soft punch.

The top gear pinion sleeve is now the only part still left in the gearbox, and if the sprocket locknut is unscrewed, after suitable attention to the tab washer, the sprocket may be removed and the pinion tapped into the gearbox with the aid of a wooden mallet.

Do not disturb the ballrace unless it is suspected of being faulty. Wash it thoroughly in paraffin, to remove all traces of oil, and any play will then be immediately detected.

Examine the various parts for wear, and if the forks which actuate the sliding pinions show signs of seizure it will be advisable to replace them. Attempts to erase the seizure marks will result in excessive side play.

The fixed pinions on the layshaft and mainshaft are pressed on, and new components must be a tight fit. Examine the selector plate for worn cam grooves and for wear on the ratchet members on the boss in which the selector claw (P) engages, and replace if necessary. The selector claw should be replaced if the teeth show signs of wear as, of course, should pinions with damaged or worn teeth.

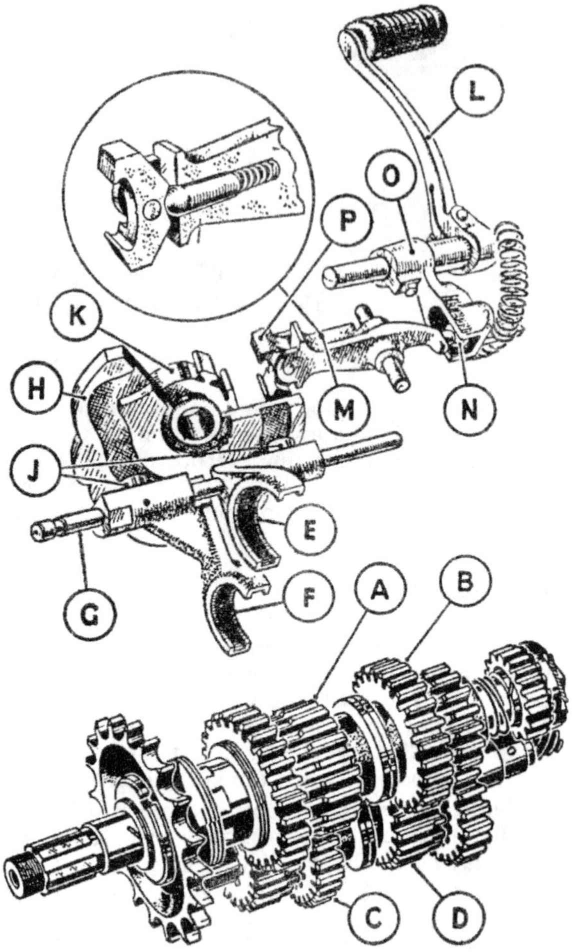

B.S.A. Service Sheet No. 209 (contd.)

Reassembly of the Gearbox and Gearbox Mechanism

If it has been decided to fit a new ballrace to the top gear pinion, remove the spring circlip and oil flinger washer with the aid of a screwdriver. In order to remove the ballrace easily, warm the gearbox shell in boiling water. If the sprocket teeth are worn hook-shaped, a new sprocket must be fitted; otherwise rapid chain wear will result. Do not forget to set the lockwasher into the grooves machined in the locknut after the latter has been tightened up. The tabs in the centre of the locknut washer must fit properly into the sprocket splines.

Assemble the layshaft with selector fork (F), with the exception of the low gear pinion (this is the largest on the shaft). Replace the selector plate and gear control plunger, rotating to the neutral position between first and second gears. Slide the layshaft complete with gears and selector fork into the box and engage the fork peg in the track of the cam plate.

Assemble the mainshaft pinions on the shaft and the selector fork (E), and insert the complete assembly into the gearbox shell engaging the peg of the selector fork in the cam plate. Slide the gear control shaft through the selector forks and press home into the

Fig. A24.

gearbox case, replace the grub screw turning the edge of the hole over to prevent loss of the screw. Replace the thrust washer and low gear pinion on the layshaft.

The inner cover should next be assembled. Coat the paper washer between the inner cover and the gearbox shell with jointing compound, hold the gearchange rocking lever in a central position, slide the inner cover on to the four studs and push it "home". The gear selector claw must engage on the ratchet members on the selector plate boss.

The ratchet mechanism may now be fitted to the mainshaft, the parts assembling in the following order—spacing washer, sleeve bush, spring, ratchet pinion, locking washer, and nut. Tighten the nut and turn over the tab on the washer as a means of locking the nut.

The outer cover can now be replaced. Coat the paper washer with jointing compound. Take up the outer cover with the kickstart lever in the left hand and the footchange lever in the right hand. Slide the cover on to the gearbox studs and press home, entering the kickstart quadrant in the ratchet pinion and the footchange slotted lever over the ball end of the rocking lever. Replace the four nuts and three screws on the outer cover.

The unit is now ready for reassembly to the engine (see Service Sheet No. 208).

A10 and AA7 Machines

After engine numbers ZA10-1215, ZA7-11192 are fitted with a modified layshaft and gear cluster to obtain improved gear selection and the engine number should be specified when ordering spares.

B.S.A. MOTOR CYCLES LTD., Service Department, Armoury Road, Birmingham 11.

B.S.A. PRESS

BSA SERVICE SHEET No. 210

October, 1948
Reprinted June 1965

A Group Models
(Without Swinging Arm Frame)
TRANSMISSION

Clutch Adjustment

Two adjustments are provided at the clutch control arm on the gearbox outer cover. The first of these is at the clutch push rod and is exposed when the inspection plate (Fig. A25) is removed. It consists of a grub screw and lock nut. Between the inner end of the screw and the clutch push rod a steel ball is inserted, and the grub screw must be adjusted so that there is just a little clearance between the ball and push rod.

To carry out this adjustment loosen the lock nut A and with the aid of a screwdriver adjust the grub screw B. Then re-tighten the lock-nut.

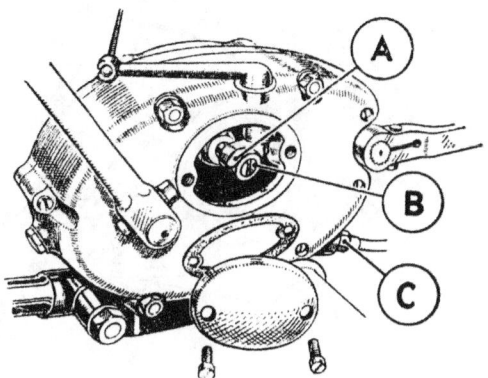

Fig. A25. Clutch control adjustment.

The other adjustment, to be used only if necessary, is provided by the cable adjuster on top of the gearbox, just under the magneto. Remember, however, that some free movement in the control arm is necessary, as if the adjustment is too tight there will be constant pressure on the clutch, with consequent wear and loss of efficiency.

Clutch Spring Pressure

After a considerable mileage it may be desirable to increase the spring pressure a little. First remove the outer half of the primary chaincase and then the domed clutch cover A (Fig. A26), which is secured to the clutch body by twelve screws. It will then be seen that the clutch plates are pressed together by springs, the tension of which is controlled by the nuts B. To increase the spring pressure tighten these nuts B a few turns. It is important that each of the six adjusting nuts be given an equal number of turns to ensure even pressure; otherwise the plates will slide unevenly and clutch drag may result. After adjustment, replace the cover and chaincase.

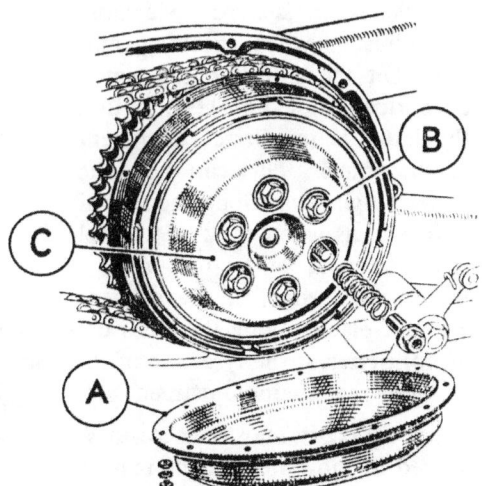

Fig. A26. Clutch spring adjustment.

B.S.A. Service Sheet No. 210 (continued).

Front Chain Adjustment

To adjust the front chain, remove the inspection plate plug A (Fig. A27) and then slacken off locknut B on the chain tensioner adjuster. Turn the adjuster C, screwing it up to reduce the slack in the chain, and down to increase it. Feel the tension by inserting the fingers through the inspection plug hole. The correct amount of slack, or up and down movement, on the front chain is half an inch. If the play is being increased, pressure on the kick starter will help to move the tensioner plate down. This is of course unnecessary when play is being reduced.

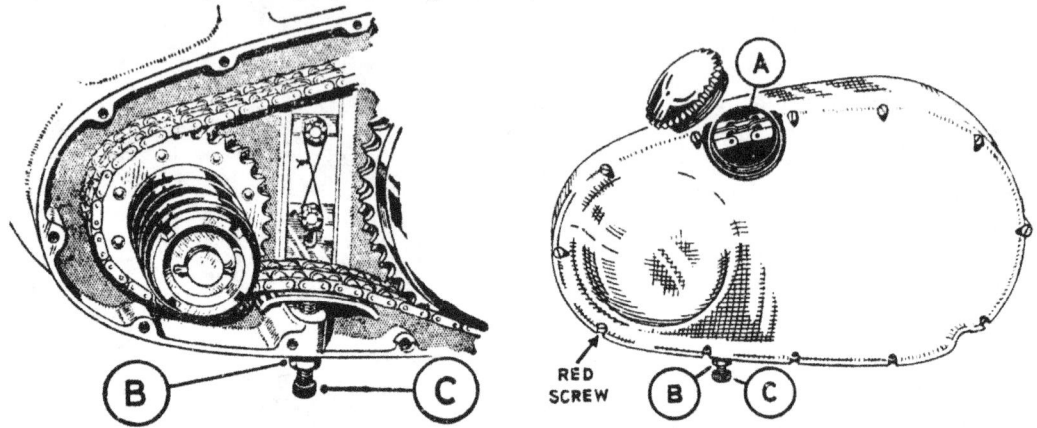

Fig. A27.

Rear Chain Adjustment (Rigid Frame)

The rear chain is adjusted by means of screw adjusters in the fork ends in front of the wheel spindle. Slacken off nut A (Fig. A29) and then unscrew the spindle a little by means of a tommy bar inserted in the hole in the spindle end B. Screw the adjusters C in or out until the chain tension is correct, with an up and down movement of three quarters of an inch. Make sure that the wheel is hard up against the adjusters when checking, and also that the adjustment is equal on both sides of the wheel, so that the latter is in correct alignment in the frame. This can be done either by glancing along the line of both wheels when the front wheel is set straight, or by means of a long straight-edge, or the edge of a plank placed along the sides of the wheels. The straight-edge should touch both walls of both tyres, if the tyres are of the same section.

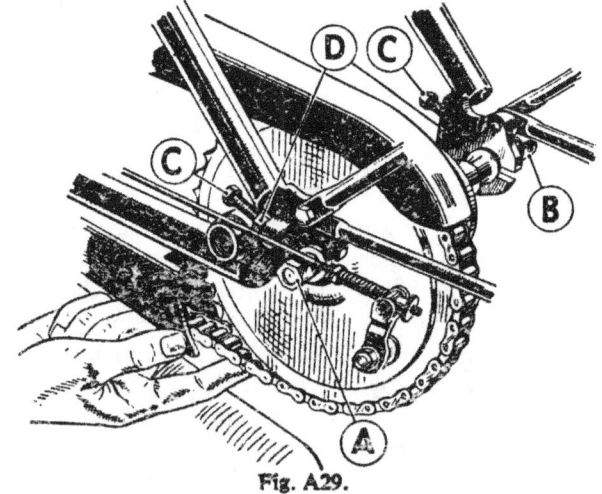

Fig. A29.

For rear chain adjustment on spring frame models see Service Sheet 212C.

NOTE. It may be necessary to re-adjust the rear brake, since this will have been altered by movement of the rear wheel.

B.S.A. MOTOR CYCLES LTD.
Service Dept., Armoury Road,
Birmingham, 11
Printed in England.

BSA SERVICE SHEET No. 211

October 1948
Reprinted October 1963

"A" GROUP
(Except Swinging Arm Models)

DISMANTLING AND RE-ASSEMBLING THE CLUTCH

Take off the nearside footrest, and then undo all the screws round the rim of the chaincase, noting the position of the red screw, which also serves as an oil level plug. The joint washer should be carefully preserved.

The clutch is revealed by removal of the cover held in position by twelve nuts and bolts. Take care not to damage the oil sealing washer between the cover and the clutch body, when the clutch cover is drawn off.

The clutch spring plate which is now revealed may be removed after the six adjusting nuts have been unscrewed and the clutch spring and spring cups withdrawn.

The clutch plates may now be withdrawn. Take note of their position so that they may be reassembled in the same order. Examine the clutch plates for oil or wear. The plates will require a thorough washing in petrol if there is any trace of oil on them. If the inserts are badly worn or glazed they must be renewed. The steel plates should be smooth and if badly scored they must be replaced.

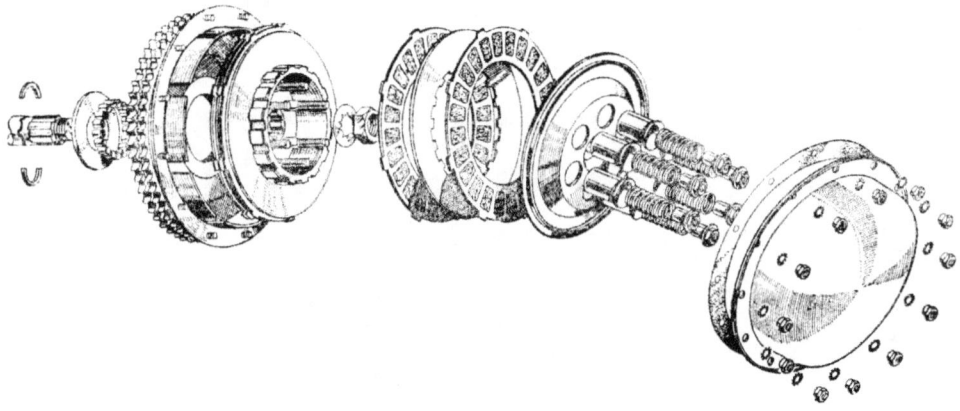

Fig. A30. *Exploded view of Clutch.*

Removal of the clutch body entails removal of the engine shaft shock absorber and sprocket, and the operation is described fully in Service Sheet No. 206.

The clutch sprocket and clutch centre can then be examined for wear. Special attention should be paid to the slots in which the steel plates slide; if any grooves or notches are worn in the sides of these, they may be filed smooth if not too deep. If the sprocket teeth are worn to a hook shape, the sprocket must be replaced; otherwise rapid chain wear

B.S.A. Service Sheet No. 211 (contd.)

will result. Finally, examine the rollers and tracks. If wear on the chainwheel bush or on the bearing boss of the clutch centre exceeds .0015 in. the bush or centre should be replaced.

Reassembly of the clutch and mainshaft sprocket is described in Service Sheet No. 208. Reference to Fig. A30 and Fig. A23, Service Sheet No. 208, will show the order and method of assembly.

It is important that the pressure plate and clutch plates should slide out evenly when the clutch is operated, and if necessary the clutch springs should be adjusted to achieve even pressure all round.

B.S.A. MOTOR CYCLES LTD., Service Department, Armoury Road, Birmingham 11.
Printed in England.

BSA SERVICE SHEET No. 212

**A Group Models
before Engine No. ZA7-101**

*Oct., 1948
Reprinted Jan., 1958*

ADJUSTMENT, DISMANTLING AND RE-ASSEMBLY OF HUBS AND BRAKES

Both wheels are of the quickly detachable type and are interchangeable.

Front Wheel Removal and Replacement

Slacken the pinch bolt A, Fig. A31, at the front of the nearside fork end. Insert a tommy bar in the hole in the spindle end B and unscrew. Note that the spindle has a left hand thread, and therefore unscrews clockwise. The spindle can then be pulled right out, and the wheel should be pulled sideways toward the nearside of the machine, so as to disengage the coupling splines on the hub from the brake. As this is done, the distance bush C will slide into the fork end. The wheel can now be dropped out.

To replace the wheel the above operations are carried out in the reverse order. The action of tightening the wheel spindle restores the bush C to its correct position. **Do not forget finally to tighten the pinch bolt A.**

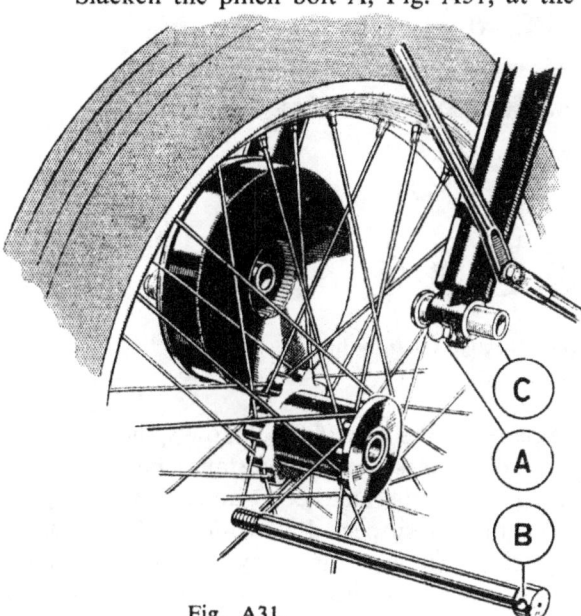

Fig. A31.

Rear Wheel Removal and Replacement

The rear wheel is removed in a somewhat similar manner. The spindle A, Fig. A32, has a right hand thread and therefore unscrews in an anti-clockwise direction. The distance bush B falls clear of the machine when the spindle is removed, or alternatively the spindle can be pulled out until it is clear of the hub and then slid backwards out of the slotted chainstay end, carrying the bush with it.

This is the most convenient way of dealing with the bush when refitting the wheel. When detaching the rear wheel, it is quite unnecessary to touch the hexagon nut C on the nearside.

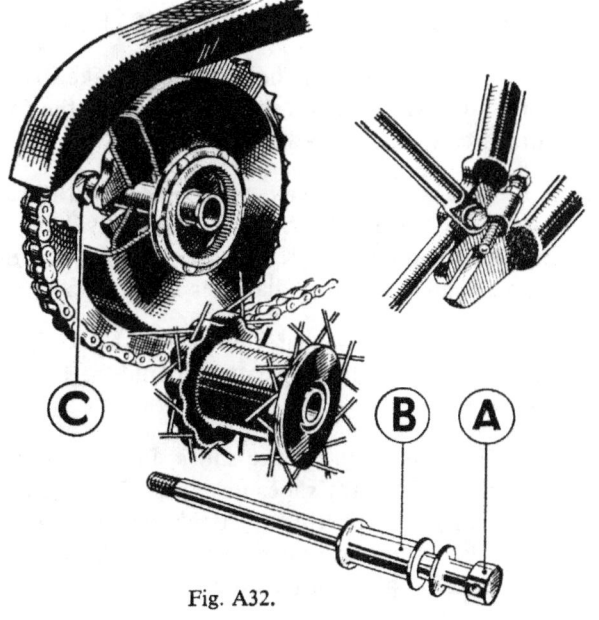

Fig. A32.

B.S.A. Service Sheet No. 212 (cont.)

Dismantling and Re-assembly of the Hubs

The hubs are fitted with two ballraces which are a light press fit on the hollow spindle and in the hub shell. Remove the dust cap A, Fig. A33 and felt washer B. Unscrew the ballrace retaining ring C. This ring has a left hand thread and therefore unscrews in a clockwise direction.

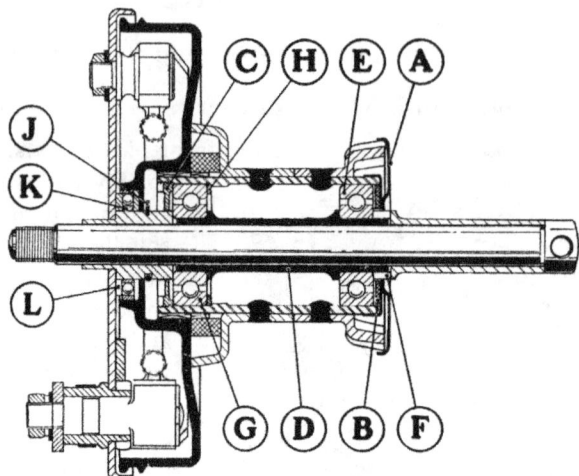

Fig. A33. Section through the front hub.

With the aid of a suitable soft drift applied to the end of the hollow spindle D, drive out the spindle and ballrace E. As the spindle comes away the distance bush F will be released. The only parts remaining in the hub are the ballrace G and the shim H, and these need not be disturbed unless the ballrace is suspected of being faulty. Wash it thoroughly in paraffin to remove all trace of grease when any play will be immediately detected. If it is decided to replace the race it can be driven from the hub shell with the aid of a soft drift.

Removal and Dismantling of the Front Brake Drum

After removal of the wheel the brake drum is held in position in the frame by means of a stud which passes through a lug on the fork leg. With the nut removed the complete drum can be withdrawn.

The brake drum cover plate can be withdrawn from the brake drum after removal of the spring circlip J, Fig. A33. The plate will be seen to carry the brake shoes together with their fulcrum pin and operating arm and a thrust race with its accompanying washers. Note that the smaller diameter washer goes next to the cover plate.

It is unlikely that the brake shoes, fulcrum pin and operating arm will require attention, although the latter should be checked for freedom of movement and greased if necessary.

To remove the brake shoes, lay the drum cover plate flat on a bench (shoes uppermost) and lever the shoes upwards. They can then be drawn over and free of the cam and fulcrum pin. To replace, attach the springs and reverse the method of removal. If the cam pads show excessive wear, new shoes should be fitted. If only the brake linings are worn, these alone need be replaced.

B.S.A. Service Sheet No. 212 (cont.)

If examination of the brake drum shows that the splines have become worn and the braking surface scored, a new drum must be fitted. The drum must not be machined to produce a new braking surface. To do so is only a temporary cure and further attention would be required later.

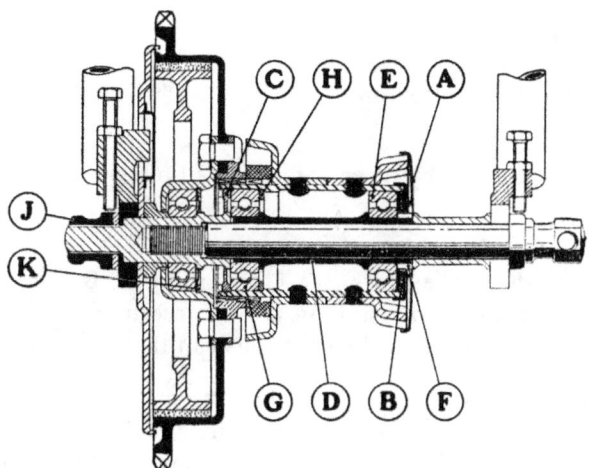

Fig. A34. Section through the rear hub.

When new linings or new shoes have been fitted, the brakes must be centralised after refitting the wheel. To do this, replace the brake cover plate, complete with shoes, fulcrum pin and cam, in the brake drum. Slacken the fulcrum pin nut, and turn the cam so as to open the brake shoes in the normal manner. The fulcrum pin will then move in its slot until both shoes are pressing equally on to the drum. Tighten the fulcrum pin nut firmly and release the brake.

Removal and Dismantling of the Rear Brake Drum

After removal of the rear wheel the brake drum is held in position in the wheel by nut J, Fig. A34. To remove the drum disconnect the chain and rear brake rod, slacken nut J, move the drum towards the offside of the machine until the lug on the frame disengages from the slot in the brake anchor plate, and then slide the drum to the rear, until it is clear of the chainstay ends.

With the brake drum removed from the frame, the brake drum cover plate, to which are attached the brake shoes, can be withdrawn, together with their fulcrum pin and operating arm. It will be seen that these are similar in construction to those of the front brake, and the instructions given for the front brake will apply.

The hub ballrace, which is totally enclosed in the brake drum, should not normally require attention. If it has been decided to replace this race, however, its housing can be removed from the brake drum by unscrewing the nuts and withdrawing the bolts that pass through the splined ring, the brake drum and the ballrace housing. Note that the nuts are locked in position by three locking strips: it is essential that these are fitted on re-assembly.

B.S.A. Service Sheet No. 212 (cont.)

The brake drum ballrace is held in position in its housing by means of a spring circlip K, which can be removed with the aid of a screwdriver. The replacement ballrace should be well greased before fitting the washer in place to prevent grease entering the brake drum. When replacing the bearing housing in the drum, make sure that its face is clean and free from burrs, as failure to do this may result in the brake drum running out of truth.

Brake Adjustment

The front brake is adjusted by means of the screwed sleeve on the cable stop, fitted to the brake cover plate.

The rear brake is adjusted by means of a knurled nut on the end of the brake rod.

Brake Re-lining

After removal of the brake shoes (see Dismantling of Brake Drums), the old lining is easily taken off by gripping the shoe in a vice, inserting a chisel under one end and shearing the rivets off in sequence. The rivet ends can then be punched out of the shoe.

New linings are die-pressed to suit the curvature of the shoes, but will require drilling and counter-boring for the rivets. Position the lining and hold it in place at one end by means of clamps. Using the holes in the shoes as guides, drill holes of the correct size ($\frac{5}{32}$ in. dia.) for the rivets adjacent to the clamp. Turn the shoe over, and counterbore the holes just drilled sufficiently deep so that the rivet heads will stand below the lining surface; this is important, since the rivets will otherwise score the brake drum.

Insert rivets into the holes and rivet them over on the inside of the shoe. This is easily accomplished by holding in a vice a short length of rod, whose diameter is equal to that of the rivet head, and using it as an anvil upon which to rest the rivet head while hammering the shank over. This will also make sure that the rivets do not stand proud of the lining.

Move the clamps to the next pair of holes, taking care that the lining is kept in firm contact with the shoe the whole time, and repeat the above procedure. When the lining is finally riveted down, bevel off the ends of the linings and file off any local high spots.

Precautions to be observed when fitting the relined shoes to the hubs are given in the chapter on 'Dismantling of the Brake Drums.'

J.U.B1283

B.S.A. MOTOR CYCLES LTD.
Service Dept., Birmingham 11
Printed in England.

BSA SERVICE SHEET No. 212A

Reprinted December 1967

A, B AND M GROUP MODELS
(for A7 models before engine number ZA7-101—see Service Sheet 212)

ADJUSTMENT, DISMANTLING AND RE-ASSEMBLY OF FRONT HUB AND BRAKE (7 in. Brake)

Wheel Removal and Replacement

To remove the front wheel, first disconnect the brake cable, then slacken the pinch bolt (*A*) Fig. A31A. Insert a tommy bar in the hole in the head of the spindle at (*B*) and unscrew the spindle, noting that it has a left-hand thread and therefore unscrews in a clockwise direction. With the spindle withdrawn the bush (*C*) should be pulled out to its fullest extent. This will leave the wheel free to be pulled away from the right-hand fork leg and withdrawn from the machine.

The wheel is replaced in the reverse order, noting that the brake plate stop must be located in its recess at the rear of the right-hand fork leg. It is most important that after the spindle has been tightened and before the pinch bolt is tightened, the forks are depressed once or twice to enable the left-hand fork end to position itself on the distance bush. If this precaution is not observed, the fork leg may be clipped out of position and will not function correctly.

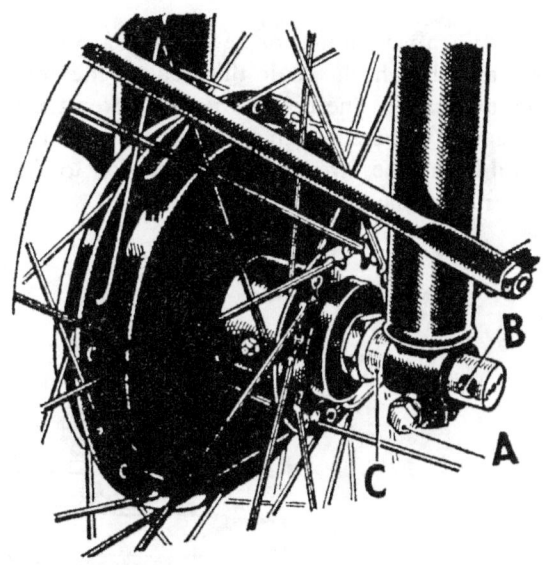

Fig. A31A. *Wheel removal.*

Dismantling and Reassembly of the Hub

This is fitted with ball journal bearings and therefore no adjustment is necessary or provided for. The only attention required is periodical grease gun lubrication.

If it becomes necessary to replace the bearings unscrew the nut retaining the brake anchor plate and remove the plate together with the brake mechanism.

Unscrew the cap (*A*) Fig. A32A, noting that this has a left-hand thread and therefore unscrews in a clockwise direction. Using a hide mallet from the brake drum side, drive out the hollow spindle (*B*) which will carry with it the nearside ballrace (*C*), dust cap (*D*), and distance piece (*E*).

Only the offside ballrace (*F*) now remains in the hub and this should be driven out with the aid of a soft drift.

B.S.A. Service Sheet No. 212A (contd.)

During reassembly ensure that the ballrace (*F*) is fully home and that the retaining collar (*A*) is quite tight.

Brake Relining

To remove the brake shoes lay the drum cover plate flat on a bench and lever the shoes upwards. They can then be drawn over, and free of the cam and fulcrum pin. If the cam pads show excessive wear the brake shoes should be renewed.

When the brake shoes are removed the linings can be replaced as described in Service Sheet 612.

When new linings or new shoes have been fitted, the brakes must be centralised after refitting the wheel. To do this, replace the brake cover plate, complete with shoes, fulcrum pin and cam in the brake drum. Slacken the fulcrum pin nut, and turn the cam so as to open the brake shoes in the normal manner. The fulcrum pin will then move in its slot until both shoes are pressing equally on to the drum. Tighten the fulcrum pin nut firmly and release the brake.

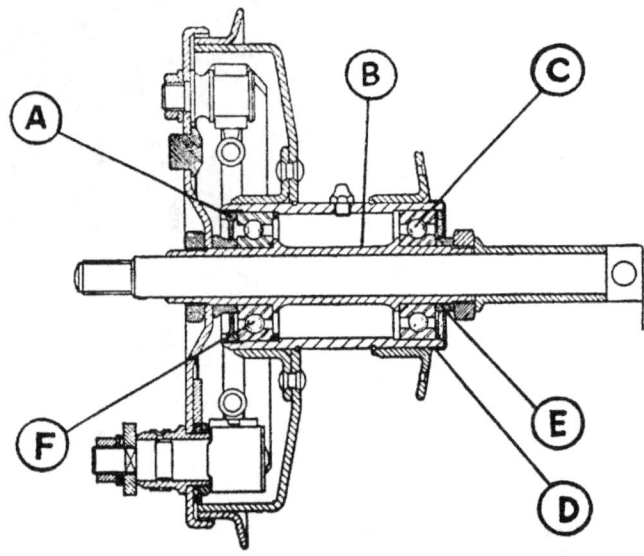

Fig. A32A. *Section of front hub (7 in. brake).*

B.S.A. MOTOR CYCLES LTD., Service Department, Armoury Road, Birmingham 11.
PRINTED IN ENGLAND—B.S.A. PRESS

BSA SERVICE SHEET No. 212B

"A", "B" AND "M" GROUP MODELS
ADJUSTMENT, DISMANTLING AND RE-ASSEMBLY OF FRONT HUB AND BRAKE (8 in. Brake)

Wheel Removal and Replacement

To detach the wheel, first disconnect the brake cable by pushing it out of the brake clip at (E) and unscrewing it from the bracket at (F). Remove the torque arm nut (C) and undo the pinch bolt (A). Insert a tommy bar in the hole in the head of the spindle at (B) and unscrew the spindle, noting that it has a left-hand thread and therefore unscrews in a clockwise direction. Support the wheel as the spindle is withdrawn, and when it is clear the wheel can be pulled away from the right-hand fork leg and removed from the machine.

After removal do not let the wheel fall on to the bush which projects from the brake drum side of the hub. Although the bush is pressed in, it may, if subjected to a sharp blow, be forced back into the hub. If this should happen the bush can be retrieved and re-positioned with the aid of the wheel spindle.

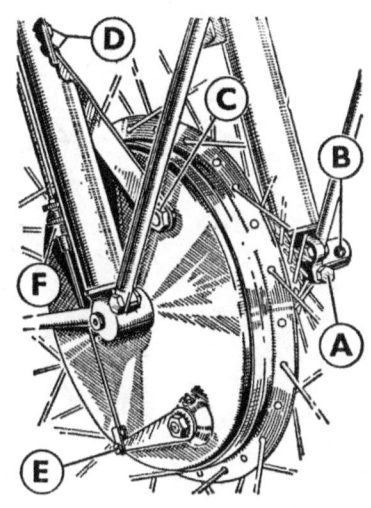

Fig. A31b. *Wheel Removal.*

The wheel is replaced in the reverse order to that for removal. It is most important that after the spindle has been tightened and before the pinch bolt is tightened, the forks are depressed once or twice to enable the left-hand fork end to position itself on the spindle shank. If this precaution is not observed, the fork leg may be clipped out of position and will not function correctly.

Dismantling and Reassembly of the Hub

Withdraw the brake plate which is a push-fit on the bush (B) Fig. A32b. Remove the locking split pins and unscrew the bearing retaining collars (C) and (D), which have normal right-hand threads. Replace the spindle and drive out the brake side ballrace (E) together with the bush (B) by striking the end of the spindle with a hide mallet. Only the ballrace (F) now remains in the hub and can be removed with a suitable soft drift.

Before replacing the bearing retaining collars ensure that the rubber oil seals in them are in good condition. The collars should be done up quite tight and if necessary fresh holes should be made for the locking split pins.

B.S.A. Service Sheet No. 212B (contd.)

Brake Relining

To remove the brake shoes lay the drum cover plate flat on a bench and lever the shoes upwards. They can then be drawn over, and free of the cam and fulcrum pin. If the cam pads show excessive wear the brake shoes should be renewed.

When the brake shoes are removed the linings can be replaced as described in Service Sheet No. 612.

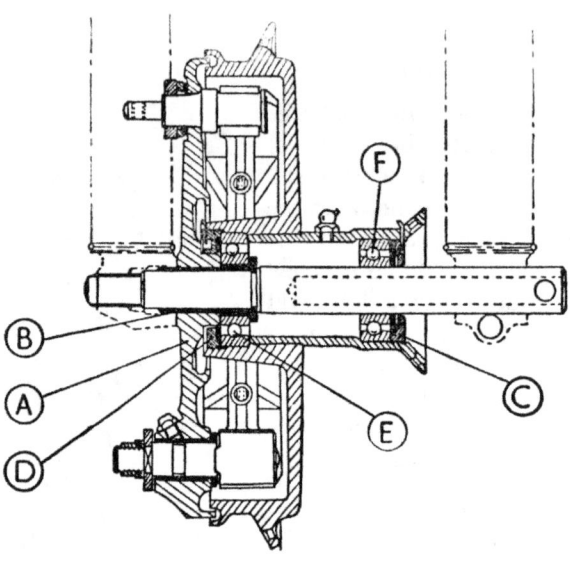

Fig. A32b. *Section of Front Hub (8 in. brake).*

B.S.A. MOTOR CYCLES LTD., Service Department, Armoury Road, Birmingham 11.
Printed in England
B.S.A. Press.

BSA SERVICE SHEET No. 212C

Reprinted December 1967

'A', 'B' AND 'M' GROUP MODELS
(with plunger-type rear suspension)

ADJUSTMENT, DISMANTLING AND RE-ASSEMBLY OF REAR HUB AND BRAKE

Rear Wheel Removal and Replacement

Remove the smaller outer nut (C) Fig. A31c, on the left-hand side of the rear wheel spindle, and withdraw the spindle (A) from the right-hand side of the machine.

The distance bush (B) will normally fall clear when the spindle is removed. The wheel should then be pulled towards the right-hand side of the machine until it is free from the spline engaging it with the brake drum. When the hub is free from the drum the wheel can be dropped out. To replace the wheel the operations are carried out in the reverse order. When detaching the rear wheel, it is quite unnecessary to touch the larger of the two hexagonal nuts on the left-hand side of the spindle.

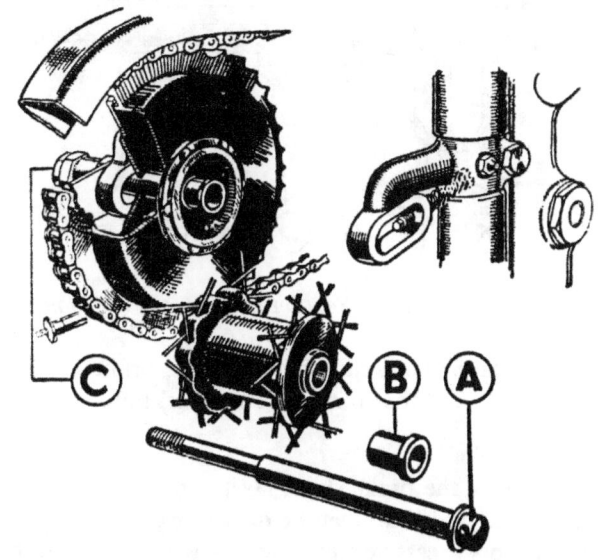

Fig. A31c. *Rear wheel removal (spring frame).*

Dismantling and Reassembly of the Rear Hub

The hub is fitted with two ballraces which are a light press-fit in the hub shell. Remove the dust cap (A) Fig. A32c. Unscrew and remove the two screwed rings (C) and (M). These rings are left-hand threaded, and therefore unscrew clockwise. Remove distance piece (F).

Place the wheel spindle through the hub from the offside. Using a hide mallet tap the head of the spindle so as to drive the offside ballrace toward the centre of the hub shell. By this means the brake drum side race will be driven out, after which the distance pieces (D) and (H) can be removed.

The only part now remaining in the shell will be the offside ballrace which can be driven out with a soft drift.

Removal and Dismantling of the Brake Drum

After removal of the rear wheel the brake drum is held in position in the wheel by nut (J) see Fig. A32c. To remove the drum disconnect the chain and rear brake rod, remove nut (J) and withdraw the drum.

With the brake drum removed from the frame, the brake drum cover plate, to which are attached the brake shoes, can be withdrawn, together with their fulcrum pin and operating arm.

B.S.A. Service Sheet No. 212C (contd.)

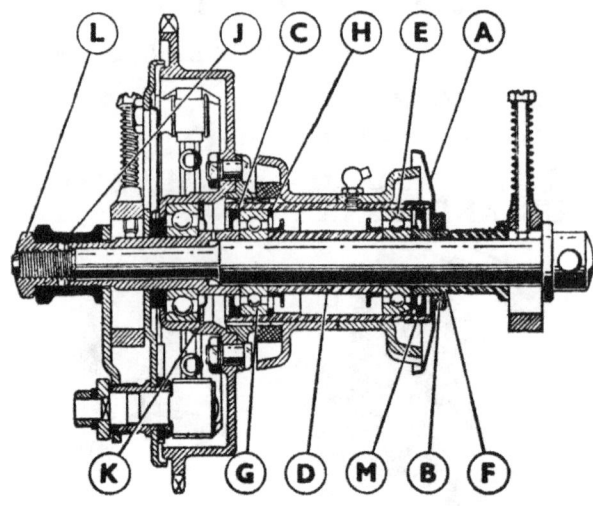

Fig. A32c. *Section through the rear hub.*

The brake drum ballrace is held in position in its housing by means of a spring circlip (*K*), which can be removed with the aid of a screwdriver. The replacement ballrace should be well greased before fitting the washer in place to prevent grease entering he brake drum.

If examination of the brake drum shows that the teeth have become worn and the braking surface scored, a new drum must be fitted. The drum must not be machined to produce a new braking surface. To do so is only a temporary cure and further attention would be required later. The spline bolted to the brake drum should be replaced if there is any play between it and the spline on the wheel hub.

Brake Relining
To remove the brake shoes lay the drum cover plate flat on a bench, and lever the shoes upwards. They can then be drawn over, and free of the cam and fulcrum pin. If the cam pads show excessive wear the brake shoes should be renewed. When the brake shoes are removed the linings can be replaced as described in Service Sheet No. 612.

Rear Chain Adjustment
Put the machine on its stand. The rear wheel must be at its lowest point in the suspension unit when the adjustment is made. Undo nut (*A*) Fig. A33c, several turns and slacken nut (*B*) just sufficient to allow the wheel to move.

Screw in the adjusters (*D*) to tighten the chain. There should be a total up and down movement of half an inch at the centre of the chain span. See that the wheel spindle is up against the adjusters and that the wheels are in line. Check the alignment by means of a taut piece of string, which should be equidistant from the front and rear of each wheel.

Tighten the large hexagon nut (*B*) very firmly, followed by the smaller nut (*A*). Re-adjust the rear brake.

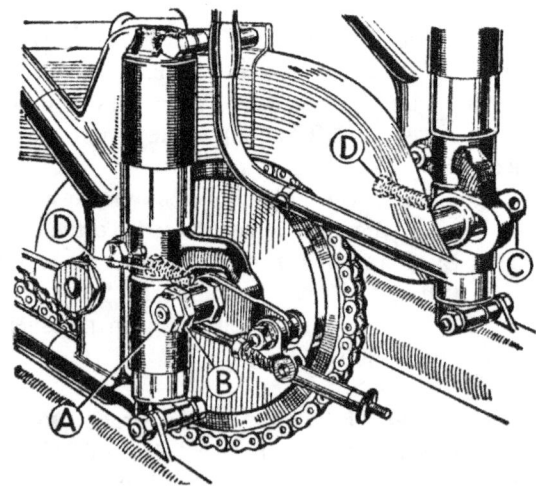

Fig. A33c. *Rear chain adjustment.*

B.S.A. MOTOR CYCLES LTD., Service Department, Armoury Road, Birmingham 11.
PRINTED IN ENGLAND — B.S.A. PRESS

BSA SERVICE SHEET No. 212D

"A" AND "B" GROUP MODELS
(with Welded Type Frame)

ADJUSTMENT, DISMANTLING AND RE-ASSEMBLY OF REAR HUB AND BRAKE

Wheel Removal

Removal of the wheel does not affect the chain or brake adjustment. Remove the spindle (B) Fig. A31d, it has a normal right-hand thread and therefore unscrews in an anticlockwise direction. The distance bush (E) falls clear when the spindle is removed and the wheel can then be pulled away from the brake drum and withdrawn from the machine.

When detaching the rear wheel it is quite unnecessary to touch the hexagon nut (A) on the left-hand side.

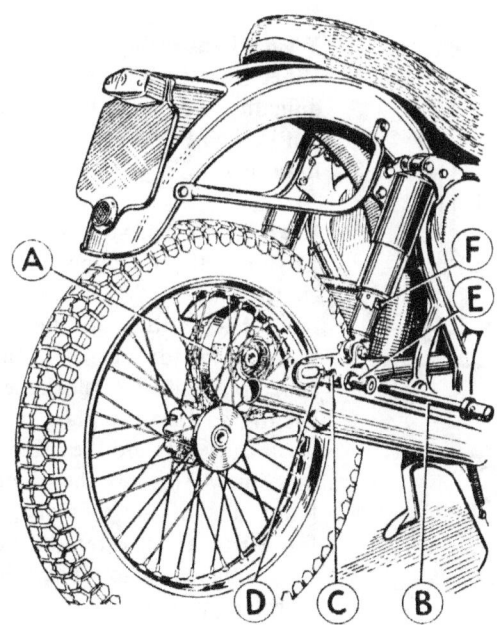

Fig. A31d. *Rear wheel removal.*

Hub Dismantling and Reassembly

The hub is fitted with two ballraces which are a light press-fit on the hollow spindle and in the hub shell. Remove the dust cap (A) Fig. A32d, and felt washer (B). Unscrew the ballrace retaining ring (C). This ring has a left-hand thread and therefore unscrews in a clockwise direction.

With the aid of a suitable soft drift applied to the brake drum end of the hollow spindle (D), drive out the spindle and ballrace (E). Then tap the spindle from the bearing, as the spindle comes away the distance bush (F) will be released. The only parts remaining in the hub are the ballrace (G) and the spacing washer (H), and these need not be disturbed unless the ballrace is suspected of being faulty. Wash it thoroughly in paraffin to remove all trace of grease when any play will be immediately detected. If it is decided to replace the race it can be driven from the hub shell with the aid of a soft drift. During reassembly ensure that this bearing is fully home and that the locking ring (C) is quite tight.

Removal and Dismantling of the Brake Drum

After removal of the rear wheel the brake drum is held in position by the nut (J) and by the nut securing the brake anchor strap. To remove the drum, first disconnect the rear chain and brake rod, then remove the nut (J) and the nut retaining the torque arm to the brake plate. The brake drum can then be pulled away from the brake plate and removed

B.S.A. Service Sheet No. 212D (contd.)

from the machine. Pivot the brake plate support strap on the cam lever boss so that the brake plate is free to be withdrawn from the fork leg.

To remove the brake shoes lay the brake plate on a bench (shoes uppermost) and lever the shoes upwards. They can then be drawn over and free of the cam and fulcrum pin. The operating cam and fulcrum pin should be inspected but it is unlikely that more than greasing will be necessary. If the cam pads on the brake shoes show excessive wear then new shoes should be fitted. To replace the shoes, attach the springs and push the shoes over the cam and pivot by reversing the dismantling procedure.

If examination of the brake drum shows that the teeth have become worn and the braking surface scored, a new drum must be fitted. The drum must not be machined to produce a new braking surface. To do so is only a temporary cure and further attention would be required later.

The brake drum ballrace, which is totally enclosed in the drum, should not normally require attention. The ballrace is held in position in its housing by a dished washer and a spring circlip (K), which can be removed with the aid of a screwdriver. The replacement ballrace should be well greased before fitting the dished washer which prevents the entry of grease into the brake drum.

Brake Shoe Relining

After removal of the brake shoes (see "Dismantling of Brake Drum") the old lining can be removed as described in Service Sheet No. 612.

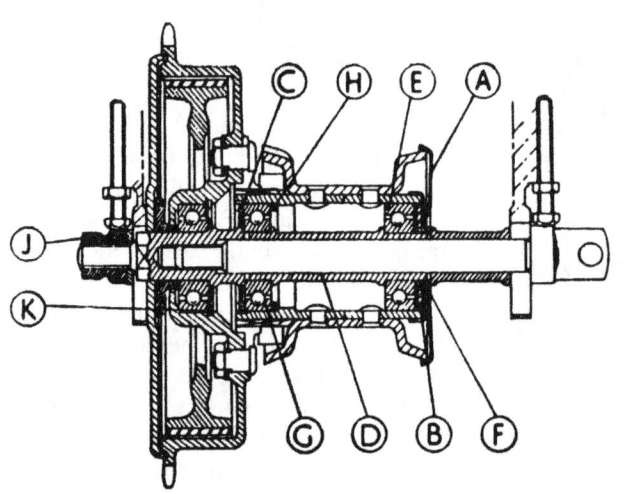

Fig. A32d. *Section through the rear hub.*

Wheel Reassembly

Wheel reassembly involves no difficulty and should be carried out in the reverse order to dismantling.

Rear Chain Adjustment

First put the machine on its centre stand. Whenever the rear wheel is adjusted, the nut securing the torque arm to the brake plate must be slackened slightly so that the plate may pivot freely. Undo the spindle (B) Fig. A31d, on the right-hand side of the machine, a few turns, and slacken nut (A) just sufficiently to allow the wheel to move.

Slacken the locknuts (C) and screw out the adjusters (D) to tighten the chain. With the wheel in its lowest position there should be a total up and down movement of 1¼ in. in the centre of the chain at its tightest point. Ensure that the wheel spindle is against the adjusters and that the wheels are in line. Check the alignment by means of a taut piece of string which should be equidistant from the front and rear of each wheel.

Tighten the nut (A), the spindle (B) and the nut securing the torque arm to the brake plate. Re-check the chain adjustment and the wheel alignment.

B.S.A. MOTOR CYCLES LTD., Service Department, Armoury Road, Birmingham 11.

BSA SERVICE SHEET No. 212E

"A" and "B" Group Models
(with Full Width Hubs)

ADJUSTMENT, DISMANTLING AND RE-ASSEMBLY OF HUBS AND BRAKES

FRONT WHEEL REMOVAL AND REPLACEMENT

To remove the wheel, place the machine on both front and centre stands, take out the two bolts securing the brake anchor strap to the fork leg, and unscrew the large nut from the right-hand side of the wheel spindle. Disconnect the brake cable completely from the brake plate. If sufficient slack cannot be obtained by screwing down the cable adjuster, the outer casing may be released from its holder at the handlebar end.

Next, slacken the pinch bolt in the left-hand fork leg and draw out the spindle by inserting a tommy bar in the hole provided, and using a pulling and twisting motion. At the same time support the weight of the wheel to avoid damaging the bush which projects through the brake plate and partly enters the right-hand fork leg. Should this bush be pushed inadvertently back inside the hub, it can be re-positioned by inserting the wheel spindle from the left-hand side.

There is no distance piece fitted outside the hub, location being maintained by means of a shoulder formed on the spindle meeting the bush already referred to. Once the spindle has been removed, the wheel can be pulled away from the right-hand fork leg and withdrawn.

Refitting is carried out by reversing the procedure for removal, except that tightening the pinch bolt must be left until the machine has been taken off the stands. The forks should then be fully depressed and released several times to ensure that the left-hand leg takes up the correct position on the wheel spindle. The inner edge of the tommy bar hole should be approximately level with the outer face of the fork leg. Finally, tighten the pinch bolt and check the tightness of all other bolts and nuts which have been disturbed.

FRONT WHEEL REMOVAL AND REPLACEMENT (models with Frame prefix letters FA or FB)

To remove the wheel, place the machine on the stand, disconnect the brake cable by removing the split pin and clevis pin on the brake arm. Unscrew the four bolts holding the fork end caps when the wheel will then drop to the ground. Note that there is a register at each end of the spindle to clear the bolts, these also serve to locate the wheel in the forks.

REFITTING

This is simply the reverse of the above procedure but care must be taken to locate the lug on the right-hand leg in the groove on the brake cover plate.

Do not omit the split pin when re-connecting the brake cable.

B.S.A. Service Sheet No. 212E (contd.)

REAR WHEEL REMOVAL AND REPLACEMENT

Place the machine on the centre stand, and remove the right-hand silencer. Unscrew the four nuts securing the sprocket to the hub. Where the rear chain is totally enclosed, access to these nuts is gained by removing the rearmost of the two rubber plugs in the chaincase. Disconnect the brake cable completely from the brake plate. It may be necessary to disengage the ferrule of the outer casing from the frame lug, in order to obtain enough slack in the inner cable. Take off the brake anchor strap by removing the nut holding it to the brake plate, and loosening the bolt fixing the forward end to the swinging arm fork.

Next, unscrew and take out the wheel spindle from the right-hand side, and extract the distance piece. The large nut on the left-hand fork end should not be disturbed as this holds the fixed spindle of the sprocket which remains in position. The wheel can now be pulled away from the sprocket. By standing on the left-hand side of the machine and tilting it in that direction, the wheel can be taken out. If the rear part of the wheel is brought clear of the mudguard first, this is a simple operation.

The wheel is replaced by reversing the order of the instructions given for removal. Make sure that the four sprocket retaining nuts are fully and evenly tightened, and that the washer beneath the head of the wheel spindle has not been omitted.

REAR CHAIN ADJUSTMENT

The chain must be adjusted while the machine is on the centre stand, with the swinging arm fork at the lower limit of its travel. When a chaincase is fitted, access to the chain is gained by removing the foremost of the two rubber plugs. Rotate the wheel several times to find the position in which the chain is tightest. The total up and down movement in the centre of the top run should be 1¼ in. If the setting varies appreciably from this, the chain should be re-adjusted as follows:—

Slacken the wheel spindle and the fixed spindle nut. Release the two locknuts and screw the adjusting screws in or out as required. Take care that both are turned an equal amount to avoid putting the wheel out of line.

When the tension is correct, secure the locknuts, press the wheel forward in the fork ends and tighten, first the fixed spindle nut and finally the wheel spindle.

B.S.A. Service Sheet No. 212E (contd.)

WHEEL ALIGNMENT

It is advisable to check the alignement of the wheels periodically, particularly after the chain, has been adjusted. A long straight-edge is placed alongside and close to, the two wheels and supported as high up from the ground as possible. The distances from the straight-edge to the rims, measured at the front and rear of each wheel, should all be equal.

Tyres are unreliable guides in checking wheel alignment, since tyres of different section will give the appearance of error when, in fact, everything is in order.

BRAKE ADJUSTMENT

A fulcrum type adjuster is provided on each brake (except those models with engine prefix letters FA or FB, where adjustment is carried out by screwing in or out, as required, the finger adjusters on the brake cables), in addition to the usual cable adjuster. The adjusting pin should be turned in a clockwise direction until it will turn no further, then slackened off until the wheel rotates freely. The adjusters have a click action, each click representing one-twelfth of a turn.

The brake shoes must not be allowed to bind even slightly, as this may generate sufficient heat to distort the drum, or cause the grease to melt and impregnate the linings.

BRAKE SHOE RECONDITIONING

After the brake plate has been taken from the hub, the adjusting pin should be slackened right off, and the plate laid flat with the shoes uppermost. They can then be levered up at right angles to the plate, pivoting on their ends, until the tension of the springs has been relieved.

Should new linings be required, full instructions for fitting are contained in Service Sheet No. 216

SPROCKET ASSEMBLY—REMOVING AND DISMANTLING

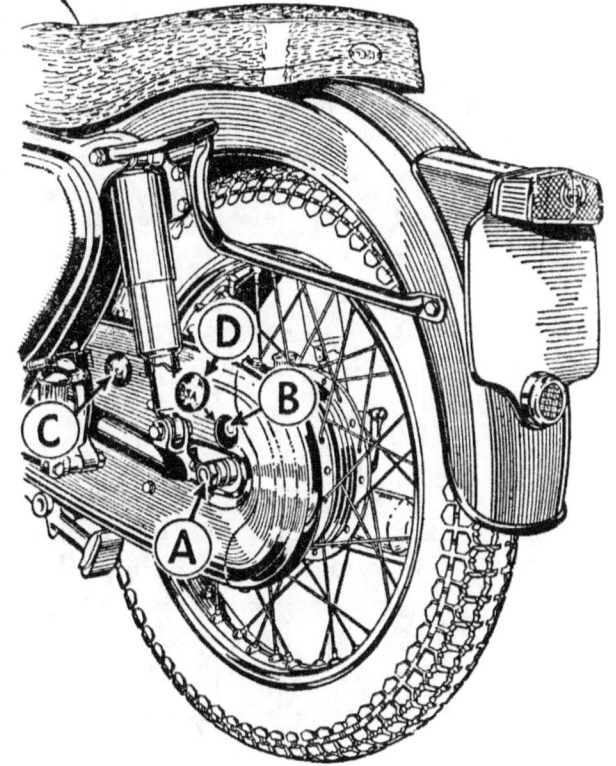

Before the sprocket assembly can be removed, the chaincase must first be taken off. The rear section is held by two hexagon-headed set screws, while the top and bottom sections are secured by two bolts in each, passing through lugs on the swinging arm fork. The large nut on the fixed spindle must also be loosened.

If a chainguard instead of a chaincase is fitted, the four bolts holding it to the swinging arm fork can be taken out to allow the guard to be raised sufficiently to clear the sprocket.

After parting the chain at the spring link, the large nut on the end of the fixed spindle is screwed off. The sprocket can then be dismounted and the spindle tapped out. The bearing and the grease retainer are pressed in, and may be driven out with a suitable drift.

When reassembling note that there should be a large washer between the sprocket and the fork end, and also a smaller washer between the fork end and the fixed spindle nut.

B.S.A. Service Sheet No. 212E (contd.)

HUB DISMANTLING AND REASSEMBLY

The front hub contains two ball journal bearings which require no adjustment. They are secured by locking rings on the outside, and are located by circlips in the hub shell on the inside. Both locking rings have a right-hand thread, the one on the brake drum side being split-pinned to the hub for additional security. A special peg spanner (part number 61-3542), is used to unscrew the locking rings, which incorporate felt grease seals. Early models had separate seals and steel retainers, the concave sides of which should face the bearings. The bearings themselves are pressed into the hub shell, and can be tapped out with a soft metal drift, taking care not to damage the circlips.

When reassembling, make sure that the circlips are properly seated in their grooves before refitting the bearings. Do not omit the bush from the right-hand bearing, as this has a shoulder on the inner end and cannot be replaced from outside the hub. Note that the locking rings have different sized centre holes, the larger being for the right-hand side.

The rear hub carries only one bearing, on the right-hand side, which is held by a locking ring and split pin in exactly the same way as already described for the front hub. It is removed and replaced in a similar manner.

On the left-hand side is a pressed in grease retainer. There is also a loose distance piece inside the hub.

If the bearing locking rings have been renewed it will be necessary to drill fresh split pin holes.

The other rear wheel bearing is housed in the sprocket itself. All four bearings are identical, the part number being 89-3022. No grease nipples are provided on these hubs; the bearings are packed with grease during assembly and they should be re-packed at intervals of 10,000 to 15,000 miles.

The brake cam spindle housings have grease nipples, but these should be used sparingly to avoid forcing grease into the brakes.

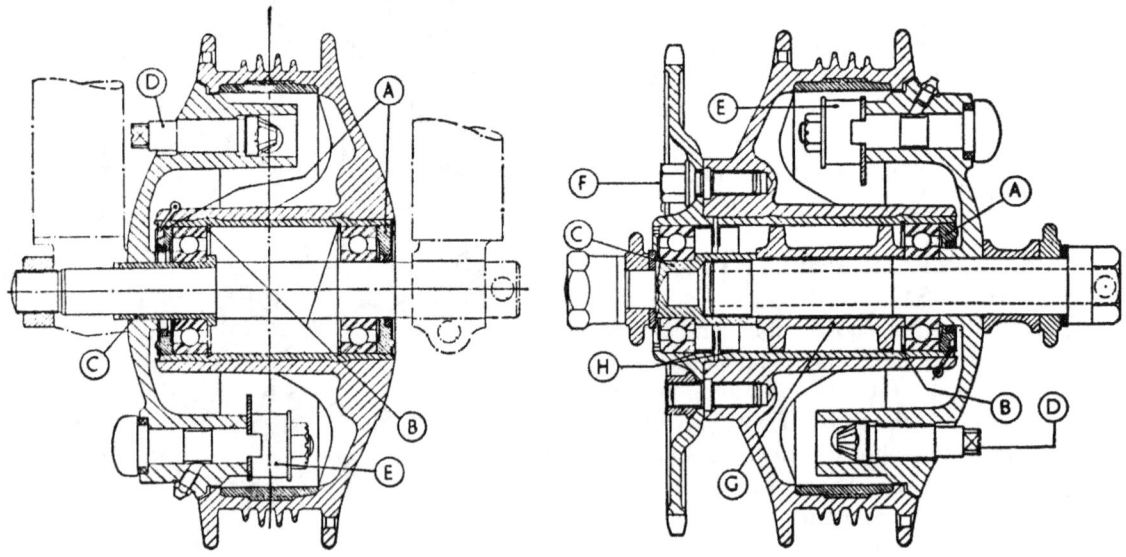

B.S.A. Service Sheet No. 212E (contd.)

HUB DISMANTLING AND REASSEMBLY (models with engine prefix letter FA or FB)

The front hub has two bearings part number 42–5819, the right-hand side can be driven out from the left-hand side using the spindle as a drift, after the brake cover plate and bearing lock-ring have been removed.

To remove the left-hand side bearing, take out the circlip and dust cover and drive out the bearing from the right-hand side using the spindle reversed.

When replacing the bearings do not omit the ring behind the bearing on the right-hand side.

REAR HUB

The rear hub is similar to the earlier type except that there is only one grease retainer on the sprocket side (bearing number 89–3022) and the right-hand bearing is part number 42–5819, no split pin being used to secure the lock-ring.

There is a smaller grease retainer midway along the centre distance tube.

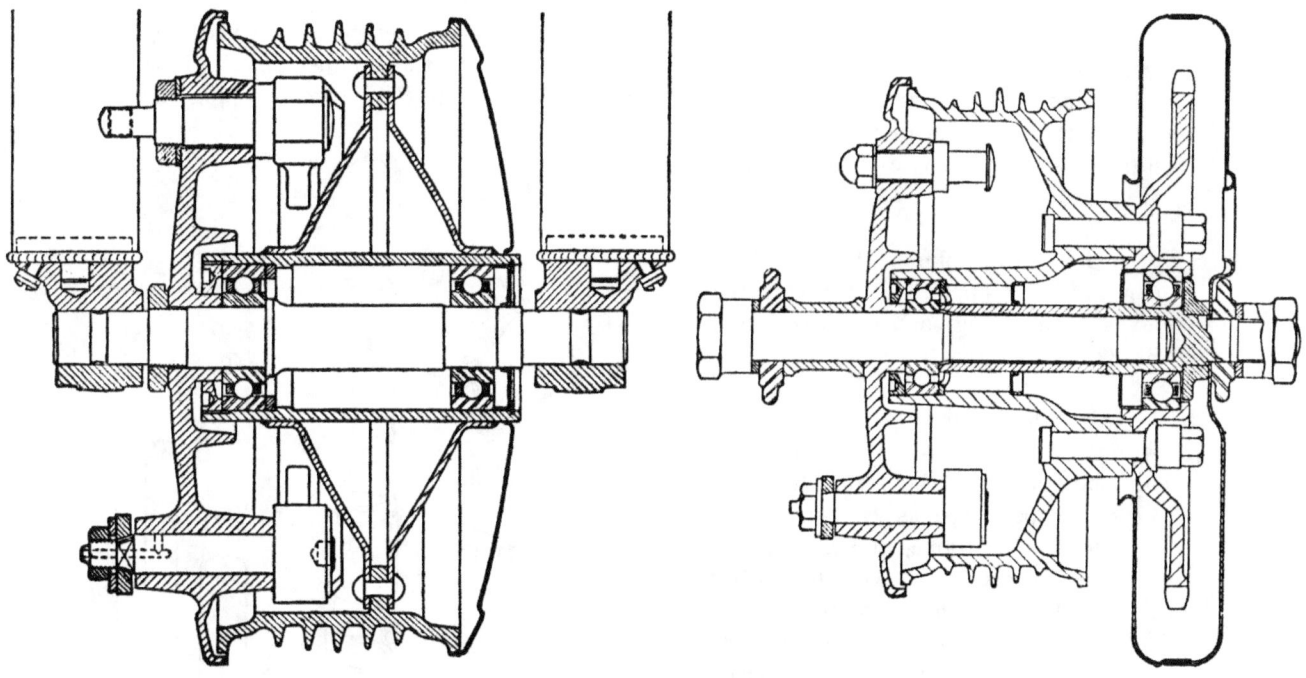

B.S.A. MOTOR CYCLES LTD., Service Department, Armoury Road, Birmingham 11.

B.S.A. PRESS

BSA SERVICE SHEET No. 213

"A," "B" and "M" Group Models

March 1950.
Reprinted Sept. 1961.

THE SPRING FRAME

The B.S.A. rear suspension is entirely automatic, and no adjustment is required or provided for. The only maintenance necessary is lubrication by grease gun every thousand miles.

TO DISMANTLE.
First remove the rear wheel (see Service Sheet No. 212A), detach the silencers by removing the nuts (A), Fig. A35, and slacken the clip bolts to the exhaust pipes. Take off the nuts (B), spring washers (C) and remove the pinch bolts (D). Remove plug (E) and in the space vacated, screw in the formed end of Service Tool 61-3222 (Fig. A36).

The centre column (F) Fig. A35, can now be tapped out through the lower frame lug and Service Tool 61-3222 withdrawn.

Grip the top and bottom suspension shrouds (G) and press the bottom shroud up and out from the frame lugs. A kick is experienced as the suspension unit leaves the frame, and a firm grip on the shrouds is necessary to control the springs. When the bottom of the column is clear the whole unit can be removed from the frame, and placed on the bench for complete dismantling. The inner and outer shrouds, springs (J), washers (K), if fitted, and locating pieces (L) may be withdrawn, carefully noting their respective positions for subsequent reassembly.

The wheel spindle brackets (M) together with the bearing sleeves (N), to which they are attached, form the spring plunger, and can be separated from the sleeves when the pinch bolts (O) are withdrawn. Note that each

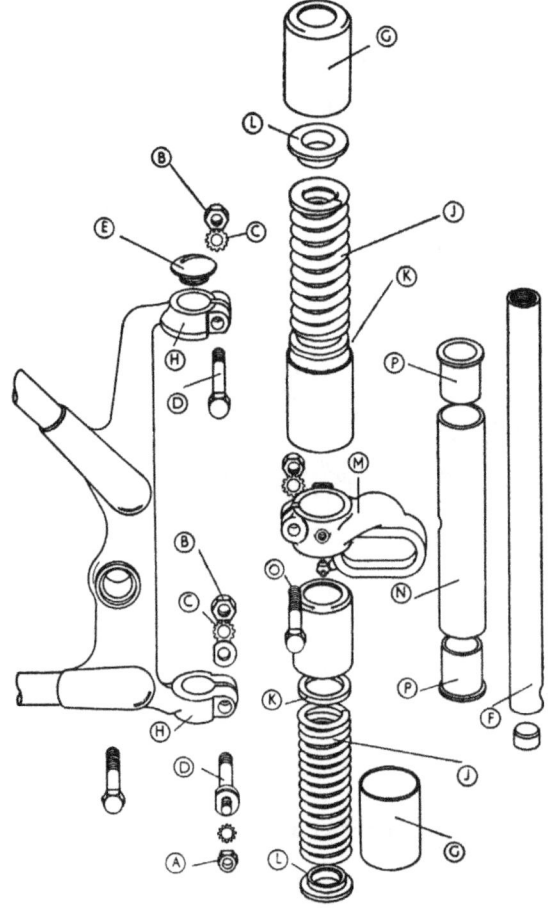

FIG A35 THE SUSPENSION COLUMN (EXPLODED VIEW)

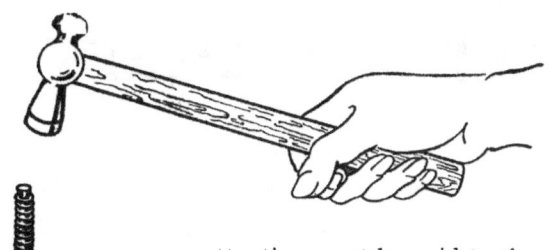

pinch bolt engages in a notch in the bearing sleeve, and also that the bottom bolts (D) similarly engage in notches in the centre column. Particular attention must be paid to the correct alignment of these notches on reassembly.

REASSEMBLY.

Reassemble all units of the suspension column, except the centre column (F) in the same order in which they were dismantled. Pass Service Tool 61–3222 through the assembly and position the top and bottom slotted plates (Fig. A37). Pass the distance piece down the shaft of the tool on to the top plate, and screw up the nut, at the same time supporting the two plates so that they do not come out of position. The nut must be screwed down until the column with the tool in position can be passed up through the top lug of the frame and the bottom of the tool dropped vertically into the bottom lug.

Now unscrew the nut until the top and bottom slotted plates are in contact with the frame lugs. Pass a tommy bar through the holes in the plates and withdraw them. As the plates come away the column will spring into position.

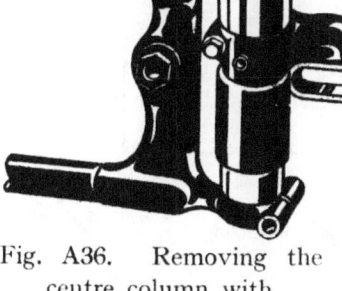

Fig. A36. Removing the centre column with Service Tool 61–3222.

Withdraw Service Tool 61–3222 from the top to ensure alignment of the suspension unit with the frame lugs.

Replace the centre column in the reverse order to that for dismantling. Refit and tighten the pinch bolts.

Replace the cap (C) and the silencers.

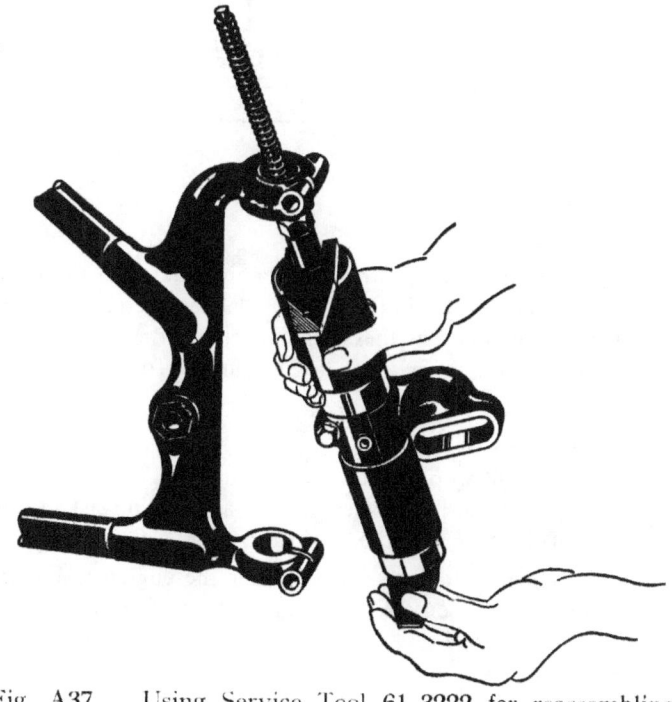

Fig. A37. Using Service Tool 61–3222 for reassembling.

B.S.A. MOTOR CYCLES LTD., Service Dept., Waverley Works, Birmingham, 10.

BSA SERVICE SHEET No. 214

"A" GROUP MODELS
(with Swinging Arm type Frame, except models A50 and A65)

ENGINE REMOVAL AND COMPLETE DISMANTLING

The dismantling procedure will be described from the point reached in Service Sheet No. 204, when the cylinder head and barrel have been removed.

Before commencing to dismantle the engine it will be advantageous to construct a fixture such as that illustrated in Fig. A38.

Drain the oil tank and disconnect the oil pipes. Detach the dynamo leads and the stop button lead from the magneto end cap.

Remove the primary chaincase as described in Service Sheet No. 310 on "Primary Transmission".

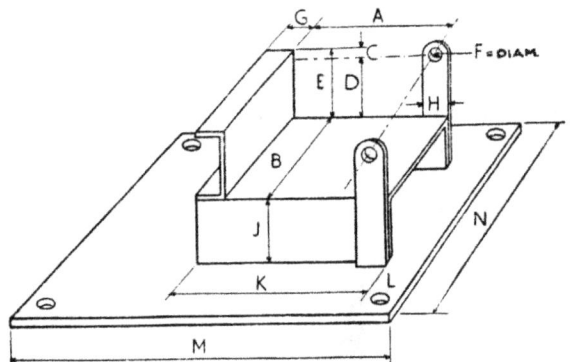

	Inches	mm
A	$4\frac{3}{4}$–5	120–125
B	$3\frac{1}{2}$	85–90
C	$\frac{3}{8}$	9
D	$1\frac{5}{8}$	41
E	2	50
F	$\frac{7}{16}$ dia.	11.5 ⌀
G	1	25
H	$\frac{3}{4}$	20
J	2	50
K	$6\frac{1}{4}$–$6\frac{1}{2}$	155–160
L	1	25
M	12	300
N	8	200

Fig. A38. *Engine Bench Fixture.*

Engine Removal
Remove the studs securing the engine plates to the crankcase, and the studs holding the front engine plates in the frame. Slacken the gearbox bolts and the lower front stud of the rear engine plate as these tend to clamp the rear engine plates on to the crankcase. The engine is now ready to be lifted from the frame.

Dismantling the Engine
Set the engine up in the bench fixture and undo the twelve timing cover securing screws, noting that the four lowest screws are the longest in the set and the three at the dynamo end of the cover are the shortest.

A pan should be placed under the engine to collect the oil which will fall from the timing chest when the cover is removed.

B.S.A. Service Sheet No. 214 (contd.)

Remove the dynamo securing strap and turn the dynamo in its housing until the chain is slack enough to permit it to be removed from the smaller sprocket. The dynamo can then be removed complete with its sprocket. To remove the larger sprocket, undo the retaining nut after prising back the lockwasher, then with the aid of a soft drift give a light tap on the side of the sprocket. This should free it, but if it does not do so then engine should be rotated slightly so that the punch is applied to another point on the sprocket. This should be repeated until the sprocket is jarred free from its taper.

Fig. A39. *Timing Pinion Extractor. number 61-3676.*

Undo the four retaining screws and withdraw the inner timing cover to expose the timing gears. The crankcase breather will probably come away with the inner timing cover, but care should be taken that the thick cork washer which separates it from the camshaft gear is not damaged.

The magneto advance and retard mechanism may now be removed by undoing its central securing nut. The mechanism is self-extracting and as the nut is unscrewed the gear will be pulled from its taper.

The camshaft pinion is keyed on and is retained by a nut and lockwasher. Prise back the tab of the washer and remove the nut. With the aid of Service Tool number 61-3256, draw the pinion off the shaft taking care not to lose the locating key.

The idler pinion with its shaft can now be pulled free with the fingers.

Remove the three securing nuts and washers holding the oil pump in position. Bend back the lockwasher and undo the locknut from the end of the mainshaft, noting that it has a right-hand thread. Remove the washer, then free the hexagon headed worm gear, which also has a left-hand thread. Withdraw the oil pump gradually from the studs and at the same time unscrew the worm gear from the mainshaft. It may be advantageous to remove the oil pump studs to prevent them being bent.

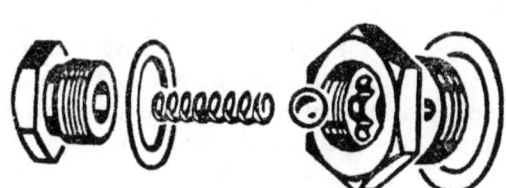

Fig. A40. *The Oil Pressure Release Valve.*

The oil pump should not be dismantled unless it is known to be faulty. If the worm shaft is worn it may be removed by simply removing the circlip and end pad.

B.S.A. Service Sheet No. 214 (contd.)

The timing gear which is keyed to the crankshaft may now be extracted with the aid of Service Tool number 61-3676, as shown in Fig. A39. Do not lose the mild steel washer which lies between the timing gear and the worm gear.

Remove the oil pressure release valve from the crankcase to clean and check it (see Service Sheet No. 202).

Three studs, the one underneath having a long nut, secure the magneto to the crankcase. After the nuts have been removed, the magneto can be pulled from its housing.

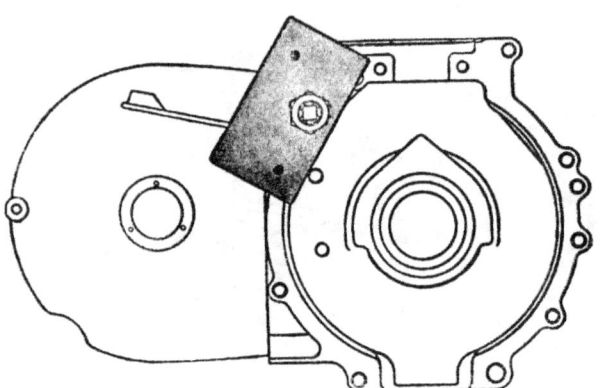

Fig. A41. *Withdrawing Blind Camshaft Bush (Service Tool number 61-3159).*

Remove the sump plate and withdraw the crankcase filter but do not attempt to withdraw the oil return pipe. The four studs should be left in position to protect the projecting part of the pipe.

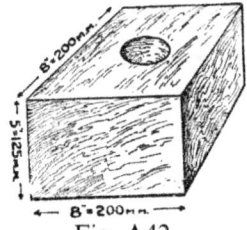

Fig. A42.

Remove the engine from the bench fixture and place it on a wooden block, simiar to that illustrated in Fig. A42, drive-side downwards. If the crankshaft splined sleeve has not already been removed it should be withdrawn from the shaft. After all the crankcase securing bolts have been removed, separate the crankcase halves by gently tapping the front and rear of the cases with a soft mallet. With the crankcase halves parted, the complete crankshaft and con-rod assembly can be detached and laid aside.

Prise the oil seal out of the drive-side crankcase. The drive-side roller-race and the gearside white metal bearing can then be pressed from their respective halves to the inside if they are in need of attention. It is advisable to warm the crankcase halves in a degreasing plant, or hot water, before attempting to remove the bearings.

Service Tool number 61-3159 will withdraw the blind camshaft bush from the drive-side crankcase (see Fig. A41).

The tappets are carried in the cylinder block and will not normally require attention. To remove them, undo the two setscrews (A) Fig. A43, and withdraw the inlet tappets (B). Remove the setscrew (C) and the steel ball which it retains. The locating pin between the two exhaust tappets can then be pushed out from the inside of the barrel and the tappets withdrawn. The inlet and exhaust tappets are not interchangeable.

B.S.A. Service Sheet No. 214 (contd.)

Withdraw the split pins and unscrew the big-end cap retaining nuts. The con-rod can then be pulled away from the crankshaft. Mark the con-rods and bearings, etc., to ensure that they are replaced in the same position and the same way round.

The flywheel is bolted to the crankshaft and need only be disturbed if a new crankshaft has to be fitted. The plugs at each end of the crankshaft should be removed and the internal oilways cleared of sludge. The inner race of the drive-side bearing should not be removed unless a replacement is required, as it may be damaged during removal. Take careful note of the shims fitted behind the bearing and ensure that they are not omitted during reassembly.

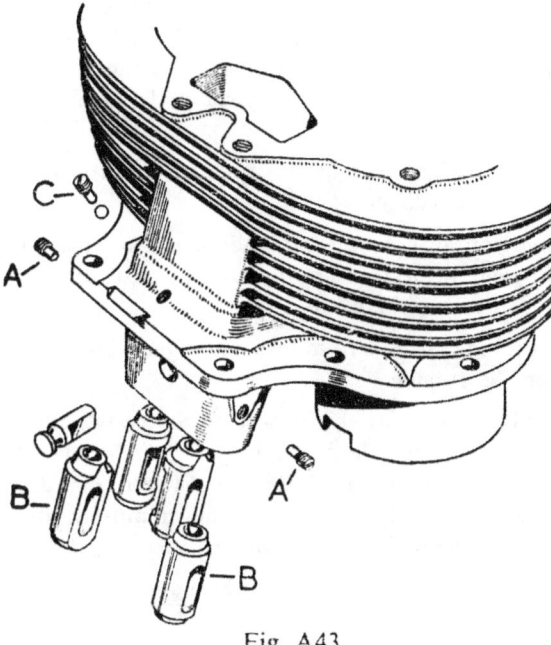

Fig. A43.

Dimensions for regrinding the crankpins, as given in Service Sheet no. 207, must be rigidly adhered to, as the bearing liners are manufactured to match these dimensions.

The return pipe from the sump is cemented into the case and should only be disturbed if it is damaged. This also applies to the non-return ball valve which is retained by a small grub screw near to the crankshaft main bearing. Check that the internal oilways are clear and if necessary flush out with petrol.

B.S.A. MOTOR CYCLES LTD., Service Department, Armoury Road, Birmingham 11

Printed in England

B.S.A. Press

BSA SERVICE SHEET No. 215

October 1948
Revised August, 1956

A GROUP MODELS
(with Swinging Arm Type Frame)
REASSEMBLY OF THE ENGINE

The need for cleanliness cannot be over emphasized; all parts should be clean and free from dirt or rust. Smear all bearing surfaces with clean engine oil during reassembly.

If the crankshaft has been replaced, the original flywheel, if serviceable, may be retained and fitted by passing it over the drive side of the crankshaft and bolting to the flange by six high tensile steel bolts. After securely tightening the bolts, they should be peined over on to the nuts to lock them.

The flywheel is positioned with the counter-weight part at the opposite side to the big end journals (see Service Sheet number 712X for balancing).

Heat the crankcase halves in a degreasing plant or hot water, then by means of an arbour press insert the bearings and bushes into their respective housings. The cases must be suitably supported during these operations to prevent damage.

Press the two camshaft bushes into the timing case, one from inside and one from outside and the idler pinion spindle bush also from the outside.

If a new camshaft or idler pinion bushes have been fitted it is now necessary to bolt the crankcase together and attach the inner cover, then with the aid of jig, part number 61-3281 use reamer 61-3167 to ream the bushes to .7495 to .7485 in. internal diameter (Fig. A42) This reaming jig should also be used to guide the mainshaft reamer if a new mainshaft bush has been fitted (see Service Sheet number 711 for details of this reamer).

Then unbolt the crankcase and detach the inner timing cover. Remove all traces of swarf left from the reaming operation.

At this point it is advisable to obtain a fixture such as shown in Fig. A38, Service Sheet number 214, and a wooden block with a hole through the centre as shown in Fig. A40.

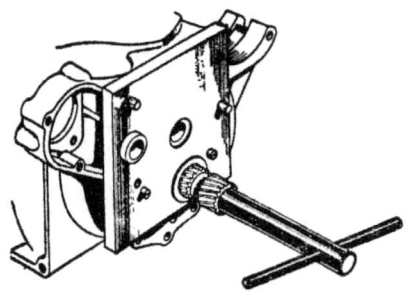

Fig. A42. Reaming Jig

The big end bearing liners should now be placed in the endcaps and connecting rods, Note that these can only be put in the correct way, because the liners are lipped, but they must, of course, be replaced in their original positions.

When fitting new liners, it will be noticed that each half has a small central drill hole. Originally, only one drilled liner was used. The left-hand con-rod has a bleed hole to supplement the lubrication of the cylinder bore. This should be positioned so that the hole faces the flywheel.

B.S.A. Service Sheet No. 215 (contd.)

No scraping is necessary with these big-end liners, and it must not be attempted or damage will result.

Connect each rod and cap to its crank journal, making sure that their marks correspond, and insert the big-end bolts and tighten them. On no account must the castellated nuts be slackened off to allow the insertion of the split pins. If one of the slots on the nut does not line up with the hole in the pin when the nut has been fully tightened, the latter must be removed and filed on its flat face until the hole and the slot coincide. A torque spanner set at $8\frac{1}{2}$ lbs. ft. should be used for tightening these nuts to ensure that they are not over-tightened.

Note:—On and after the following engine numbers, the torque spanner setting must be 22 lbs.

BA10-13830   CA10-7998   CA10R-2006   CA7-2686   CA7SS-2256

The maximum crankshaft end float should be .003 in. and this is controlled by the shims between the inner race of the drive side roller bearings and the crankshaft web.

If the original crankshaft is to be replaced, then it is merely necessary to ensure that the original shims are used. Where a new crankshaft is fitted it should be assembled into the crankcase and the two halves bolted tightly together to enable the end float to be checked. The shims should then be regulated to ensure that the end float is correct.

Place the crankshaft assembly on a thick wooden block through which a hole large enough to take the gear side mainshaft has been bored. Then place the drive side crankcase half over the drive shaft and push into position, making sure that the bearing enters the race squarely and goes right home.

Reverse the whole assembly on the block, and then insert the camshaft into the blind phosphor bronze bush in the drive side crankcase half. Smear both joint faces of the crankcase with jointing compound, and after it has become tacky, place the gear side crankcase in position and bolt the crankcases together, making sure that each nut has a shakeproof washer.

When the cases are bolted securely together, the camshaft and crankshaft must rotate freely; otherwise the case alignment is incorrect.

Attach the sump plate filter and its paper washer, making sure that the pump suction pipe from the inside of the crankcase passes freely through the hole in the filter gauze. Replace the oil release valve unit after assembly, as shown in Fig. A43.

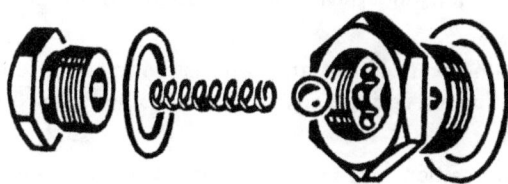

Fig. A43.

The dynamo securing straps and timing side front engine plate, if previously removed, should now be attached to the gear side case. The left-hand engine plate was removed when the engine was taken from the frame, and will be replaced when the engine is being rebuilt into the frame cradle.

The keyed timing pinion should be pushed on to the crankshaft, concave side to crankcase, followed by the mild steel plain washer. Before mounting the pump, replace the thick washer so that the holes match, and the round fibre washer on the third stud. Slide the pump and the driving worm on together, turning the worm anti-clockwise. The driving worm is left-hand threaded and care must be taken to avoid damage to the worm gears during assembly.

B.S.A. Service Sheet No. 215 (contd.)

The driving worm is secured by a keyed washer and a left-hand nut, the outside edge of the washer being subsequently turned over on to the nut to form a locking device.

Place a screwdriver inside the engine against one of the cams and the inside top crankcase lug, to prevent the camshaft from sliding inwards and so disturbing the key when putting the cam pinion on the shaft. Now, holding the screwdriver, the cam pinion may be inserted, with the breather actuating stud outwards, on to the keyed end of the camshaft, and secured by its locknut and special locking washer, the tabs of which must be turned down on to the nut after tightening.

Check to see that the camshaft key has not become dislodged from the pinion.

Rotate the crankshaft until the dot on the timing or crankshaft pinion is upwards, and insert the idler pinion so that the dot on the crankshaft pinion meshes with the dot on the idler pinion and the dash mark on the camshaft pinion meshes with the corresponding dash mark on the idler pinion (Fig. A44).

Fig. A44. Valve Timing.

The magneto should now be fixed in position by its three securing nuts, the two short nuts on top and the long nut underneath the magneto, with a paper washer between the magneto and crankcase.

Timing of the magneto is carried out at a later stage in the assembly, and the magneto drive pinion with its automatic ignition advance device should now be only loosely attached to the magneto spindle.

Place the dynamo in position in its securing carrier on the front of the engine without tightening the securing strap. Smear the inner joint face of the inner timing cover with jointing compound, and place its paper joint washer in position so that it is held by the jointing compound.

The crankcase breather should now be placed on the cam pinion, with the cork washer between the pinion and breather. Smear the breather with engine oil, and place the inner cover in position, securing with the screws. Check end float on the breather and correct if necessary by fitting a thicker cork washer to eliminate any play.

Now fit the pistons to the connecting rods, making sure by the marks previously scribed on the inside of each piston, if they are the original ones that they are in the correct positions. The split portion of the skirt should face towards the front.

Replace the tappets in the reverse order to that for dismantling (see Service Sheet number 206).

B.S.A. Service Sheet No. 215 (contd.)

Place the paper cylinder base washer in position on the top of the crankcase, and **rotate** the engine to bring the connecting rods to top dead centre. Turn the piston rings so that the gaps, which should be .011 to .013 in., are not in line with each other. Smear the pistons with engine oil.

Place two thin wooden strips across the mouth of the crankcase so that they support the front and rear of the piston skirts. Compress the piston rings with the aid of two slipper rings, part number 61-3334 (A7) or 61-3262 (A10), noting that the bevelled edge of the slipper should be at the bottom (see Fig. A45). Now lower the cylinder barrel over the pistons until the full length of the pistons is in the cylinder bore. Raise the barrel and pistons to permit the wooden strips and piston ring slippers to be removed. The block can then be lowered into position on the crankcase and secured with the holding down nuts and shakeproof washers.

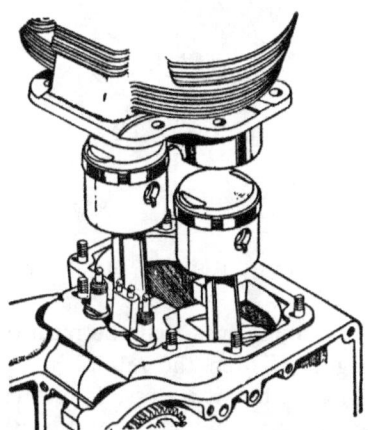

Fig. A45. Replacing the Cylinder Block.

Replace the four push rods through the tunnel on to their tappets. The two long rods are the inner ones and the two short rods the outer ones.

The magneto should now be timed. To do this, see Service Sheet number 203.

Place the chain on the dynamo driven sprocket and the dynamo driving sprocket, which should now be inserted on to the shaft, the concave side of the sprocket inwards, a cork washer being placed between the sprocket and the inner timing cover. Fit the nut and a plain washer, turning the edge of the washer on to the nut to lock it after securely tightening.

Adjust the dynamo chain by rotating the dynamo in its cradle to give approximately $\frac{1}{8}$ in. to $\frac{3}{16}$ in. up and down play on the chain, but not sufficient to foul the inner case retaining screw boss in the centre of the cover, near which the chain passes. Then tighten up the dynamo in its cradle. The dynamo will tend to rotate as the strap is tightened and the adjustment must be checked when the strap is quite tight.

The aperture in which the dynamo chain drive runs should now have approximately $\frac{1}{4}$ lb. of light grease inserted, as not other means of lubrication is provided.

Smear the inner side of the outer cover joint face with jointing compound, and position a paper washer on the face when the compound is tacky. Place the cover on to its dowels and secure it with the twelve securing screws, the longest screws at the lower end of the case, and the three shortest screws at the dynamo end of the case.

Next replace the valves into their respective ports, place the springs over the stems and with the top collars in position, and using Service Tool number 61-3340 as before, com-

B.S.A. Service Sheet No. 215 (contd.)

press the springs until the split collets can be inserted. A dab of grease on the inside of the collets will serve to hold them in position, until the spring is released. Make quite sure that the collets are correctly located.

Check that the push rods are on their respective tappets, position the cylinder head gasket and then lift the cylinder head into position. Replace and tighten the cylinder head bolts, commencing with the centre bolt and then working diagonally in order to secure even tightness, as shown in Fig. A46. Tighten each bolt a little at a time, and when they are all right down give them a final wrench to make certain that they are really tight.

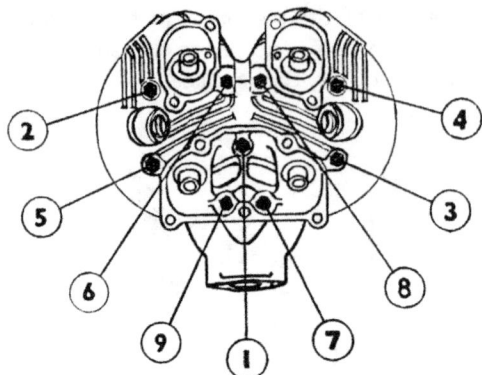

Fig. A46. Cylinder Head Bolts.

Now replace the rocker box making sure that the push rods are correctly inserted into the rocker ends, and thoroughly tighten the retaining nuts and bolts. Unless care is exercised when replacing the rocker box it is possible to cause damage to the valve stems. When fitting, place it in position over the valves, and gently ease the four holding down studs through their locating holes in the cylinder head. Check that the rocker box is well clear of the valve spring collars and then push it firmly down to its seating on the cylinder head. No force must be used in this operation.

Failure to use this method may result in the valve stems being bent, by fouling the rocker box. Although not noticeable in the test run of the engine, this will result in sticking valves and loss of power at high speeds. Do not forget the engine steady plates which are retained by the rocker box bolts.

A special push rod locating tool part number 67–9114 is available which facilitates the location of the push rods while replacing the rocker box. The tool should be inserted between the cylinder head and the rocker box from the right-hand side, with the shaped edge to the rear and with the outside recesses located by the two rear rocker box holding down bolts, as shown in Fig. A47. Rotate the engine until the push rods are level. The rocker box should then be tightened down and the tool removed just before it is gripped between the rocker box and cylinder head.

Before replacing the rocker box covers, check the tappet clearances and adjust if necessary. For correct clearances, see Service Sheet number 203.

The engine is now completely assembled and ready to be replaced in the frame. Lower the engine into position in the frame and move it backwards into its position between the rear engine plates and secure with the aid of the fixing studs.

Slide the left-hand front engine plate into position and secure with the frame and engine studs. Later models have both the distance pieces attached to the left-hand engine plate, but on some early models the lower distance piece is separate and must be slid into position before replacing the lower frame stud.

B.S.A. Service Sheet No. 215 (contd.)

Replace the nuts and washers and tighten all the engine plate securing nuts.

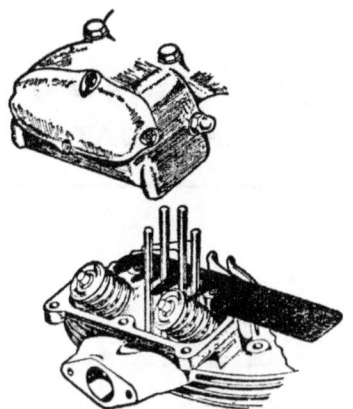

Fig. A47. Push Rod Assembly Tool.

Refit the primary chaincase as indicated in Service Sheet number 310.

Replace the exhaust pipes and electrical connections, noting that the dynamo plug should be replaced with its convex side facing outwards. Reconnect the rocker box oil supply pipes.

Screw the pipes from the oil tank on to the crankcase unions noting that the outside union is the inlet and the inner union the return. The oil return pipe on the oil tank can be identified by the rocker box supply pipe leading from it.

B.S.A. MOTOR CYCLES LTD., Service Dept., Armoury Road, Birmingham 11.
(Printed in England)

BSA SERVICE SHEET No. 216

A Group (Swinging Arm Frame)
USEFUL DATA

MODEL	A7	A7 Shooting Star	A10	A10 Road Rocket & Super Rocket
Engine Stroke (mm.)	72.6	72.6	84	84
Engine Bore (mm.)	66	66	70	70
Engine Capacity (mm.)	479	497	646	646
Petrol Tank Capacity (galls.)	2 or 4	2 or 4	2 or 4	2 or 4
Oil Tank Capacity (pints)	5½	5½	5½	5½
Gearbox Capacity (pint)	1	1	1	1
Gearbox Capacity—after 1956: (fluid ozs. and c.c.)	14 (400)	14 (400)	14 (400)	14 (400)
Front Fork Capacity—each leg (fl. ozs.) (c.c.)	7½ (213)	7½ (213)	7½ (213)	7½ (213)
Chaincase Capacity (fluid ozs) (c.c.) Note:—¼ pint — 5 fl. ozs. — 8 tablespoons	8 (225)	8 (225)	8 (225)	8 (225)
Tappet Clearance—engine cold (see note below) Inlet (in.) Exhaust (in.)	.010 .016	.008 .012	.010 .016	.008 .008
Piston Ring Gap—compression (in.)	.013	.013	.013	.013
Piston Ring Gap—oil control (in.)	.011	.011	.011	.011
Piston Ring Side Clearance (in.)	.002	.002	.002	.002
Piston Clearance—split skirt (in.)	.0011—.0031	.0011—.0031	.0011—.0031	.0011—.0031
Piston Clearance—solid skirt (in.)	.002—.004	.0035—.005	.0035—.005	.004—.0055
Ignition Advance before T.D.C. (in.)	5/16	⅜	11/32	⅜
Ignition Advance—for machines with frame number prefixed "G.A." (in.)	5/16	⅜	13/32	13/32
Contact Breaker Gap (in.)	.012	.012	.012	.012
Compression Ratio	6.6 : 1	7.25 : 1	6.5 : 1	8.0 : 1
Compression Ratio—after 1957	6.6 : 1	8.0 : 1	7.25 : 1	8.26 : 1 S.R.
Compression Ratio—after 1959	7.25 : 1	8.0 : 1	7.25 : 1	8.26 : 1 S.R.
Sparking Plug—Champion	L.7	N.3	L.7	N.3
Sparking Plug Gap (in.)	.018—.020	.018—.020	.018—.020	.018—.020
Valve Timing—Inlet (deg.): Opens before T.D.C. Closes after B.D.C.	30 70	42 62	30 70	42 62
Valve Timing—Exhaust (deg.): Opens before B.D.C. Closes after T.D.C.	65 25	67 37	65 25	67 37

Note:—After engines numbers CA7—5232 and DA10—1647, the valve timing for the A7 and A10 is the same as the Shooting Star and Rocket machines. Tappet clearances for quiet running should be .008 in. Inlet; .010 in. Exhaust, but for maximum power .010 in. Inlet and .016 in. Exhaust.

B.S.A. SERVICE SHEET No. 216 (Cont'd)

MODEL	A7		A7 Shooting Star		A10		A10 Road Rocket & Super Rocket	
Carburetter—up to 1959	Std.	Mono.	Std.	Mono.	Std.	Mono.	R.R. 10TT9	S.R. Mono.
Bore (in.)	15/16	15/16	1	1	1-1/16	1-1/16	1-1/16	1-1/16
Main Jet	140	210	160	270	170	246	360	250
Throttle Valve	6/4	376/3½	6/4	376/3½	6/4	376/3½	6	376/3½
Needle Position	4	2	3	3	2	3	4	3
Needle Jet (in.)	.107	.1065	.107	.1065	.107	.1065	9	.1065
Carburetter—1960:								
Bore (in.)	—	15/16	—	1	—	1⅛	1-5/32	1-5/32
Main Jet	—	210	—	270	—	250	410	420
Throttle Valve	—	376/3½	—	376/3½	—	389/3½	7	389/3
Needle Position	—	2	—	3	—	3	4	2
Needle Jet	—	.1065	—	.1065	—	.106	.109	.106
Gear Ratios:								
Top	5.28		5.28		4.52		4.52	
3rd	6.38		6.38		5.47		5.47	
2nd	9.28		9.28		7.95		7.95	
1st	13.62		13.62		11.67		1.67	
Rear Chainwheel— No. of Teeth	42		42		42		42	
Engine Sprocket— No. of Teeth	Solo 18 S/car 18		Solo 18 S/car 18		Solo 21 S/car 18		21	
Clutch Sprocket— No. of Teeth	43		43		43		43	
Gearbox Sprocket— No. of Teeth	Solo 19 S/car 17		Solo 19 S/car 17		Solo 19 S/car 19		19	
Front Chain ½ × .305 in.	Solo 67 S/car 67		Solo 67 S/car 67		Solo 69 S/car 67		69	
Rear Chain ⅝ × ⅜ in.	Solo 98 S/car 97		Solo 98 S/car 97		Solo 97 S/car 98		97	
Tyres:—front	3.25 × 19		3.25 × 19		3.25 × 19		3.25 × 19	
rear	3.50 × 19		3.50 × 19		3.50 × 19		3.50 × 19	
Tyre Pressures (Solo)—front (lbs. p.s.i.)	17		17		17		17	
rear (lbs. p.s.i.)	19		19		20		19	
Total Front Fork Movement (in.)	5¾		5¾		5¾		5¾	
Rear Suspension Movement (in.)	4		4		4		4	
Brake Dimensions:— front (in.) (1954 and 1955)	8 × 1⅜		8 × 1⅜		8 × 1⅜		8 × 1⅜	
rear (in.)	7 × 1⅛		7 × 1⅛		7 × 1⅛		7 × 1⅛	
Brake Dimensions:— front (in.) (1956 and 1957)	7 × 1½		7 × 1½		7 × 1½		7 × 1½	
rear (in.)	7 × 1½		7 × 1½		7 × 1½		7 × 1½	
Brake Dimensions:— front (in.) (1958 to 1960)	7 × 1⅛		7 × 1⅛		7 × 1⅛		7 × 1⅛	
rear (in.)	7 × 1⅛		7 × 1⅛		7 × 1⅛		7 × 1⅛	

BSA MOTOR CYCLES LTD., SERVICE DEPT., ARMOURY ROAD BIRMINGHAM 11   B.S.A. PRESS

BSA SERVICE SHEET No. 302A

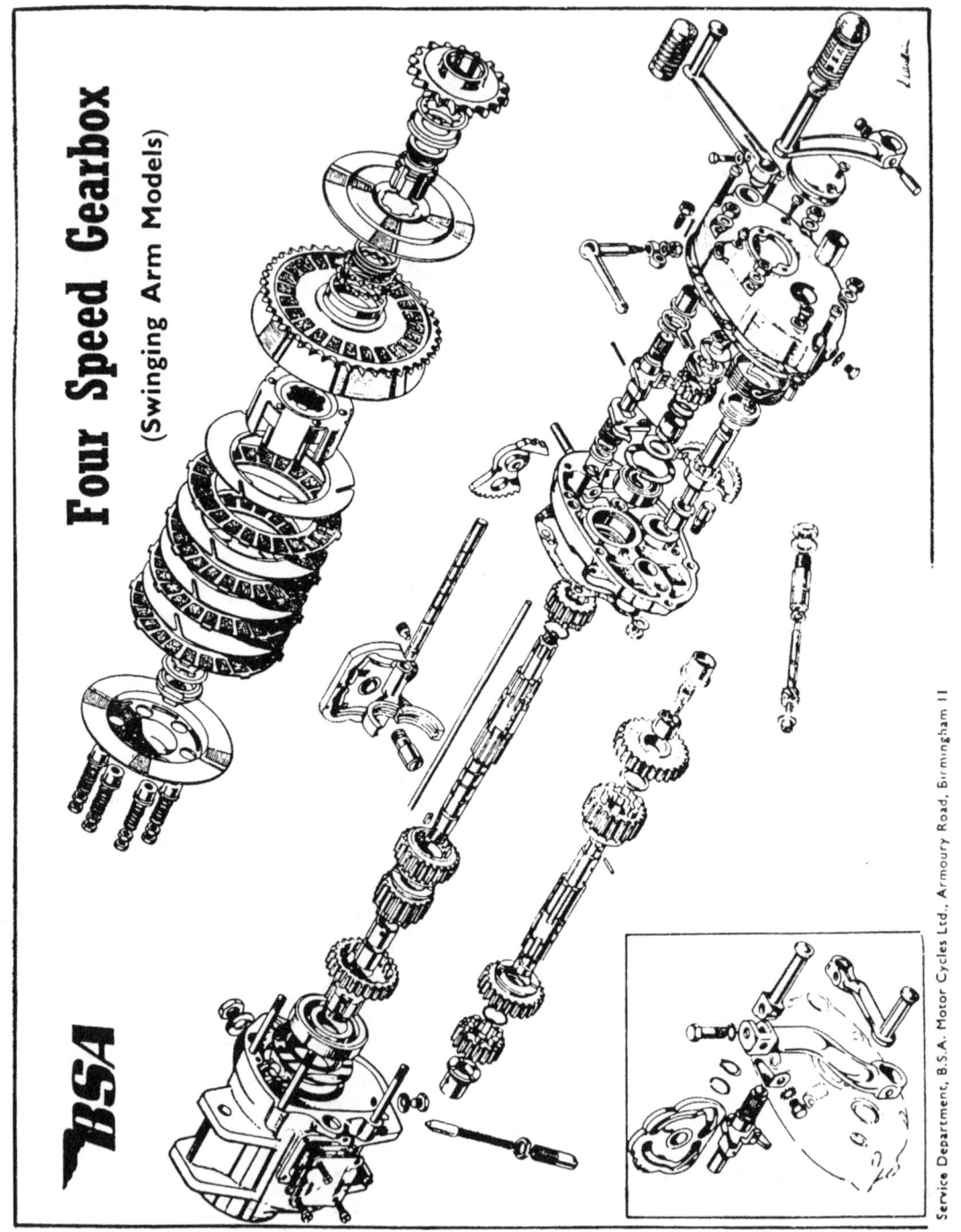

Four Speed Gearbox (Swinging Arm Models)

BSA SERVICE SHEET No. 302B

INTERNAL GEARBOX RATIOS FOR SWINGING ARM FRAME MODELS

The following gearbox ratios are available for models fitted with swinging arm type frame

Description	Marking	Top	Third	Second	Bottom
Extra Close Ratio	R.R.(T2)	1	1.099	1.326	1.754
Extra Close Ratio	R.R. or R.R.(T)	1	1.099	1.326	1.929
Close Ratio	DAY or DAY(T)	1	1.101	1.460	2.124
Scrambles	SC. or SC.(T)	1	1.325	1.754	2.343
Standard	STD. or STD.(T)	1	1.210	1.758	2.580
Wide Ratio (Trials)	TRI. or TRI.(T)	1	1.459	2.339	3.167
Standard	STB or ST. BT.	1	1.325	1.754	2.877

Marking suffix (T) denotes needle roller layshaft bearings. Suffix (T32) denotes needle roller mainshaft and layshaft bearings.

The part numbers and number of teeth for the relative pinions are listed overleaf.

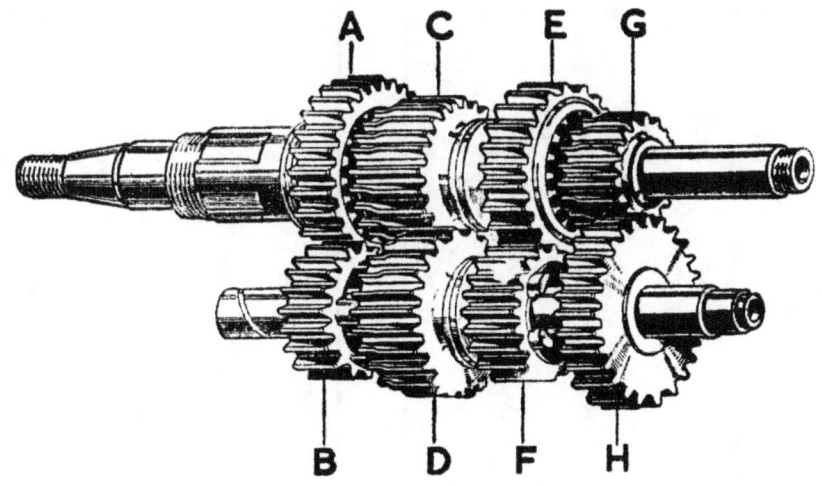

B.S.A. Service Sheet No. 302B (contd.)

PART NUMBERS

Ratios	A	B	C	D	E	F	G	H	M/shaft	Layshaft
R.R.	67-3184	42-3022	67-3361	42-3026	67-3187	67-3198	67-3221	67-3216	67-3330	42-3019
R.R.(T)	67-3184	42-3086	67-3361	42-3026	67-3187	67-3198	67-3221	42-3087	67-3330	42-3094
R.R.(T2)	42-3133	42-3086	67-3361	42-3026	42-3136	67-3198	42-3137	42-3138	42-3131	42-3094
DAY	67-3207	42-3020	67-3361	42-3026	67-3223	67-3226	67-3221	67-3216	67-3330	42-3019
DAY(T)	67-3207	42-3081	67-3361	42-3026	67-3223	67-3226	67-3221	42-3087	67-3330	42-3094
SC.	42-3088	42-3022	67-3302	42-3024	67-3305	67-3212	67-3191	42-3097	67-3315	42-3019
SC.(T)	42-3088	42-3086	67-3302	42-3024	67-3305	67-3212	67-3191	67-3210	67-3315	42-3094
STD.	67-3192	42-3020	67-3201	42-3023	67-3202	67-3198	67-3191	42-3097	67-3330	42-3019
STD.(T)	42-3076	42-3081	67-3201	42-3025	67-3202	67-3198	67-3191	67-3210	67-3330	42-3094
TRI.	67-3309	42-3020	67-3301	42-3025	67-3210	67-3212	67-3313	67-3213	67-3313	42-3019
TRI.(T)	42-3091	42-3081	67-3301	42-3025	67-3210	67-3212	67-3313	42-3093	67-3313	42-3094
ST.B	42-3088	42-3022	67-3302	42-3024	67-3210	67-3212	67-3313	67-3213	67-3313	42-3019
ST. BT.	42-3088	42-3086	67-3302	42-3024	67-3210	67-3212	67-3313	42-3093	67-3313	42-3094

NUMBER OF TEETH

Ratios	A	B	C	D	E	F	G	H	Speedo. Gears Driving	Driven
R.R. & R.R.(T)	25	18	22	21	24	19	18	25	42-3033	42-3032
R.R.(T2)	25	18	22	21	24	19	19	24	42-3033	42-3032
DAY & DAY(T)	26	17	22	21	25	18	18	25	67-3088	67-3175
SC. & SC.(T)	25	18	19	24	22	21	16	27	67-3088	67-3175
STD. & STD.(T)	26	17	20	23	24	19	16	27	67-3088	67-3175
TRI. & TRI.(T)	26	17	17	26	22	21	14	29	67-3088	67-3175
ST. B	25	18	19	24	22	21	14	29	42-3033	42-3032
ST. BT.	25	18	19	24	22	21	14	29	42-3303	42-3032

The forward footchange cam plate is part number 67-3332. The reverse footchange cam plate is part number 42-3011.

B.S.A. MOTOR CYCLES LTD., Service Department, Armoury Road, Birmingham 11.

Printed in England.

BSA SERVICE SHEET No. 308

'M' GROUP, C10, C11, 'A' GROUP (S.A.), AND 'B' GROUP
(Except those engine with prefix letters G.B. or 'A' Group after engine
numbers CA7-8623, CA755-8112 and DA10-13298)

DISMANTLING AND RE-ASSEMBLING THE CLUTCH

Take off the nearside footrest and then undo all the screws round the rim of the chaincase. As the outer half of the chaincase cover is taken off, careful note should be made of the positioning of the washers, etc., for replacement purposes. The joint washer should be carefully preserved.

Remove the six adjusting nuts, the springs and spring cups, and take off the clutch pressure plate so exposing the mainshaft nut which holds the clutch body in position.

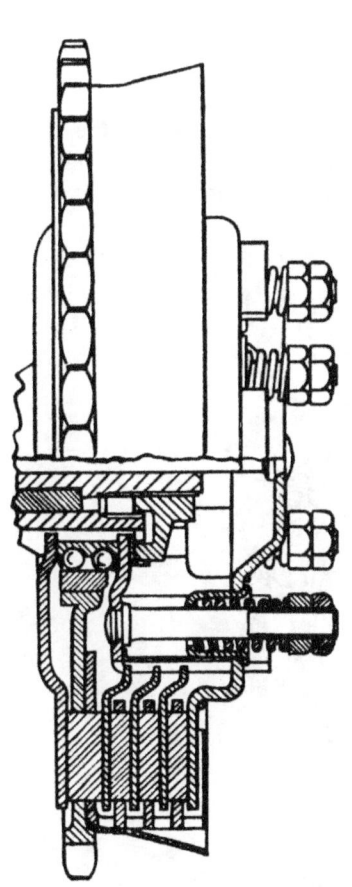

Fig. B18. *Section through clutch.*

The mainshaft nut is prevented from undoing by a locking washer which is turned over a flat on the nut. Flatten out the turned over edge of the washer and remove the nut. The clutch centre can now be withdrawn from the taper on the mainshaft using an extractor (part number 61-3362). Take care that the mainshaft key is not mislaid.

When the clutch is removed from the mainshaft it can be completely dismantled and the various components examined for wear. Special attention should be paid to the slots in which the clutch plates slide and any grooves should be removed with the aid of a fine file. If the grooves are very deep their removal will mean that the plates have excessive clearance and rapid wear will ensue. If the sprocket teeth are worn to a hook shape the sprocket must be replaced, otherwise rapid chain wear will result.

The steel plates should be smooth and if badly scored they should be replaced, while the fabric and cork inserts will require a thorough washing in petrol if there is any trace of oil on them. If the inserts are glazed or saturated in oil they should be replaced.

Finally, examine the balls, ball cages and tracks. If wear on the chainwheel bush or on the bearing boss of the clutch centre exceeds .0015 in. the bush or centre should be replaced (see Service Sheet No. 702 for correct dimensions).

NOTE.—When fitted to certain models this clutch is provided with additional plates, thus necessitating the use of a wider chainwheel and clutch centre, but the method of dismantling and reassembly is unaltered. C10 and C11 models have less plates than shown in the diagram but dismantling and assembly remain the same.

B.S.A. Service Sheet No. 308 (contd.)

Reassembly of the Clutch
The clutch is of straightforward construction and a study of Fig. B18 will show how the parts are assembled. Do not forget the mainshaft key when replacing the clutch centre.

The plates must be fitted in their proper order as follows: drive plate (tongues on inner diameter), fabric insert plates, drive plate, etc. Before refitting the pressure plate it is advisable to smear a small quantity of grease on the centre button at the point of contact with the clutch push rod.

The clutch springs should be replaced if they have shortened appreciably. The spring retaining nuts should be tightened initially until the outer nut (A) Fig. B19, is just fully engaged on its thread.

It is most important that the clutch spring pressure is evenly distributed, and this should be checked by ensuring that the clutch pressure plate does not tilt when the clutch is withdrawn. If the plate does tilt the nuts should be adjusted until the spring pressure is even. Unequal spring pressure may cause clutch drag and noisy gearchange. When the adjustment is complete tighten the locknuts firmly.

Clutch Re-adjustment
After a considerable mileage has been covered it may be necessary to screw the spring retaining nuts in further to allow for wear on the clutch inserts. Release the locknuts (A), and tighten the nuts (B) by a few turns. After the adjustment has been carried out, check that the clutch lifts evenly and then tighten the locknuts.

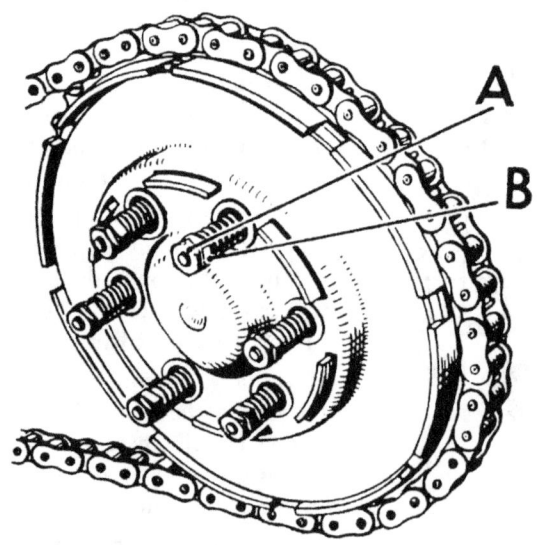

Fig. B19. *Clutch spring adjustment.*

B.S.A. MOTOR CYCLES LTD., Service Department, Armoury Road, Birmingham 11.

BSA SERVICE SHEET No. 310

A AND B GROUP MODELS
(with welded type frame, except those with engine prefix letters GB)

PRIMARY TRANSMISSION

Clutch Adjustment

Two adjustments are provided for the clutch control arm on the gearbox outer cover. The first of these is at the clutch push rod and is exposed when the inspection plate is removed. It consists of a grub-screw (*H*) Fig. B22, and locknut (*G*). Between the inner end of the screw and the clutch push rod a steel ball is inserted, and the grub-screw must be adjusted so that there is just a little clearance between the ball and push rod.

To carry out this adjustment loosen the locknut and with the aid of a screwdriver adjust the grub-screw. Then retighten the locknut.

The other adjustment is provided by the cable adjuster on top of the gearbox. Remember that some free movement in the control arm is necessary as, if the adjustment is too tight, there will be constant pressure on the clutch with consequent wear and loss of efficiency. The control arm pivot should be greased occasionally by means of the grease nipple (*F*).

Primary Chain Adjustment

Adjustment of the front chain is achieved by pivoting the gearbox backwards and forwards on the bottom support bolt. To adjust the chain, remove the knurled inspection cover on the primary chaincase and slacken the nuts (*A*) and (*B*) Fig. B22, which clamp the top and bottom gearbox lugs in the rear engine plates. An adjuster is attached to the right-hand side of the top gearbox bolt. Slacken the locknut (*C*) and screw the adjuster (*D*) back-

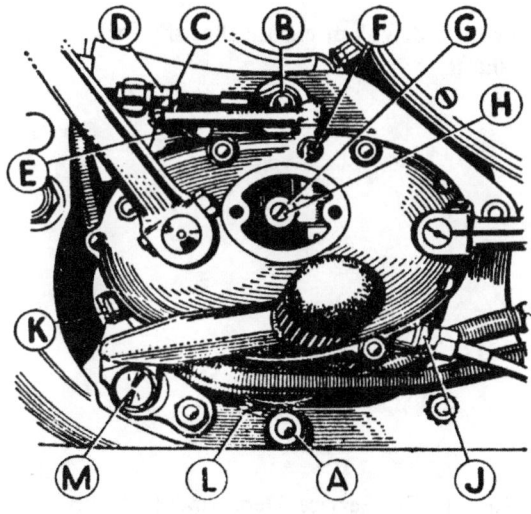

Fig. B22.

B.S.A. Service Sheet No. 310 (contd.)

wards or forwards until the chain tension is correct. This is when the maximum up and down movement of the chain at the tightest point is ½ in. Tighten the gearbox bolt nuts (*A*) and (*B*), also the adjuster locknut, and re-check the adjustment. Note that after re-adjusting the primary chain, the rear chain will be in need of adjustment.

Chaincase Removal

Drain off the oil in the case by removing the drain screw in the lower edge of the primary chaincase. Two of the screws retaining the primary chaincase outer cover have red painted heads. The front one of these is the chaincase oil level screw, and the rear one the drain screw. Remove the left-hand footrest. This may be rather tight, but a few light blows on the front of the footrest should free it. Undo the small screws round the rim of the chaincase and pull off the outer half.

To dismantle the cush drive assembly, bend back the cush drive nut locking washer by inserting a small screwdriver through the coils of the spring, and remove the nut. Withdraw the locking washer, the spring and the cush drive sliding sleeve. If any difficulty is experienced in unscrewing the cush drive nut due to the engine rotating, place the machine in gear and apply the back brake.

Remove the clutch in the manner described in Service Sheet No. 308.

Remove the engine sprocket and pull the cush drive bearing off the mainshaft. Unscrew the bolts which hold the inner half of the chaincase to the crankcase, after breaking the locking wire which passes through the heads of the bolts. There now remains only one bolt which secures the rear of the chaincase to the frame, and its removal will allow the chaincase to be detached.

Reassembly of the primary transmission and chaincase should be carried out in the reverse order to dismantling.

Before replacing the cush drive nut ensure that the lockwasher is correctly located in the splines on the mainshaft.

B.S.A. MOTOR CYCLES LTD., Service Department, Armoury Road, Birmingham 11.

BSA SERVICE SHEET No. 311

Reprinted November, 1966

A and B Group Models with Swinging Arm Frame

DISMANTLING AND RE-ASSEMBLY OF GEARBOX AND GEARCHANGE

Gearbox Removal

In most cases it will be found convenient to dismantle the gearbox while it is still in position. However, if attention to the final drive pinion sleeve bearing is required it may be advisable to remove the complete gearbox. The primary transmission, clutch and chaincase must be removed in either case and this should be carried out as described in Service Sheet 310.

To remove the gearbox from the frame, slacken the retaining bolts and remove the two right hand rear engine plates. The gearbox is then free to be withdrawn from the right hand side of the machine.

Dismantling

Remove the clutch and speedometer cables. Move the gears to the neutral position between first and second. Undo the four nuts and three screws round the rim of the outer cover but do not slacken the screw and nut which are not on the edge of the cover as these do not prevent its removal. The outer cover can then be removed complete with the kickstarter, gearchange and clutch lever. As the cover is withdrawn the kickstarter lever will tend to rotate under the action of the return spring and the clutch lever should be pulled out to the fullest extent so that the kickstarter lever may be rested against it, thus preventing the complete release of the spring.

The gearchange mechanism can be dismantled by removing the gearchange lever and the circlip which retains the gearchange spindle in the outer cover. Withdraw the spindle complete with change mechanism which can then be completely dismantled after removing the split pin. Examine the operating claw 'A' for wear and if the ends are no longer well formed the claw should be replaced.

Before the inner cover is removed the clutch push rod should be withdrawn and the single screw to the left of the top right stud, must be undone. The inner cover together with the mainshaft and gearchange rocking lever 'B' can then be withdrawn, leaving the gear cluster in position. To remove the rocking lever the gear lever spindle bush must first be pushed out of the inner cover. This will reveal the end of the rocking lever spindle which is threaded internally $\frac{1}{4}$ in. C.E.I. Screw in a suitable screw or bolt, then use this to pull out the spindle.

If it is necessary to remove the mainshaft from the inner cover the shaft should be held in a soft jawed vice so that the kickstart ratchet nut can be undone after its locking washer has been bent back. The kickstart ratchet, ratchet pinion, spring and bush should

B.S.A. Service Sheet No. 311 (contd.)

then be removed, leaving the shaft free to be pushed from its bearing. This bearing can be removed by pulling out the retaining circlip and then warming the cover in hot water before tapping the bearing from its housing with a suitable soft drift.

The rod 'D' on which the two gear operating claws slide is pressed into the gearbox shell at the clutch end and is secured by a small grub screw on the outside of the case. Release the grub screw and pull out the rod. It is then possible to withdraw the gear cluster and operating claws together with the layshaft so that the only components remaining in the gearbox shell are the final drive pinion sleeve assembly and cam plate 'C'.

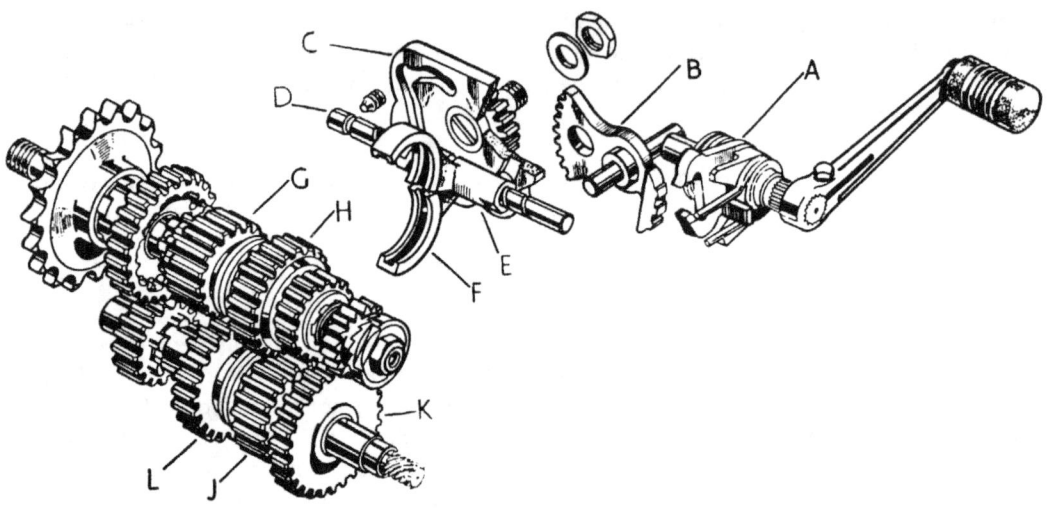

Unscrew the selector plunger housing locknut and remove the plunger housing from the gearbox shell. The gear selector cam plate will now slide from its pivot and the latter can also be removed after unscrewing the retaining nut and warming the case. The layshaft bearings are a press fit in the gearbox and if necessary can be driven out with the aid of a soft punch.

Run a length of old chain round the gearbox sprocket and hold the chain in a vice to prevent the sprocket rotating. Flatten the locking tab washer and undo the retaining nut. Withdraw the sprocket from its spline, then tap the pinion into the gearbox with a soft mallet. To remove the pinion sleeve bearing, prise out the retaining circlip, withdraw the oil seal, then warm the case in hot water before tapping the bearing out of the case. Do not disturb the ballrace unless it is suspected of being faulty. Wash it thoroughly in petrol to remove all traces of oil and any play will then be immediately detected.

Examine the various parts for wear, and if the forks which actuate the sliding pinions show signs of seizure it will be advisable to replace them. Attempts to erase the seizure marks will result in excessive side play.

B.S.A. Service Sheet No. 311 (contd.)

The fixed pinions on the layshaft and mainshaft are pressed on, and new components must be a tight fit. Examine the selector plate for worn cam grooves, and replace if necessary. The rocking arm should be replaced if the teeth show signs of wear as, of course, should pinions with damaged or worn teeth.

Re-assembly

Re-assembly is carried out in the reverse order to dismantling. The aluminium case should always be warmed before a bearing is pressed in. When replacing the gearbox sprocket ensure that the oil seal is in good condition and that the retaining nut locking washer is correctly seated in the spline. Tighten the nut fully and turn the lockwasher over into the slots on the nut. If the teeth on the sprocket are worn to a hook shape a new sprocket must be fitted otherwise rapid chain wear will result.

Replace the cam plate and selector plunger making sure that the plunger is in the neutral position between first and second gear. Place the layshaft in position and then feed in the first pair of gears 'J' and 'L' together with their selector claw 'F.' These claws are interchangeable but if the original components are to be used then they should be replaced in their original positions. Replace the second pair of gear wheels 'G' and 'H' together with selector claw 'E' and make sure that the guide pins of both selector claws are correctly engaged in the cam groove. Replace the selector claw rod and secure it in position by means of its grub screw. Position the spacing washer and the large pinion on the layshaft. Assemble the mainshaft, kickstart ratchet mechanism and rocking lever into the inner cover. The mainshaft and inner cover can then be pushed into the gearbox, but before they are completely home the rocking lever must be correctly set so that the red dots on the lever and on the cover are in line. Replace the single inner cover retaining screw.

Note that when a reverse cam plate 42-3001 is fitted the red dots will not coincide as described above. Correct meshing of the rocking lever must be obtained by trial and error.

Assemble the gearchange and kickstarter mechanism in the outer cover, then push the latter on to the four studs, rotating the kickstarter slightly so that the quadrant does not jam on its stop.

Replace the four nuts and three screws in the outer cover. The gearbox is now completely re-assembled.

B.S.A. MOTOR CYCLES LTD.,
Service Dept., Armoury Road, Birmingham, 11.

BSA SERVICE SHEET No. 313

"A" and "B" Group Models
with Swinging Arm Frame

REAR SUSPENSION

REMOVING AND DISMANTLING THE SUSPENSION UNITS

Support the machine on the central stand. Take out the top and bottom bolts securing the suspension units and pull them away from the mounting lugs.

The upper shroud is retained by split collets, and the spring must be compressed before the collets can be removed. The assistance of a second person may be necessary for this operation. Alternatively, Service Tool number 61-3503 can be used, as shown in Fig. B24.

Place the tool in position on the shroud, insert the pin through the top lug and turn the handle until the shroud has been pressed down far enough to allow the collets to be withdrawn. After the tool has been released, the spring and both shrouds can be removed

No further dismantling is possible, and if the damper units are damaged, they must be replaced.

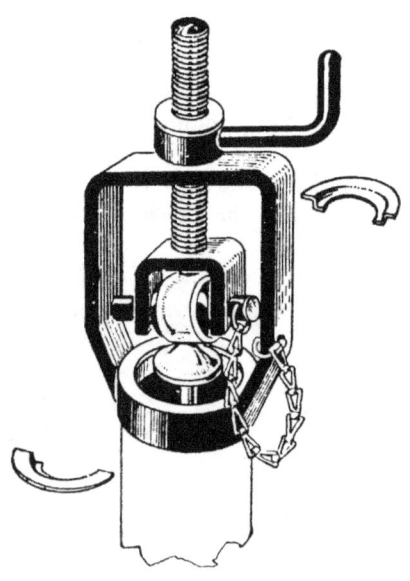

Fig. B24.

B.S.A. Service Sheet No. 313 (contd.)

REMOVING AND REPLACING THE SWINGING ARM FORK

With the machine on the centre stand, take out the rear wheel in the normal manner. Detach the chainguard, or chaincase, and remove the chain and sprocket assembly. Remove the brake pedal and, on 1956 models, withdraw the crossover shaft. Take out the two bottom bolts from the suspension units, and pull these clear of the mounting lugs. Unscrew the large nut on the offside end of the fork spindle, and also the small bolt from the spindle locking plate on the nearside. Drive out the spindle with a suitable drift, taking care not to damage the threaded end.

Now take hold of the two fork ends and twist the whole fork in a clockwise direction. It can then be drawn away towards the rear.

On some models, the rear mudguard extends down between the arms of the fork, behind the pivot. In this case, the mudguard also must be removed before the fork can be taken out.

The "silentbloc" spindle bushes have a very long life, and replacement is rarely necessary.

Reassembly of the fork into the frame is carried out in the reverse order to dismantling, except that the final tighteneing of the spindle nut should be left until all other parts have been refitted. Then, take the machine off the stand and load it with the weight normally carried. Tighten the spindle nut fully so as to clamp the centre sleeves of the bushes to the frame members in the correct position.

B.S.A. MOTOR CYCLES LTD., Service Department, Armoury Road, Birmingham 11.

BSA SERVICE SHEET No. 612

Reprinted Sept. 1960

All Models

BRAKE RELINING

Brake Shoe Removal and Replacement

After the brake plate has been removed from the wheel, the brake cam lever A (Fig. M40) should be detached and the cam spindle B pushed in slightly to allow the shoes to clear the brake plate. Insert a screwdriver between the brake shoes at the fulcrum pin C and twist the screwdriver.

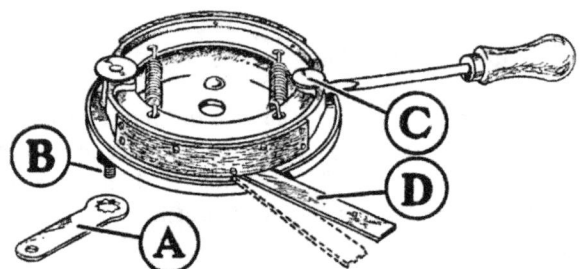

Fig. M40. Removing the Brake Shoes

Place a small lever D between one of the shoes and the cover plate and lever the shoe away from the cover plate until the spring pressure is released. Both shoes can then be lifted from the brake plate.

The shoes can be replaced by the reverse procedure. Hook the springs on to the shoes and place the ends of the shoes in position on the fulcrum pin and cam lever. Then push the shoes outwards until the springs pull them into their correct position.

NOTE: The brake shoe springs are quite strong and care should be taken that the fingers are not trapped by the brake shoes during these operations.

Brake Shoe Relining

With the shoes removed the linings can best be removed by drilling away the heads of the rivets and punching the shanks out to the inside of the shoe with a suitable drift.

New linings are die pressed to suit the curvature of the shoes, but will require drilling and counter-boring for the rivets. Position the lining and hold it in place at one end by means of clamps. Using the holes in the shoes as guides, drill holes of the correct size for the rivets adjacent to the clamp. Turn the shoe over, and counterbore the holes just drilled sufficiently deep so that the rivet heads will stand below the lining surface; this is important, since the rivets will otherwise score the brake drum.

B.S.A. Service Sheet No. 612 (continued)

Insert the rivets into the holes and rivet them over on the inside of the shoe. This is easily accomplished by holding in a vice a short length of rod, whose diameter is equal to that of the rivet head, and using it as an anvil upon which to rest the rivet head while hammering the shank over. (See Fig. M41.) This will also make sure that the rivets do not stand proud of the lining.

Move the clamps to the next pair of holes, taking care that the lining is kept in firm contact with the shoe the whole time, and repeat the above procedure. When the lining is finally riveted down, bevel off the ends of the linings and file off any local high spots.

Precautions to be observed when fitting the relined shoes to the hubs are given in the Service Sheet on Hubs and Brakes.

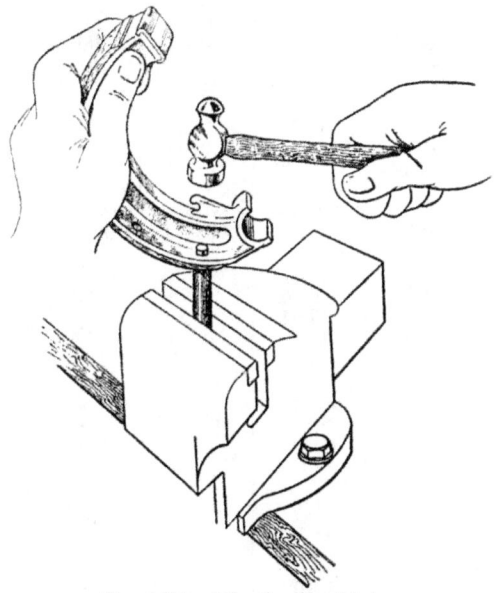

Fig. M41. Riveting the Linings

Works reconditioned brake shoes can be obtained through the medium of your Dealer from the B.S.A. Exchange Replacement Service.

U/B5305

B.S.A. MOTOR CYCLES LTD.
Service Dept., Waverley Works, Birmingham 10
Printed in England.

BSA SERVICE SHEET No. 701

ALL MODELS — USEFUL DATA

MODEL	C10	C11	C12	C15 Std.	B31	B32	B33	B34	M20
Engine bore (mm.)	63	63	63	67	71	71	85	85	82
Engine stroke (mm.)	80	80	80	70	88	88	88	88	94
Engine capacity (c.c.)	249	249	249	249	348	348	499	499	496
Petrol tank capacity (galls.)	2½	2½	2¾	2½	3	3	3	3	3
Oil tank capacity (pints)	4	4	4	4	4	4	4	4	5
Gearbox capacity (pint)	*½	*½	½	½	1	1	1	1	1
Tappet clearance cold:									
inlet (in.)	.004	.003	.010	.008	.003	.003	.003	.003	.010
exhaust (in.)	.006	.003	.012	.010	.003	.003	.003	.003	.012
Tyres—front	3.00×19	3.00×20†	3.00×19	3.25×17	3.25×19	2.75×21	3.25×19	2.75×21	3.25×19
Tyres—rear	3.00×19	3.00×20†	3.00×19	3.25×17	3.25×19	4.00×19	3.25×19	4.00×19	3.25×19
Piston ring gap:									
plain (in.)	.010	.010	.010	.010	.010	.010	.010	.010	.010
oil control (in.)	.010	.010	.010	.010	.010	.010	.010	.010	.010
Piston ring side clearance (in.)	.002–.004	.002–.004	.002–.004	.002–.004	.002–.004	.002–.004	.002–.004	.002–.004	.002–.004
Piston clearance:									
bottom of skirt	.0045–.0065	.0035–.0055	.0035–.0055	.0025–.004	.0040–.0055	.0040–.0055	.0045–.0065	.0045–.0065	.0040–.0060
Gear ratios:									
Top	6.6	6.6	6.26	5.98	5.6	7.1	5.0	5.6	5.3
third	—	—	7.64	7.65	7.3	9.2	6.5	7.4	7.0
second	9.8	9.8	11.1	10.54	11.1	14.2	10.0	11.5	10.9
first	14.5	14.5	16.15	15.96	15.9	20.2	14.2	16.8	15.8
Ignition setting (in. before T.D.C.):									
fully advanced	—	—	—	11/32	7/16	7/16	7/16	7/16	7/16
fully retarded	1/32	1/32	T.D.C.	—	—	—	—	—	—
Carburetter:									
jet	90	80	140	—	150	150	200	200	170
with air cleaner	90	80	100	140	150	150	170	170	—
Sparking plug:									
C.I. cylinder head	L.10	L.10S	L.10S	—	L.10S	L.10S	L.10S	L.10S	—
Al. alloy cylinder head	N.8	—	—	N.5	—	NA.8	—	NA.8	N.8
Compression ratio	5.1:1	6.5:1	6.5:1	7.25:1	6.5:1	6.5:1	6.8:1	6.8:1	4.9:1
Valve timing—inlet (deg.):									
opens before T.D.C.	25	25	34	26	25	25	25	25	25
closes after B.D.C.	70	70	78	70	65	65	65	65	65
Valve timing—exhaust (deg.):									
opens before B.D.C.	70	70	74	61½	65	65	65	65	65
closes after T.D.C.	25	25	38	34½	25	25	25	25	25
Distributor points gap (in.)	.012	.012	.015	.012	—	—	—	—	—
Magneto points gap (in.)	—	—	—	—	.012	.012	.012	.012	.012
Plug points gap (in.)	.015–.018	.015–.018	.018–.020	.020–.025	.015–.018	.015–.018	.015–.018	.015–.018	.015–.018
Tyre pressures:									
front (lb. per sq. in.)	20	20	18	16	16	—	16	—	17
rear (lb. per sq. in.)	28	28	26	22	20	—	17	—	22

For Swinging Arm and other models not listed see appropriate series.

*Four-speed gearbox, 1 pint. †3.00 × 19 on later models.

B.S.A. SERVICE SHEET No. 701 (contd.)

MODEL	M21	M33	A7 (up to Eng. No. ZA7-11192)	A7 ST 2 carburetters)	A7 (on and after Eng. No. AA7-101)	A7 S/T & S/S (on & Eng. No. AA7S-101)	A10	R/R & S/R
Engine bore (mm.)	82	85	62	62	66	66	70	70
Engine stroke (mm.)	112	88	82	82	72.6	72.6	84	84
Engine capacity (c.c.)	591	499	495	495	497	497	646	646
Petrol tank capacity (galls.)	3	3	3	3½	3½	3½	4¼	2 or 4
Oil tank capacity (pints)	5	5	4	4	4	4	4	5½
Gearbox capacity (pint)	1	1	1	1	1	1	1	14 fl. oz.
Tappet clearance—cold:								
inlet (in.)	.010	.003	.015	.015	.010	.008	.010	.008
exhaust (in.)	.012	.003	.015	.015	.016	.012	.016	.008
Tyres—front	3.50×19	3.25×19	3.25×19	3.25×19	3.25×19	3.25×19	3.25×19	—
Tyres—rear	3.50×19	3.50×19	3.50×19	3.50×19	3.50×19	3.50×19	3.50×19	—
Piston ring gap:								
plain (in.)	.010	.010	.013	.013	.013	.013	.013	—
oil control (in.)	.010	.010	.011	.011	.011	.011	.011	—
Piston ring side clearance	.002–.004	.002–.004	.002–.004	.002–.004	.002–.004	.002–.004	.002–.004	.002–.004
Piston clearance:								
bottom of skirt (in.)	.0040–.0060	.0045–.0065	.0030–.0050	.0030–.0050	.0030–.0050	.0030–.0050	.0030–.0050	.0030–.0050
Gear ratios:						S/T S/S		
Top	5.9	4.8	5.1	5.1	5.1	5.0 5.28	4.42	4.53
third	7.8	6.3	6.2	6.2	6.2	6.05 6.38	5.36	5.48
second	12.2	9.9	9.0	9.0	9.0	8.8 9.28	7.77	7.96
first	17.8	14.3	13.2	13.2	13.2	12.9 13.62	11.41	11.68
Ignition setting (in. before T.D.C. fully advanced)	7/16	7/16	3/8	3/8	5/16	3/8	11/32	3/8
Carburetter:								
jet	170	200	—	110	—	—	—	250
with air cleaner	—	170	140	—	140	160	170	240
Sparking plug:								
C.I. cylinder head	L.10	L.10S	L.10S	L.10S	L.10S	L.10S	L.10S	NA.10
Al. alloy cylinder head	N.8	—	—	—	—	—	—	—
Compression ratio	5 : 1	6.8 : 1	6.6 : 1	7 : 1	6.6 : 1	7.25 : 1	6.5 : 1	R/R 8 : 1 S/R 8.26:1
Valve timing—inlet (deg.):								
opens before T.D.C.	25	25	24	24	30	42	30	42
closes after B.D.C.	65	65	65	65	70	62	70	62
*Valve timing—exhaust (deg.):								
opens before B.D.C.	65	65	60	60	65	67	65	67
closes after T.D.C.	25	25	21½	21½	25	37	25	37
Distributor points gap	—	—	—	—	—	—	—	—
Magneto points gap (in.)	.012	.012	.012	.012	.012	.012	.012	.012
Plug points gap (in.)	.015–.018	.015–.018	.015–.018	.015–.018	.015–.018	.015–.018	.015–.018	.018–.020
Tyre pressures:								
front (lb. per square inch)	16	17	17	17	17	17	17	17
rear (lb. per square inch)	18	18	18	18	18	18	18	19

*NOTE.—Standard A7's after engine number CA7-5232 and Standard A10's after engine number DA10-1647 have the same camshaft as the S/S and R/R machines and valve timing is therefore the same.

B.S.A. MOTOR CYCLES LTD., Service Department, Armoury Road, Birmingham 11.
PRINTED IN ENGLAND—B.S.A. PRESS

BSA SERVICE SHEET No. 702

Reprinted June, 1959.

ALL MODELS

WORKSHOP DATA

ENGINE, BUSH AND SHAFT DIAMETERS

(All Dimensions in Inches, after Reaming or Grinding).

	D1	C10, C11	B31, B32	M33 B33, B34	M20, M21	A7 Up to Engine No. ZA7 11192	A7 On and After Engine No. AA7 101	A10
Overhead Rocker Arm	— —	.569 .567 C10 only	.562 .563	.562 .563	— —	.4995 .5005	.4995 .5005	.4995 .5005
Inlet Valve Guide	— —	.313 .314	.313 .314	.3525 .3515	.3525 .3515	.313 .314	.313 .314	.313 .314
Exhaust Valve Guide	— —	.313 .314	.352 .353	.3785 .3795	.3525 .3535	.313 .314	.313 .314	.313 .314
Inlet Tappet Guide	— —	.3125 .3135 C10 only	.3745 .3755	.3745 .3755	.3745 .3755	.3125 .3135	— —	— —
Exhaust Tappet Guide	— —	.3125 .3135 C10 only	.3745 .3755	.3745 .3755	.3745 .3755	.3125 .3135	— —	— —
Cam Pinion Bush	— —	— —	.6255 .6245	.6255 .6245	.6255 .6245	— —	— —	— —
Cam Shaft Bush	— —	.687 .688	— —	— —	— —	.7485 .7495	.7485 .7495	.7485 .7495
Idler Pinion Shaft Bush	— —	— —	— —	— —	— —	.7485 .7495	.7485 .7495	.7485 .7495
Idler Pinion Bush	— —	— —	.7505 .7495	.7505 .7495	.7505 .7495	.7485 .7495	.7485 .7495	.7485 .7495
Cam Shaft Bush T/Cover	— —	1.0005 .9995	— —	— —	— —	— —	— —	— —
Crankshaft Bush G/S	— —	.983 .982	— —	— —	— —	1.375 1.3745	1.375 1.3745	1.375 1.3745
Conrod Big End	— —	— —	1.7704 1.7702	1.7704 1.7702	1.7704 1.7702	1.4495 1.4500	1.4495 1.4500	1.4495 1.4500
Gudgeon Pin Bush	.4697 .4692	.6255 .625	.7506 .7503	.7506 .7503	.7506 .7503	.6881 .6878	.6881 .6878	.7506 .7503

B.S.A. Service Sheet No. 702 (Contd.).

GEARBOX—BUSH DIAMETERS

(All Dimensions in Inches, after Reaming or Grinding)

	D Group	C Group	B Group 1945/48	M Group 1945/48	A Group	B & M 1949 on
Pinion Sleeve Bush	.4975 .4965	—	.7505 .7495	.8755 .8745	.812 .813	.8755 .8745
Layshaft Bush (Shell)	.501 .500	—	.687 .688	.687 .688	.687 .688	.687 .688
Mainshaft Bush (I/Cover)	—	.751 .752	.687 .688	—	—	—
Layshaft Bush (K/S Quadrant)	—	—	—	.687 .688	.7495 .7505	.687 .688
Layshaft 1st Gear Bush	—	—	.8125 .8135	.8765 .8755	.7495 .7505	.8765 .8755
Layshaft Pinion/s Bush	—	.562 .563	—	—	—	—
M/Shaft 3rd L/Shaft 2nd Gear Bush	—	—	.9375 .9385	1.0005 1.0015	—	1.0005 1.0015
K/S Quadrant Bush I/Cover	—	.9995 1.0005	1.1245 1.1255	—	.561 .563	—
K/S Quadrant Bush O/Cover	—	.812 .813	.812 .813	1.187 1.188	.7495 .7505	1.187 1.188
Control Shaft Bush (Shell)	—	—	.562 .563	.562 .563	—	.562 .563
Control Shaft Bush (I/Cover)	—	.689 .688	—	.562 .563	—	.562 .563
Control Quadrant Bush (I/Cover)	—	—	—	.562 .563	—	.562 .563
Pedal Spindle Bush (I/Cover)	—	.7495 .7505	.6245 .6255	.6245 .6255	.467 .468	.6245 .6255
Pedal Spindle Bush (O/Cover)	—	.7495 .7505	.8745 .8755	.8745 .8755	.6245 .6255	.8745 .8755
Speedo Spindle Small Bush	—	—	.218 .219	—	.218 .219	.218 .219
Speedo Spindle Long Bush	—	—	.281 .282	—	.281 .282	.281 .282
Clutch Push Rod Bush	—	.257 .258	—	—	—	—

B.S.A. MOTOR CYCLES LTD., Service Dept., Waverley Works, Birmingham, 10.   *Printed in England.*

BSA SERVICE SHEET No. 703

Revised Dec. 1958.

All Models
WORKSHOP DATA (BEARINGS) 1956

B.S.A. Part No.	Hoffman No.	Skefko No.	Ransome & Marles No.	British Timkin No.	Fischer No.
24-722	RM.9L	CFM7/C2	MRJA.$\frac{7}{8}$	—	RFM.9
24-724	R.325L	402454.B	MRJA.25	—	MFM.25
24-732	325	6305	MJ.25	—	6305
24-4065	135	6207	LJ.35	—	6207
24-4217	LS.8	RLS.6	LJ$\frac{3}{4}$	—	LS.8
24-6860	—	2K.1178X 2K.1130N1	—	1178X 1130.N1	—
27-261	MS.9	RM.S7	MJ.$\frac{7}{8}$	—	MS.9
27-4027	LS.11	RL.S9	LJ.$1\frac{1}{8}$	—	—
29-3857	130	6206	LJ.30	—	6206
29-6211	MS.7	RM.S5	MJ.$\frac{5}{8}$	—	MS.7
42-5819	120	—	—	—	—
65-1388	RMS.11	CRM.9	MRJ.$1\frac{1}{8}$	—	RMS.11
65-2045	125	6205	LJ.25	—	6205
65-5883	LS.9	RLS.7	LJ.$\frac{7}{8}$	—	LS.9
67-670	R.130L	NFL.30	LRJA.30	—	NFL.30
89-3022	LS.10	RLS.8	LJ.1	—	LS.10
89-3023	LS.8	RLS.6	LJ.$\frac{3}{4}$	—	LS.8
90-10	117	6203	LJ.17	—	6203
90-11	LS.7	RLS.5	LJ.$\frac{5}{8}$	—	LS.7
90-12	S.9	EE.8J	KLNJ.$\frac{7}{8}$	—	EE.8
90-5525	112	6201	LJ.12	—	6201
90-5559	—	—	—	A.2126	—
90-6063	115	6202	LJ.15	—	6202

B.S.A. SERVICE SHEET No. 703 (continued)

LOCATION OF BEARINGS

Model	Crankcase Roller Bearing Driveside	Crankcase Ball Bearing Driveside	Crankcase Roller Bearing Gearside	Crankcase Ball Bearing Gearside	Crankcase Ball Bearing (Small)	Crankcase Ball Bearing (Large)	Gearbox Pinion Sleeve Ball Bearing	Gearbox Mainshaft Ball Bearing	Front Hub Ball Bearing	Rear Hub Ball Bearing	Rear Hub Brake Drum and C/Wheel Ball Bearing
Dandy	—	—	—	—	90–6063	24–4217	90–6063 (Output shaft)	90–6063 (Input shaft)	—	—	—
D1, D3 & D5	—	—	—	—	90–10	24–4217	90–12	90–11	90–5525	90–6063	
D1, D3 (Comp.)									90–5559		
C10L	—	24–732	—	—			29–3857	90–11	—	90–6063	
C12	—	24–732	—	—			29–3857	90–11	65–5383	90–11 O/S 29–6211 N/S	
C15	—	24–782	—	—			29–3857			90–10 O/S 42–5819 N/S	
B31 S/A	24–724	65–2045	24–722				24–4065	24–4217	89–3022	89–3022	89–3022
B31 S/A (1958)	—	—	—						42–5819	42–5819	89–3022
B32 Comp. Rigid	24–724	65–2045	24–722	—	—		24–4065	24–4217	65–5883	65–5883	65–5883
B32/34 Gold Star	65–1338	65–2045	24–722				24–4065	24–4217	65–5883	65–5883	65–5883
B33 S/A	24–724	65–2045	24–722				24–4065	24–4217	89–3022	89–3022	89–3022
B33 S/A (1958)	—	—	—						42–5819	42–5819	89–3022
B34 Comp. Rigid	24–724	65–2045	24–722				24–4065	24–4217	65–5883	65–5883	65–5883
M21 Rigid	24–724	65–2045	24–722	27–261			24–4065	24–4217	65–5883	24–6860 (Tapered Roller)	—
M21 Plunger	24–724	65–2045	24–722	27–261			24–4065	24–4217	65–5883	65–5883	89–3022
M33	24–724	65–2045	24–722				24–4065	24–4217	65–5883	65–5883	89–3022
A7 and Shooting Star	67–670	—	—				24–4065	24–4217	89–3022	89–3022	89–3022
A7 & S/S (1958)	—	—	—						42–5819	42–5819	89–3022
A10 S/A	67–670	—	—				24–4065	24–4217	89–3022	89–3022	89–3022
A10 S/A (1958)	—	—	—						42–5819	42–5819	89–3022
A10 Plunger	67–670	—	—				24–4065	24–4217	65–5883	65–5883	89–3022
A10 Road Rocket	67–670	—	—				24–4065	24–4217	65–5883	89–3022	89–3022
A10 Super Rocket	67–670	—	—				24–4065	24–4217	42–5819	42–5819	89–3022

Printed in England   B.S.A. MOTOR CYCLES LTD., Service Dept., Birmingham 11.

BSA SERVICE SHEET No. 704

ALL MODELS
PISTON CLEARANCES

To avoid the possibility of seizure or piston tap, pistons must be fitted with adequate but not excessive clearance.

The following are the recommended total clearances between the bottom of the piston and the cylinder wall.

MODEL			Tolerances
Dandy 70		7.25 : 1	.003—.004″
D1			.0027—.0045″
D3, C15			.0025—.004″
D5, D7			.003—.005″
C10, C10L			.0045—.0065″
C11, C11G, C12			.0035—.0055″
C15	(Star Group)	6.4 : 1 to 10 : 1	.0017—.0033″
B31			.004—.0055″
B31	(Split skirt)		.0005—.0016″
B32A			.002—.004″
BB32	Gold Star	8 : 1	.003—.0045″
		6.5 : 1	.004—.0055″
		7.5 : 1	.002—.004″
		9 : 1	.003—.0045″
CB32	Gold Star	6.5 : 1	.002—.004″
		8 : 1	.003—.0045″
		8.5 : 1	.003—.0045″
		9 : 1	.003—.0045″
		12.25 : 1	.004—.0055″
		13 : 1	.004—.0055″
DB32	Gold Star	7.25 : 1	.0025—.004″
		8 : 1	.003—.0045″
		9 : 1	.003—.0045″
B40	(Star Group)	7.0 : 1 to 8.7 : 1	.0015—.003″
B33			.0045—.0065″
B33	(Split skirt)		.0006—.00275″
B34A			.0045—.0065″
BB34	Gold Star	7.5 : 1 Standard	.0045—.0065″
		8 : 1	.0025—.0045″
		9 : 1	.0025—.0045″
		6.8 : 1	.0045—.0065″
		11.1	.0025—.0045″
CB34	Gold Star	7.25 : 1	.003—.0045″
		8 : 1	.003—.0045″
		9 : 1	.003—.0045″
DB34	Gold Star	8 : 1	.003—.0045″
DBD34	Gold Star	8.75 : 1	.003—.0045″

B.S.A. Service Sheet No. 704 (contd.)

MODEL			Tolerances
M20			.004—.006"
M21			.004—.006"
M33			.0045—.0065"
M33	(Split skirt)		.0006—.00275"
A7		6.7 : 1	.002—.004"
	(Split skirt)	6.7 : 1	.0011—.0031"
		7.25 : 1	.002—.004"
	(Split skirt)		.0011—.0031"
A7	(Star Twin)		.002—.004"
A7	(Split skirt)	(Star Twin and Shooting Star)	.001—.0031"
A7	(Shooting Star)	8 : 1 (after Engine No. CA7SS-4501)	.0035—.005"
A50	(Star Twin)	8.0 : 1 to 9.0 : 1	.0011—.0025"
A10	(Golden Flash)	6.5 : 1	.003—.0045"
	(Split skirt)	6.5 : 1	.0025—.0045"
	(Split skirt)	7.25 : 1	.0025—.0045"
A10	(Super Flash and Road Rocket)	8 : 1	.003—.0045"
A10	(Golden Flash)	7.5 : 1 (after Engine No. DA10-651)	.0035—.005"
A10	(Super Rocket)	8.5:1 (after Engine No. CA10R-6001)	.004—.0055"
A10	(Rocket Gold Star)	8.75 : 1	.001—.0025"
A65	(Star Twin)	7.5 : 1 to 9.0 : 1	.0012—.0027"

B.S.A. MOTOR CYCLES LTD., Service Department, Armoury Road, Birmingham 11

B.S.A. PRESS

BSA SERVICE SHEET No. 705

All Models
October, 1948
Reprinted April, 1960

PERIODICAL ATTENTIONS.

HUBS. **Every 1,000 miles.**

Inject grease through the nipples located in the centres of the hubs. Do not overdo this, otherwise grease will penetrate to the brake linings and cause ineffective brakes. Three or four strokes of the gun should be ample. Where no grease nipple is provided the bearings should be removed and packed with grease when the machine is in need of complete overhaul.

BRAKE CAM SPINDLES.

Grease sparingly. Two or three strokes of the gun only, or if no grease nipple is provided, apply a few drops of engine oil between the brake arm and the spindle.

SPEEDOMETER DRIVE.

Grease well. Three or four strokes of the gun regularly.

ENGINE OIL. **Every 2,000 miles (except 2-stroke models).**

The oil tank and sump should be drained (preferably when the engine is warm after a longish run), and the tank refilled with fresh oil.

In case of new or re-conditioned engines, the oil should be drained and renewed after the first 250 miles, and again after 1,000 miles.

REAR CHAIN.

Remove the rear chain, clean thoroughly in paraffin, and soak in engine oil or molten grease and graphite.

CONTACT BREAKER (except A and C Group Models).

A very small quantity of thin oil should be injected into the lubrication wick, and the face cam smeared with oil. The wick is accessible after removing the spring contact arm (held by the round-headed screw at the opposite end to the contact point) and is located in the hollow end of the round-headed screw which is revealed when the spring arm is removed.

When replacing the arm, it is important that the small curved backing spring is refitted correctly, i.e., with the bent portion facing outwards.

DYNAMO ARMATURE BUSH (A and C Group Models fitted with lubricator).

A few drops of oil injected through the lubricator are sufficient.

Every 5,000 miles.

Drain the gearbox and refill with new oil up to the level of the filler plug.
Drain the telescopic forks and refill each leg with correct amount of new oil.
In the case of new or re-conditioned gearboxes, change the oil after the first 1,000 miles.

New Machines.

CYLINDER HEAD BOLTS (except B and M O.H.V. engines).

Examine the cylinder head joint daily, and if leakage becomes apparent, tighten the bolts, working diagonally so as to pull the head down evenly. Do not over-tighten otherwise there is a possibility of distortion or bolt stretch.

CYLINDER BASE NUTS (except B and M O.H.V. engines).

There are five of these—one at each of the four corners outside, and one inside the tappet chest on the single cylinder models. A Group Models have eight cylinder base nuts and Model C11 six nuts. Tighten after the first 100 miles.

CYLINDER BARREL AND HEAD FIXING (B and M O.H.V. engines).

The barrel and head are both secured to the crankcase by four long bolts coupled to bushes screwed into the latter. Apply a spanner to the upper hexagon for tightening. These bolts have right-hand threads, and, being inverted, are tightened by turning the spanner to the right.

B.S.A. MOTOR CYCLES LTD.,
Service Dept., Waverley Works, Birmingham, 10

(PRINTED IN ENGLAND)

BSA SERVICE SHEET No. 706

TELESCOPIC FORKS

'A', 'B' AND 'M' GROUP, C10, C11G AND C12 MODELS

Of robust design B.S.A. telescopic forks require the minimum of maintenance it being necessary only to replenish the oil occasionally between major overhauls.

For normal use each fork leg should contain a quarter pint of oil (142 c.c.) or three-eighths of a pint (213 c.c.) according to model as detailed below.

Quarter-pint Capacity
Models C10, C10L (1956 onwards), C11, C11G, C12, B31-33 (up to 1956), B32-34 and Gold Stars (up to 1952), M20, M21, M33, 'A' Group (up to 1952).

Three-eighth Pint Capacity
Models B31-33 (1956 onwards), B32-34 and Gold Stars (1952 onwards), 'A' Group (1952 onwards).

Oil Changes
To replenish the oil remove the drain plugs at the base of the fork tubes and remove the fork top nuts. Allow the oil to drain off. Replace the plugs and pour either a quarter or three-eighths pint of oil into the hollow tubes revealed when the top plugs are removed.

Dismantling
Before beginning to overhaul the forks have the following tools and replacement parts available in case they are required:—

61-3001	Fork top nut spanner.
61-3003	Fork plug spanner.
61-3005	Oil Seal holder assembly tool.
61-3006	Oil seal extractor.
61-3007	Oil seal assembly tool.
61-3350	Fork leg assembly and removal tool.
29-5334	Packing shim (.005 in.).
29-5335	Packing shim (.010 in.).
29-5336	Packing shim (.020 in.).
29-5337	Packing shim (.030 in.).
65-5424 (2)	Fork top bush ('A' and 'B' Group).
29-5347 (2)	Fork bottom bush ('A', 'B', C11G and C12).
29-5346 (2)	Fork top bush (C10L, C11G and C12).
29-5313 (2)	Fork oil seal (all models).
	Number 5 twine (approx 18 in.).

B.S.A. Service Sheet No. 706 (contd.)

Remove the front wheel and front mudguard. Take out the fork top cap (A) Fig. X1, screw service tool part number 61-3350 into the thread at the top of the fork shaft using the larger of the fine threads.

Slacken off the pinch bolt (B) Fig. X1.

Take a firm grasp of the lower fork sliding tube and strike the top of the tool smartly with a hammer. This will release the shaft from its taper and the complete fork leg can be drawn down and removed from the machine.

Repeat the operation on the other leg.

To dismantle the lower section of the fork hold the fork sliding tube by gripping the wheel spindle lug in a soft-jawed vice and lift off the spring (see Fig. X2).

Enter service tool part number 61-3005 until the dogs on the tool engage in the slots at the bottom of the oil seal holder (D) Fig. X2. Pressing the tool down and turning at the same time unscrew the oil seal holder. Slide the holder up the shaft until it becomes tight on the tapered section of the shaft. Do not use excessive force or the oil seal may be damaged.

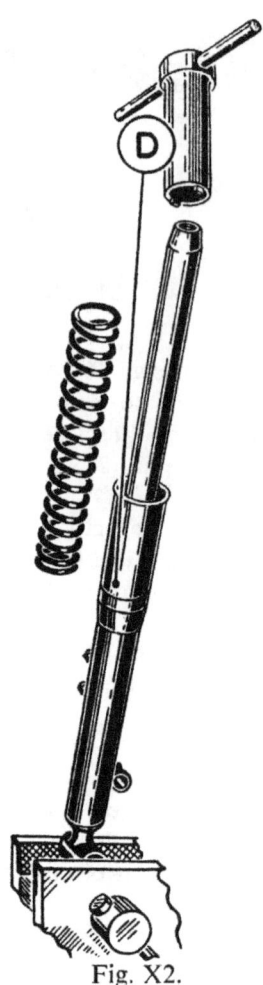

Fig. X2.

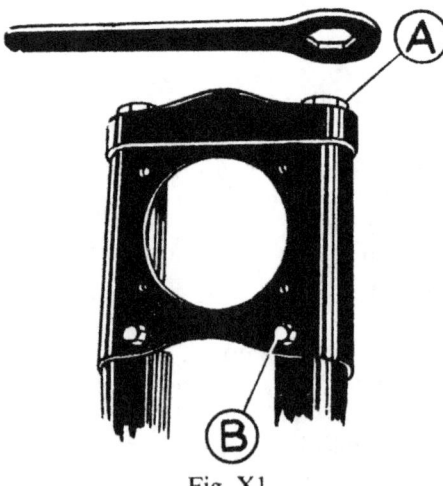

Fig. X1.

The top fork bearing is retained in the fork leg by a circlip (E) Fig. X3, which can be prised out with a sharp tool such as the tang end of a file. There may be a number of shims fitted between the circlip and the top bearing. These must be replaced if the bushes are not renewed when assembling.

Grip the shaft in a vice using soft-jaw clamps on the unground portion of the shaft and unscrew the gland nut (F) Fig. X4. Service tool part number 61-3003 is designed for this purpose. Remove the gland nut which secures the lower bearing and both bearings, shims, circlip and oil seal holder will then slide off the shaft.

B.S.A. Service Sheet No. 706 (contd.)

If it is necessary to remove the oil seal place the lower edge of the holder on a soft wooden block and enter service tool part number 61-3006 into the top of the holder. Give this tool a sharp tap with a hammer and the oil seal will be driven out.

Reassembly

Reassembly is carried out in the reverse order. Cleanliness is essential and before attempting to reassemble clean all parts thoroughly and clean down the bench on which the forks have been dismantled.

If the oil seal is to be replaced care must be taken that the feather edge of the seal is not damaged. Enter the oil seal (*I*) Fig. X6 into the holder, metal part first, and drive home using B.S.A. service tool part number 61-3007 (*H*) Fig. X6. Place the oil seal holder over the shaft and pass it up the shaft until it is firmly held on the tapered section. Do not use excessive force or the oil seal may be damaged. Place the circlip over the shaft followed by the shims and top bearing and then the bottom bearing. Place the steel washer over the thread of the gland nut, screw up the gland nut and holding the shaft firmly in a soft-jawed vice as described in dismantling procedure firmly tighten the gland nut.

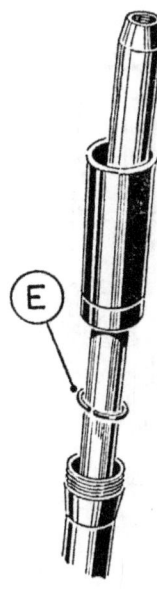

Fig. X3.

Place the lower sliding tube in a vice and enter the fork shaft with parts assembled into the lower sliding tube. Fit the circlip and check for up and down movement on the

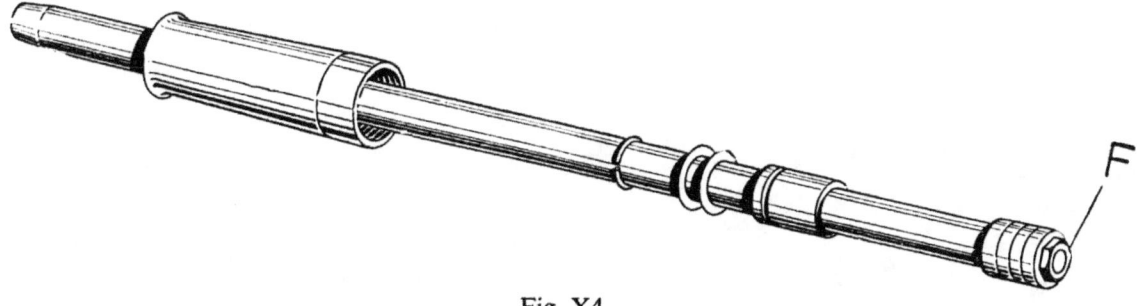

Fig. X4.

top bush. If a new bush has been fitted it may be necessary to add to, or take from, some of the existing shims. Packing shims are available in the following sizes:—

.005 in.   Part Number 29-5334
.010 in.   Part Number 29-5335
.020 in.   Part Number 29-5336
.030 in.   Part Number 29-5337

B.S.A. Service Sheet No. 706 (contd.)

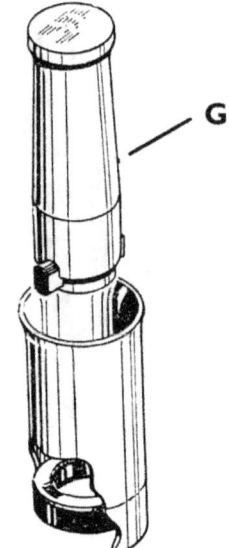

Fig. X5.

If the bush is not properly shimmed a tapping noise may be heard when the machine is ridden.

Having shimmed up the bush correctly and fitted the circlip firmly in position, screw down the oil seal holder and take one turn of number five twine around the base of the thread to provide an additional seal. Screw down the oil seal firmly using B.S.A. service tool part number 61-3005.

To fit the main tubes to the fork yokes screw B.S.A. service tool part number 61-3350 into the top of the tube and pass it up through the two yokes, then fit the collar and nut and draw the tube firmly home into the yokes. When the tube is fully home the pinch bolts on the lower yoke should be tightened. The tool may then be removed and after filling the legs with the correct amount of oil the top plugs can be replaced and fully tightened. Finally slacken the pinch bolt. position the top outer shroud centrally over the lower leg Check that the top nuts are completely tight and retighten the pinch bolts.

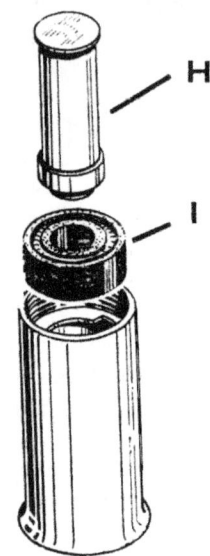

Fig. X6.

B.S.A. MOTOR CYCLES LTD., Service Department, Armoury Road, Birmingham 11.
PRINTED IN ENGLAND — B.S.A. PRESS

BSA SERVICE SHEET No. 708

ALL MODELS

CARBURATION. Monobloc and Seperate Float Chamber Type

How the Carburetter Works

The function of the carburetter is to atomise the petrol and proportion it correctly with the air drawn in through the intake on the induction stroke. The action of the float and needle in the float chamber maintains the level of fuel at the needle jet, and when the engine is stopped and no further fuel is being used the needle valve cuts off the supply.

The twist-grip controls, by means of a cable, the position of the throttle slide and the throttle needle and so governs the volume of mixture supplied to the engine.

The mixture is correct at all throttle openings, if the carburetter is correctly tuned.

The opening of the throttle brings first into action the mixture supply from the pilot jet, then as it progressively opens, via the pilot by-pass the mixture is augmented from the needle jet. Up to three-quarter throttle this action is controlled by the tapered needle in the needle jet, and from three-quarters onwards the mixture is controlled by the main jet.

The pilot jet (J), which in the older type of carburetter is embodied in the jet block, has been replaced in the Monobloc carburetter by a detachable jet (9) Fig. X5, assembled in the carburetter body and sealed by a cover nut.

The main jet does not spray directly into the mixing chamber, but discharges through the needle jet into the primary air chamber and goes from there as a rich petrol/air mixture through the primary air choke into the main air choke.

Although the maintenance and tuning instruction contained in this Service Sheet apply equally well to the Monobloc and separate float chamber types of carburetter, the new instrument has been designed with a view to giving improved performance, and certain constructional changes have been made.

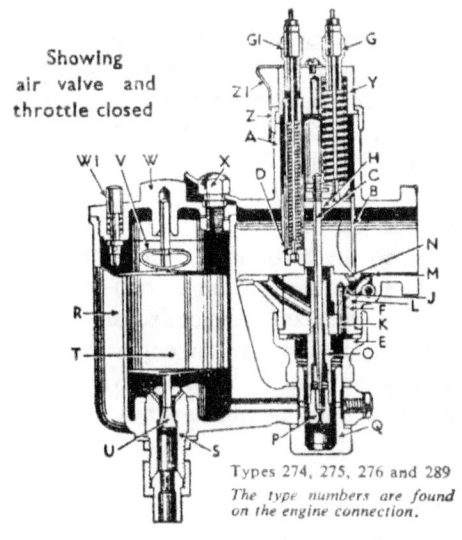

Showing air valve and throttle closed

Types 274, 275, 276 and 289
The type numbers are found on the engine connection.

A. Mixing Chamber.
B. Throttle Valve.
C. Jet Needle and Clip above.
D. Air Valve.
E. Mixing Chamber Union Nut.
F. Jet Block.
G/G1. Cable Adjusters.
H. Jet Block Barrel.
J. Pilot Jet.
K. Passage to Pilot.
L. Pilot Air Passage.
M. Pilot Mixture Outlet.
N. Pilot by-pass.
O. Needle Jet.
P. Main Jet.
Q. Float Chamber Holding Bolt.
R. Float Chamber.
S. Needle Valve Seating.
T. Float.
U. Float Needle Valve.
V. Float Needle Clip.
W. Float Chamber Cover.
W1. Tickler.
X. Float Chamber Lock Screw.
Y. Mixing Chamber Top Cap.
Z. Mixing Chamber Lock Ring.
Z1. Mixing Chamber Security Spring.

Fig. X4. *A sectioned illustration of Needle Jet Carburetter.*

B.S.A. Service Sheet No. 708 (contd.)

The float chamber is a drum-shaped reservoir, die cast in one piece with the mixing chamber. The material used being zinc-alloy. The float is designed to pivot instead of rising and falling, as in the separate float chamber type, and as it does so, it impinges on a nylon needle controlling the inflow of fuel.

Variations of up to 20° in the angle of the carburetter when fitted, do not affect the working of the float, therefore it lends itself to use for down draught carburation and is not so greatly effected by the degree of lean when cornering. Access to the float (Fig. X6) is gained by removing a plate held in place by three screws.

Compensation for over-rich mixture which results from snap throttle openings, is provided by bleed holes in the needle jet (Fig. X5). A compensatory air bleed is provided, this is the larger of the two holes at the mouth of the air intake, which leads to the space around the needle jet (Fig. X5).

The pilot intake is the smaller of the two holes, and operates in conjunction with the detachable pilot jet (Fig. X5). This pilot mixture is adjusted as before, by an adjusting screw (Fig. 8a).

Hints and Tips—Starting from Cold
Flood the carburetter by depressing the tickler and close the air control, set the ignition say, half-retarded. Then open the throttle about ⅛ in., then kick-start. If the throttle is too far open, starting will be difficult.

Starting—Engine Hot
Do not flood the carburetter, but it may be found necessary with some engines to close the air lever, set the ignition to half-retarded, the throttle to ⅛ in. open and kick-start. If the carburetter has been flooded and won't start because the mixture is too rich—open the throttle wide and give the engine several turns to clear the richness, then start again with the throttle ⅛ in. open, and air valve wide open. Generally speaking it is not advisable to flood at all when an engine is hot.

Starting—General
By experiment, find out if and when it is necessary to flood, also note the best position for the air lever and the throttle for the easiest starting. Excessive flooding, particularly when the engine is hot, will make starting more difficult. It is necessary only to raise the level of petrol in the float chamber, by depressing the tickler.

Starting—Single Lever Carburetters
Open the throttle very slightly from the idling position and flood the carburetter more or less according to the engine being cold or hot respectively.

B.S.A. Service Sheet No. 708 (contd.)

SECTIONAL ILLUSTRATIONS OF CARBURETTERS. Types 375, 376 and 389

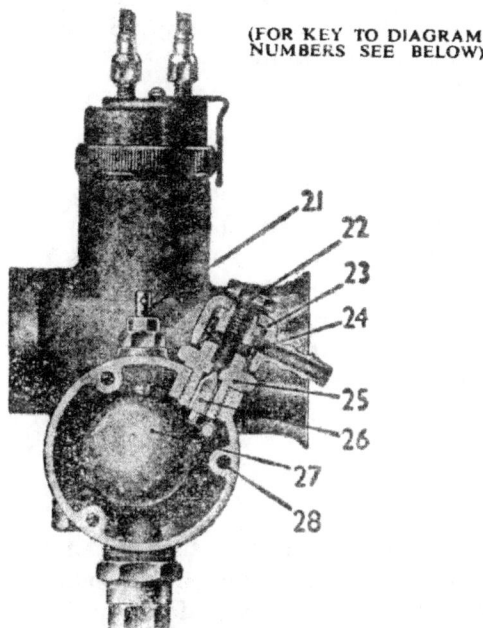

(MONOBLOC)
Fig. X6. *Section through Float Chamber.*

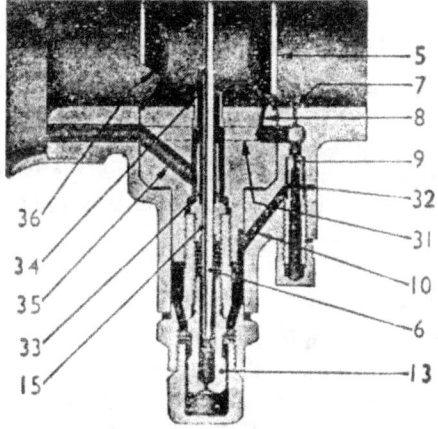

Diagrammatic section of Carburetter showing only the lower half of the throttle chamber with the throttle a little open—and the internal primary air passages to the main jet and pilot system.

FOR KEY TO DIAGRAM NUMBERS SEE BELOW
Fig. X5.

1. Mixing Chamber Top.
2. Mixing Chamber Cap.
3. Carburetter Body.
4. Jet Needle Clip.
5. Throttle Valve.
6. Jet Needle.
7. Pilot outlet.
8. Pilot by-pass.
9. Pilot Jet.
10. Petrol Feed to Pilot Jet.
11. Pilot Jet Cover Nut.
12. Main Jet Cover.
13. Main Jet.
14. Jet Holder.
15. Needle Jet.
16. Jet Block.
17. Air Valve

18. Mixing Chamber Cap Spring.
19. Cable Adjuster (air).
20. Cable Adjuster (throttle).
21. Tickler.
22. Banjo Bolt.
23. Banjo.
24. Filter Gauze.
25. Needle Seating.
26. Needle.
27. Float.
28. Side Cover Screws.
31. Air to Pilot Jet.
32. Feed Holes in Pilot Jet.
33. Bleed Holes in Needle Jet.
34. Primary Air Choke.
35. Primary Air Passage.
36. Throttle Valve Cut-away

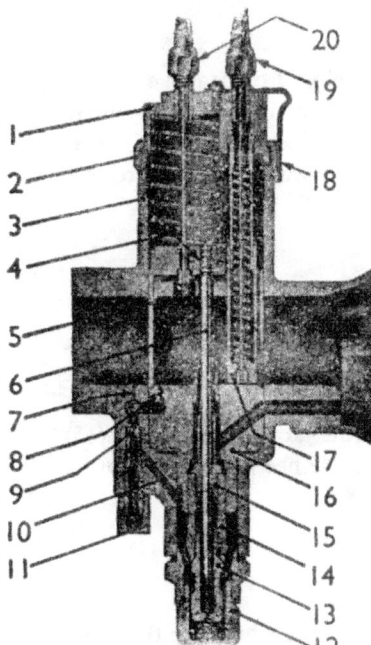

Fig. 7. *Secttion through Mixing Chamber, showing Air Valve and Thaottle closed.*

29. PILOT AIR ADJUSTING SCREW
This screw regulates the strength of the mixture for "idling" and for the initial opening of the throttle. The screw controls the depression on the pilot jet by metering the amount of air that mixes with the petrol.

30. THROTTLE ADJUSTING SCREW
Set this screw to hold the throttle open sufficiently to keep the engine running when the twist-grip is shut off.

B.S.A. Service Sheet No. 708 (contd.)

Cable Controls

See that there is a minimum of backlash when the controls are set back and that any movement of the handlebar does not cause the throttle to open; this is done by the adjusters on the top of the carburetter. See that the throttle shuts down freely.

Petrol Feed

Verification. Detach petrol pipe union at the float chamber end; turn on petrol tap momentarily and see that fuel gushes out. Avoid petrol pipes with vertical loops as they cause air-locks. Flooding may be due to a worn or bent needle or a leaky float, but nearly all flooding with new machines is due to impurities (grit, fluff, etc.) in the tank—so clean out the float chamber periodically till the trouble ceases. If the trouble persists the tank might be drained, swilled out, etc. Note that if the carburetter, either vertical or horizontal, is flooding with the engine stopped, the overflow from the main jet will not run into the engine but out of the carburetter through a hole at the base of the mixing chamber.

Fixing Carburetter and Air Leaks

Erratic slow running is often caused by air leaks, so verify there are none at the point of attachment to the cylinder or inlet pipe—check by means of oil placed around the joint, if there are leaks the oil will be sucked in, and eliminate by new washers and the equal tightening up of the flange nuts. Also in old machines look out for air leaks caused by a worn throttle or worn inlet valve guides.

Explosions in Exhaust

May be caused by too weak a pilot mixture when the throttle is closed or nearly closed—also, it may be caused by too rich a pilot mixture and an air leak in the exhaust system; the reason in either case is that the mixture has not fired in the cylinder and has fired in the hot silencer. If the explosion occurs when the throttle is fairly wide open the trouble will be ignition—not carburation.

Excessive Petrol Consumption

On a new machine may be due to flooding, caused by impurities from the petrol tank lodging on the float needle seat and so preventing its valve from closing. If the machine has had several years use, flooding may be caused by a worn float needle valve. Also excessive petrol consumption will be apparent if the throttle needle jet (o) Fig. X4. or (15) Fig. X5, has worn; it may be remedied or improved by lowering the needle in the throttle, but if it cannot be, then the only remedy is to get a new needle jet.

Air Filters

These may affect the jet setting, so if one is fitted afterwards to the carburetter the main jet may have to be smaller. If a carburetter is set with an air filter and the engine is run without it, take care not to overheat the engine due to too weak a mixture; testing with the air control will indicate if a larger main jet and higher needle position are required.

B.S.A. Service Sheet No. 708 (contd.)

Faults

The trouble may not be carburation; if the trouble cannot be remedied by making mixtures richer or weaker with the air control, and you know the petrol feed is good and the carburetter is not flooding, the trouble is elsewhere.

Fault Finding

There are only *two* possible faults in carburation, either *richness* of mixture or *weakness* of mixture, so in case of trouble decide which is the cause, by:—

1. Examining the petrol feed ...
   - Verify jets and passages are clear.
   - Verify ample flow.
   - Verify there is no flooding.

2. Looking for air leaks ...
   - At the connection to the engine.
   - Or due to leaky inlet valve stems.

3. Defective or worn parts ...
   - As a slack throttle-worn needle jet.
   - The mixing chamber union nut not tightened up, or loose jets.

4. *Testing with the air control* to see if by richening the mixture the results are better or worse.

Indications of

Richness:

Black smoke in exhaust.
Petrol spraying out of carburetter.
Four strokes, eight-stroking
Two strokes, four-stroking.
Heavy, lumpy running.
Heavy petrol consumption.
? If the jet block (F) is not tightened up by washer and nut (E) richness will be caused through leakage of petrol.
? Air cleaner choked up.
? Needle jet worn large.
Sparking plug sooty.

Weakness:

Spitting in carburetter.
Erratic slow running.
Overheating.
Acceleration poor.
Engine goes better if:—
Throttle not wide open, or air control is partially closed.
? Has air cleaner been removed.
? Jets partially choked up
Removing the silencer or running with a racing silencer requires a richer setting and large main jet.

Note

Verify correctness of fuel feed, stop air leaks, check over ignition and valve operation and timing. *Decide by test whether richness or weakness is the trouble and at what throttle position.* See throttle opening diagrams, Fig. X6.

B.S.A. Service Sheet No. 708 (contd.)

Procedure

If at a particular throttle opening you partially close the air control, and the engine goes better, weakness is indicated; or on the other hand the running is worse, richness is indicated. *Then you proceed to adjust the appropriate part as indicated for that position.*

Fault at Throttle Positions indicated on Fig. X9

To Cure Richness:		To Cure Weakness:
Fit smaller main jet.	1st	Fit larger main jet.
Screw out pilot air screw.	2nd	Screw pilot air screw in.
Fit a throttle with larger cut-away.	3rd	Fit a throttle with smaller cut-away.
Lower needle one or two grooves.	4th	Raise needle one or two grooves.

Notes

It is not correct to cure a rich mixture at half-throttle by fitting a smaller main jet because the main jet may be correct for power at full throttle: the proper thing to do is to lower the needle.

Information on throttle slides and needle position is given in paragraphs (*f*) and (*e*) respectively in the next section entitled "Tuning".

Changing from Standard Petrols to Special Fuels.

Such as alcohol mixtures will, with the same setting in the carburetter, certainly cause weakness of mixture and possible damage from overheating.

TUNING

(*a*) Figs. X8 and 8a are two diagrammatic sections of the carburetter to show:
1. The throttle stop screw.
2. The pilot air screw.

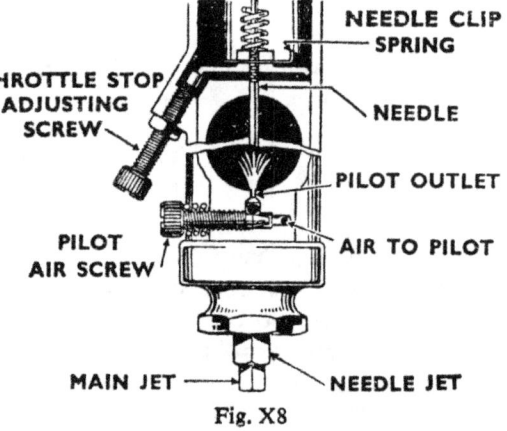

Fig. X8

(*b*) **Throttle Stop Screw**

Set this screw to prop the throttle open sufficiently to keep the engine running when the twist-grip is shut off.

(*c*) **Pilot Air Screw**

This screw regulates the strength of the mixture for "idling" and for the initial opening of the throttle. The screw controls the suction on the pilot petrol jet by metering the amount of air that mixes with the petrol.

NOTE:—The air for the pilot jet may be admitted internally or externally according to one or other of the designs, but there is no difference in tuning.

(*d*) **Main Jet**

The main jet controls the petrol supply when the throttle is more than three-quarters open, but at smaller throttle openings although the supply of fuel goes through the main jet, the amount is diminished by the metering effect of the needle in the needle jet.

Each jet is calibrated and numbered so that its exact discharge is known and two jets of the same number are alike.

B.S.A. Service Sheet No. 708 (contd.)

Never reamer a Jet out, get another of the right size
The bigger the number the bigger the jet. Spare jets *are sealed*.

To get at the main jet, undo the float chamber holding bolt (Q) Fig. X4, or main jet cover number 12 (Fig. X7). The jet is screwed into the needle jet so if the jet is tight, hold the needle jet also carefully with a spanner whilst unscrewing the main jet.

(e) Needle and Needle Jet

The needle is attached to the throttle and being tapered either allows more or less petrol to pass through the needle jets as the throttle is opened or closed throughout the range, except when idling or nearly full throttle. The needle jet is of a defined size and is only altered from standard when using alcohol fuels.

The taper needle position in relation to the throttle opening can be set according to the mixture required by fixing it to the throttle with the needle clip spring in a certain groove (see illustration above), thus either raising or lowering it. Raising the needle richens the mixture and lowering it weakens the mixture at throttle openings from quarter to three-quarter open (see illustration, Fig. X9).

(f) Throttle Valve Cut-away

The atmospheric side of the throttle is cut away to influence the depression on the main fuel supply and thus gives a means of tuning between the pilot and needle jet range of throttle opening. The amount of cut-away is recorded by a number marked on the throttle, viz.: 6/3 means throttle type 6 with number 3 cut-away; larger cut-aways, say 4 and 5, give weaker mixtures, and 2 and 1 richer mixtures.

(g) Air Valve

Is used only for starting and running when cold, and for experimenting with, otherwise run with it wide open.

(h) Tickler

A small plunger located in the float chamber lid. When pressed down on the float, the neddle valve is pushed off its seat and so "flooding" is achieved. Flooding temporarily enriches the mixture until the level of the petrol subsides to normal.

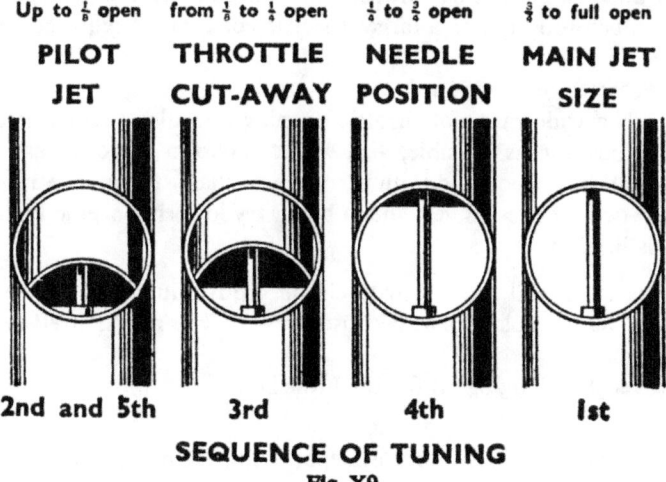

Phases of Amal Needle Jet Carburettor Throttle Openings

Fig. X9

B.S.A. Service Sheet No. 708 (contd.)

Sequence of Tuning
Tune up. In the following order only, by so doing you will not upset good results obtained.

Note.—The carburetter is automatic throughout the throttle range—the air control should always be wide open except when used for starting or until the engine has warmed up. We assume normal petrols are used.

Read remarks on "Fault Finding" and "Tuning" for each tuning device and get the motor going perfectly on a quiet road with a slight up gradient so that on test the engine is pulling.

1st Main Jet with Throttle in position
Test the engine for full throttle; if when at full throttle, the power seems better with the throttle less than wide open or with the air valve closed slightly the main jet is too small. If the engine runs "heavily" the main jet is too large. If testing for speed work note the jet size is rich enough to keep engine cool, and to verify this, examine the sparking plug by taking a fast run, declutching and stopping engine quickly. If the plug body at the end has a bright black appearance, the mixture is correct; if sooty, the mixture is rich; or if a dry grey colour, the mixture is too weak and a larger jet is necessary.

2nd Pilot Jet with Throttle in positions 2 and 5
With engine idling too fast with the twist-grip shut off and the throttle shut down on to the throttle stop screw, and ignition set for best slow running: (1) Loosen stop screw nut and screw down until engine runs slower and begins to falter, then screw the pilot air screw in or out to make engine run regularly and faster. (2) Now gently lower the throttle stop screw until the engine runs slower and just begins to falter, then lock the nut lightly and begin again to adjust the pilot air screw to get best slow running; if this second adjustment makes engine run too fast, go over the job again a third time. Finally, lock up tight the throttle stop screw nut without disturbing the screw's position.

3rd Throttle Cut-away with Throttle in position
If, as you take off from the idling position, there is objectionable spitting from the carburetter, slightly richen the pilot mixture by screwing the air screw in about half a turn, but if this is not effective, screw it back again and fit a throttle with a smaller cut-away. If the engine jerks under load at this throttle position and there is no spitting, either the throttle needle is much too high or a larger throttle cut-away is required to cure richness.

4th Needle with Throttle in position 4
The needle controls a wide range of throttle opening and also the acceleration. Try the needle in as low a position as possible, viz., with the clip in a groove as near the end as possible; if acceleration is poor and with air valve partially closed the results are better, raise the needle by two grooves; if very much better try lowering needle by one groove and leave it where it is best.

Note:—If mixture is still too rich with clip in groove number 1 nearest the end—the needle jet probably wants replacement because of wear. The needle itself never wears out.

5th Finally go over the idling again for final touches.

B.S.A. MOTOR CYCLES LTD., Service Department, Armoury Road, Birmingham 11.
Printed in England
B.S.A. Press.

BSA SERVICE SHEET No. 708B

ALL MODELS
CARBURATION AT HIGH ALTITUDES

The carburetter settings of all B.S.A. motor cycles are designed to give the best all round performance at altitudes of a few thousand feet.

At greater altitudes the air becomes rarefied with the result that the mixture is incorrect.

To overcome this difficulty it is necessary to reduce the size of the main jet, the reduction depending on the altitude at which the machine is mainly used.

The table below shows the percentage of reduction at given altitudes, but it must be emphasised that while the alteration to jet size will correct the mixture, it will not replace the lost power. This can only be corrected by "blowing" or super-charging.

It may also be advisable to re-tune the carburetter for smaller throttle openings this should be done in accordance with Service Sheet 708.

Altitude.	Percentage of reduction in jet size.
3,000 feet	5%
6,000 feet	9%
9,000 feet	13%
12,000 feet	17%

B.S.A. MOTOR CYCLES LTD., Service Dept., Armoury Road, Birmingham 11.
B.S.A. Press.

BSA SERVICE SHEET No. 709

ALL MODELS
FAULT FINDING

No adjustments should be made, or any part tampered with, until the cause of the trouble is known. Otherwise adjustments which are correct may be deranged.

Engine Stops Suddenly:
    Petrol shortage in tank, or choked petrol supply pipe or tap.
    Choked main jet, or water in float chamber.
    Oiled up or fouled sparking plug.
    Water on high-tension pick-up or on sparking plug.

Engine Fails to Start, or is difficult to start:
    Lack of fuel, or insufficient flooding if cold.
    Excessive flooding, allowing neat petrol to enter the cylinder.
    Oil sparking plug, or stuck-up valve or valve stem sticky.
    Weak valve spring, or valve not seating properly.
    Throttle opening too large, or pilot jet choked.
    Contact points dirty, or gap incorrect.
    Flat battery, if coil ignition, or faulty electrical connections in ignition circuit.

Loss of Power:
    Valve, or valves, not seating properly.
    Weak valve spring or springs, or sticking valve.
    No tappet clearance, or excessive clearance.
    Lack of oil in tank.
    Brakes adjusted too closely.
    Badly fitting or broken piston rings.
    Punctured carburettor float.
    Incorrect ignition timing.

Engine Overheats:
    Lack of proper lubrication.
    Weak valve springs, or pitted valve seats.
    Worn piston rings, or late ignition setting.
    Carburettor setting too weak, or partly choked petrol pipe.

Engine Misses Fire:
    Weak valve spring.
    Defective or oiled sparking plug, or oil on contact points.
    Incorrectly adjusted contact points or tappets.
    Faulty condenser.
    Defective sparking plug or high-tension cable.
    Loose sparking plug terminal.
    Carburettor flooding, due to stuck or defective float.
    Partly choked main jet.
    Choked vent hole in petrol tank filler cap.

Excessive Oil Consumption:
    Stoppage, or partial stoppage, in pipe returning oil from engine to tank.
    Clogged, or partially clogged, filter in sump, or oil tank.
    Badly worn or stuck-up piston rings, causing high pressure in engine crankcase.
    High crankcase pressure, caused by release valve (breather) action.
    Air leak in dry sump oiling system.
    Non-return valve in system not seating.
    Ball valve in oil pump stuck on its seat.

B.S.A. MOTOR CYCLES LTD., Service Department, Armoury Road, Birmingham 11

B.S.A. PRESS

BSA SERVICE SHEET No. 710

ALL MODELS
CHAIN ALTERATIONS AND REPAIRS

A chain rarely breaks if it is kept properly lubricated and adjusted. Usually it is worn out long before it reaches breaking point. The rear chain is the most heavily stressed and is therefore the one most likely to give trouble. Spare parts should be carried to enable the rider to carry out a repair on the road with the aid of a chain rivet extractor (see Fig. X7). The front chain will probably be worn out before it requires shortening.

How to use the Chain Rivet Extractor

First press down lever (A) Fig. X7 to open the two jaws (B). Insert the link to be removed so that the jaws grip the roller and support the uppermost inner side plate. The punch (C) is then screwed on to the rivet head until the rivet is forced through the outer plate.

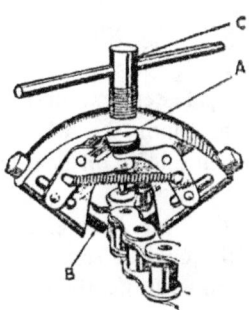

Fig. X7.

To shorten a worn Rear Chain

After a big mileage, the rear chain may have stretched so that no further adjustment is possible by the usual method. In this case it is possible to shorten the chain by one link or pitch, so increasing its useful life. First remove the single connecting spring link (A) securing the two ends of the chain, Fig. X8. If the chain terminates in two ordinary links as in Fig. X8 (in which case the chain will be an even number of pitches) extract the third and fourth rivets (B) from the end and replace the detached three pitches by a single connecting link (C). The connection is made with an additional spring link (D). If one end of the chain has a double cranked link, Fig. X9—in which case the chain will have an odd

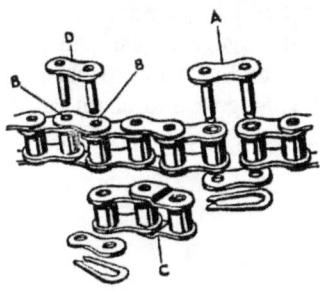

Fig. X8.

Printed in England

B.S.A. Service Sheet No. 710 (contd.)

number of pitches—extract the second and third rivets (A), releasing the cranked link unit complete, which can be retained for further use. Replace with one inner link (B) and again connect up with an additional single connecting link (C).

To repair a damaged Chain

If a roller or link has been damaged (X) Fig. X9, remove rivets (D), take out the damaged link and replace with one inner link, secured by two single connecting links.

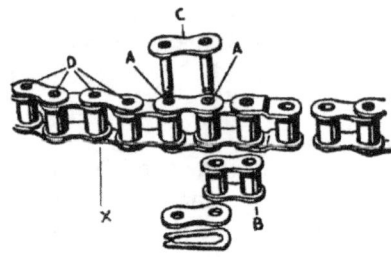

Fig. X9.

It is important that the spring clip fastener should always be put on so that the *closed* end faces the direction of travel of the chain—i.e. when clip is on top run of chain, closed end is toward front of machine—when clip is on bottom run, closed end is towards rear of machine.

It should be noted that once a rivet has been extracted it must not be used again, so that it is important to check that the correct rivet is being removed before actually removing it. In the case of double cranked links, the complete unit comprises an inner link and the cranked outer link—three rollers in all—and these must never be separated.

Fitting Rear Chain

To fit a new rear chain, turn wheel until the spring link of the old chain is located on rear sprocket. Disconnect, and allow the lower run to drop down. Join the top run of the old chain to the new chain by means of the connecting link, and then by pulling on the bottom run of the old chain the new one will be carried round the gearbox sprocket. Then the old chain can be disconnected and the ends of the new one joined together.

When the rear chain breaks and falls from its sprockets, the new or repaired chain can be replaced without taking off the chainguards. One end of the chain must be fed (from the rear) under the front end of the rear top chainguard on to the gearbox sprocket. A long bladed screwdriver or a piece of stiff wire may assist this operation. When the chain has located on the sprocket teeth, engage a gear and gently turn gearbox over with the kickstarter. This will feed chain round gearbox sprocket. When sufficient length of chain is hanging below sprocket, disengage gear and chain can then be pulled round until both runs can be fed inside rear chainguard and engaged on rear wheel sprocket.

B.S.A. MOTOR CYCLES LTD., Service Department, Armoury Road, Birmingham 11.

SERVICE SHEET No. 710x

MARCH, 1969

FRAME REPAIRS

ALL MODELS

Frame repairs must not be attempted unless adequate workshop facilities are available.

The information given in this sheet is intended for the use of Dealers who are unable to take advantage of the B.S.A. repair service and who have frame repair facilities.

Spotting points to enable frame trueing to be carried out can be determined by making use of the dimensions given.

B.S.A. Motor Cycles Ltd., Armoury Road Birmingham 11.

PRINTED IN ENGLAND

IT IS DIFFICULT TO UNDERSTAND WHY B.S.A. ISSUED THE FOLLOWING FRAME DRAWINGS IN VARYING SCALES AND AT SUCH SMALL SIZES - MAKING SOME OF THE DIMENSIONS ALMOST IMPOSSIBLE TO READ. HOWEVER, THEY ARE INCLUDED FOR THE SAKE OF COMPLETENESS

A7-10 RIGID FRAME

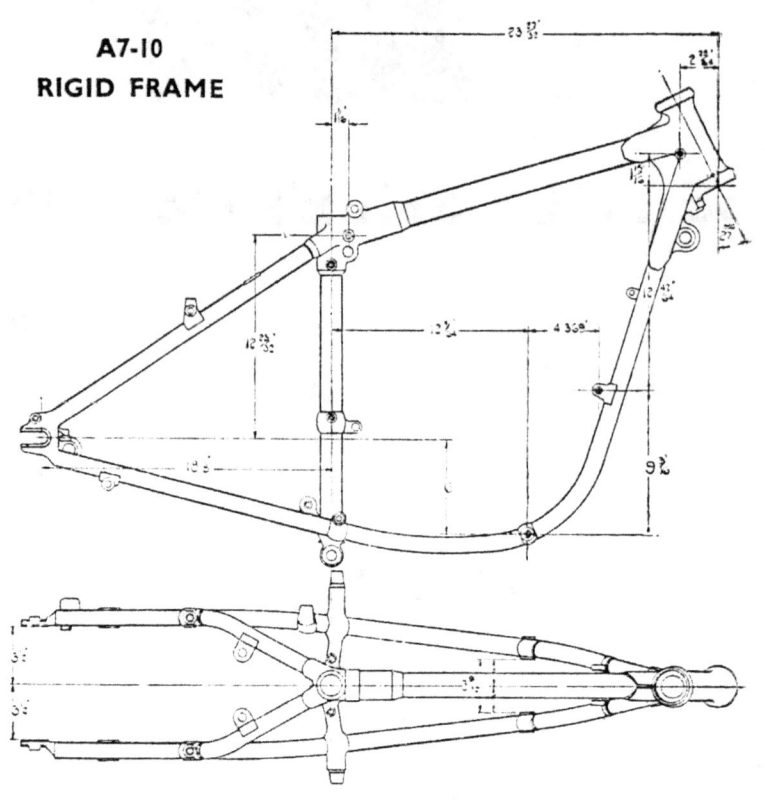

A7-10 SPRING FRAME

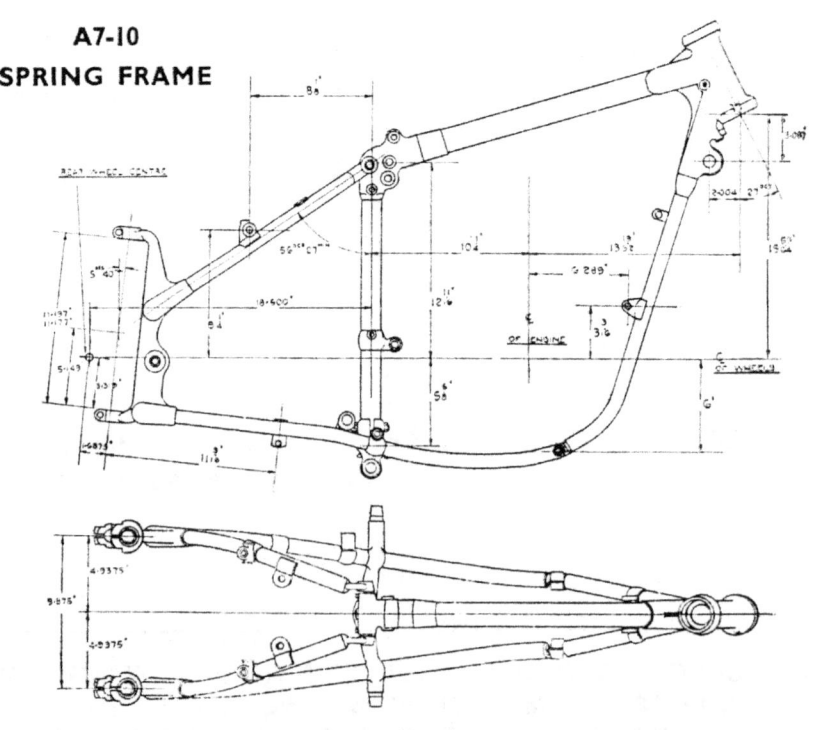

1953 SUPER FLASH SPRING FRAME

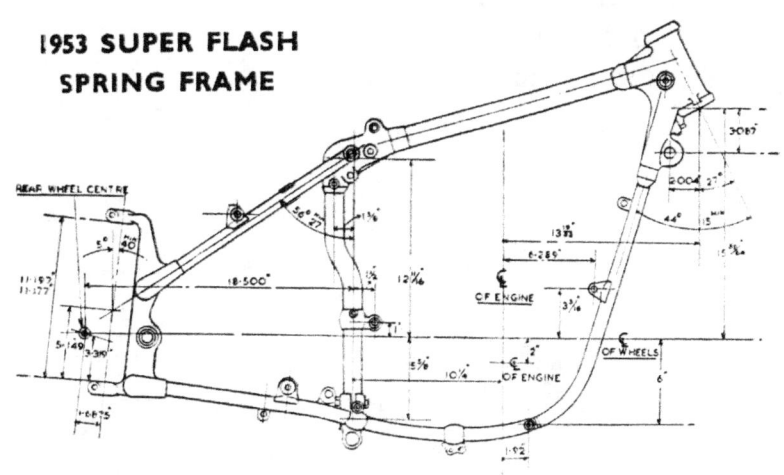

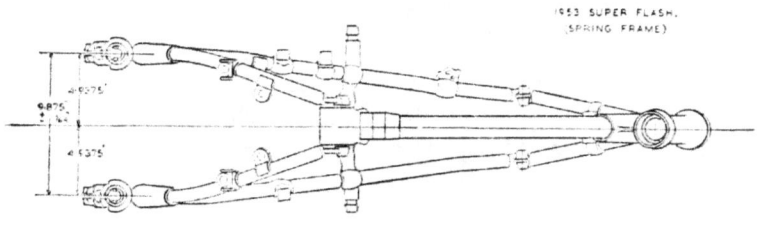

M20, M21 and M33 RIGID FRAME 1945 - 1948

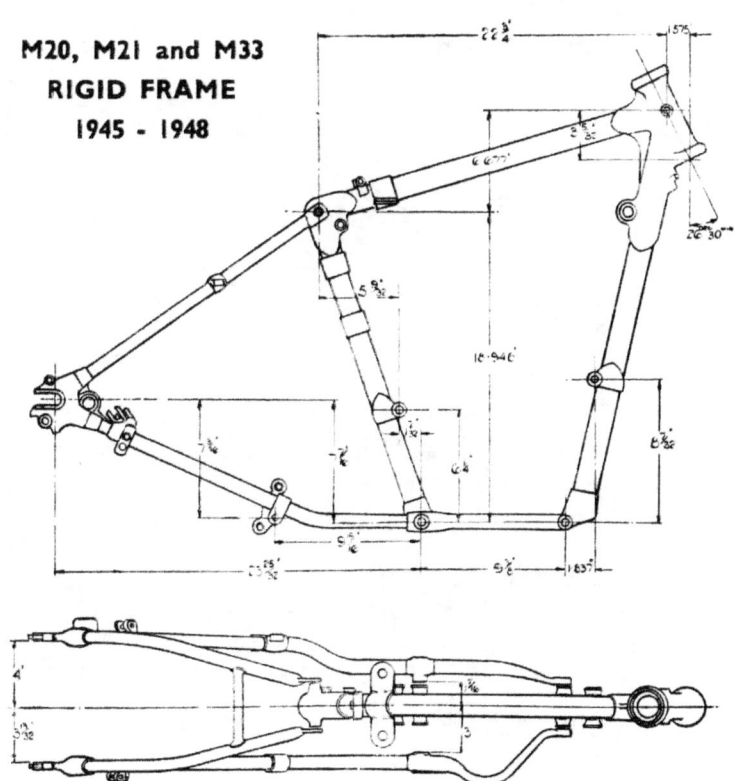

M20, M21 and M33 RIGID FRAME
1949 onwards

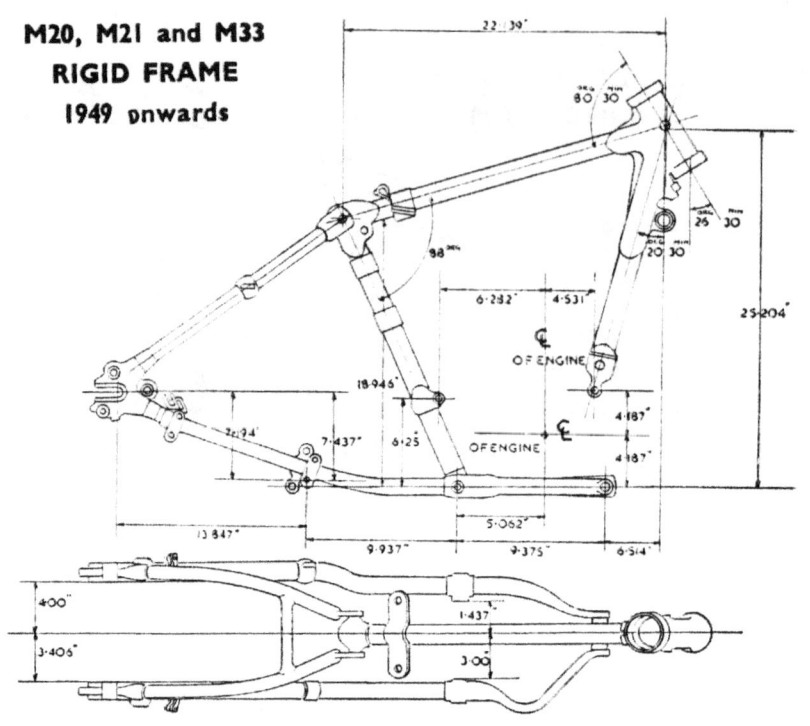

M20, M21 and M33 SPRING FRAME

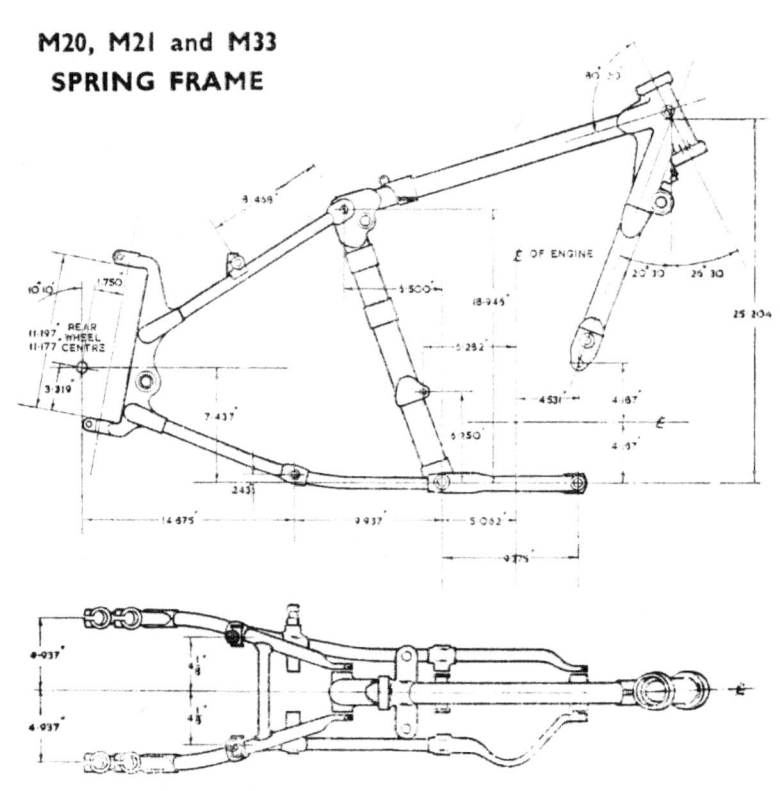

B31-32-33-34 RIGID FRAME

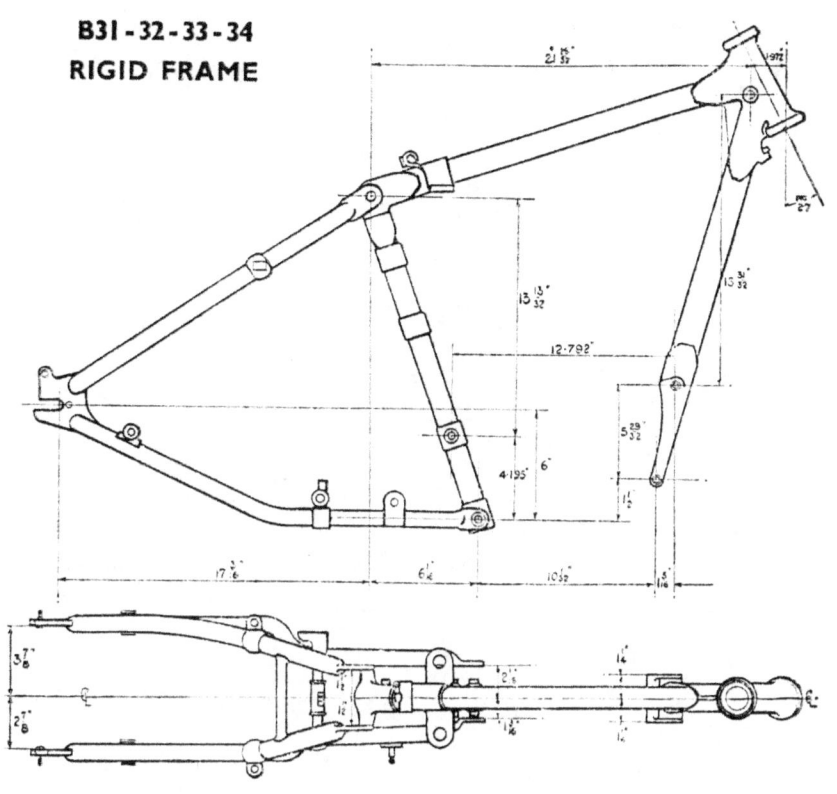

B31-32-33-34 SPRING FRAME

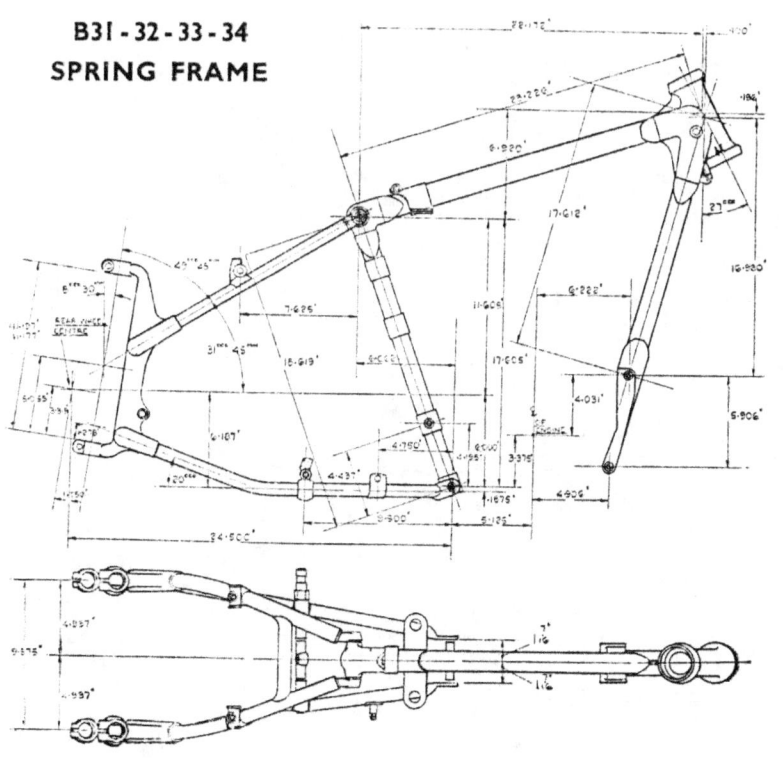

D1 and D3
RIGID FRAME

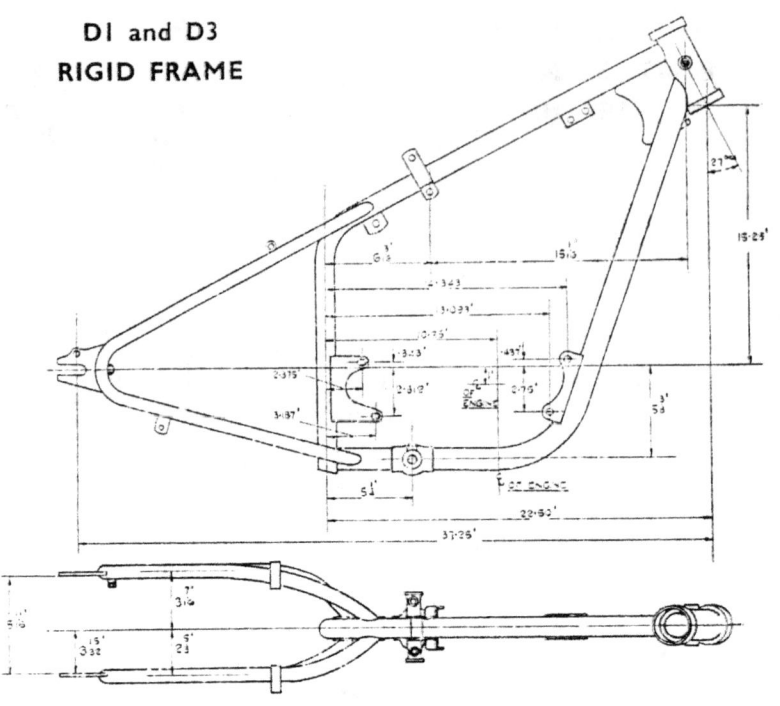

D1 and D3
SPRING FRAME

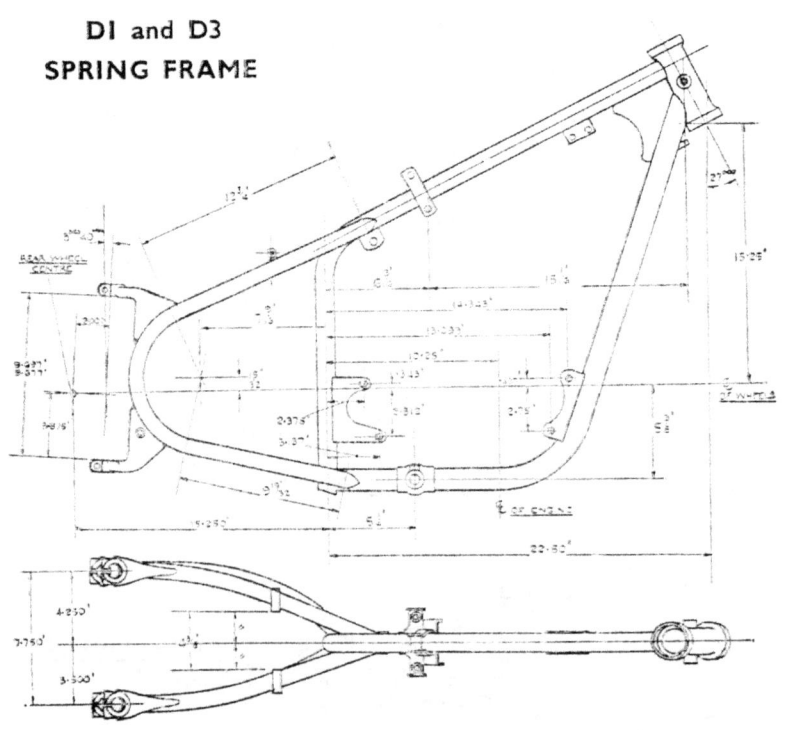

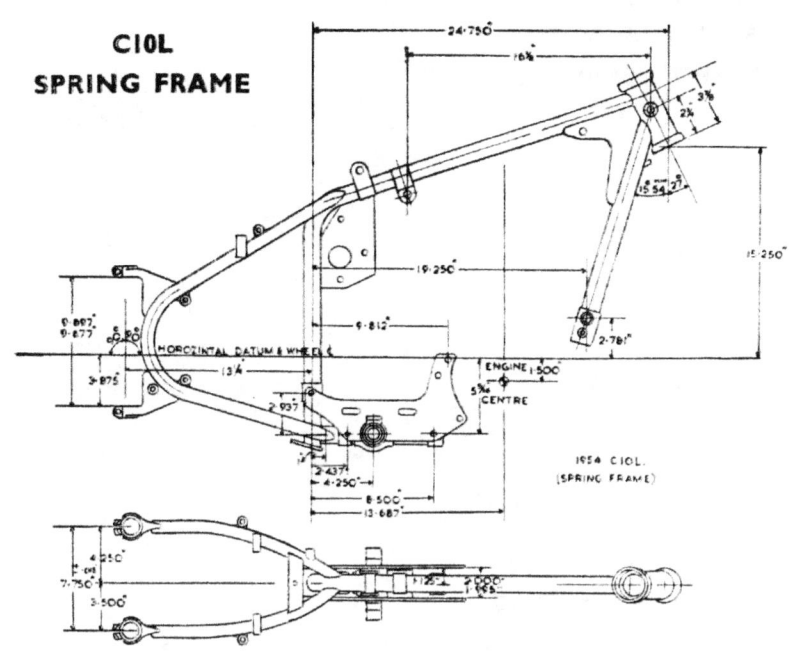

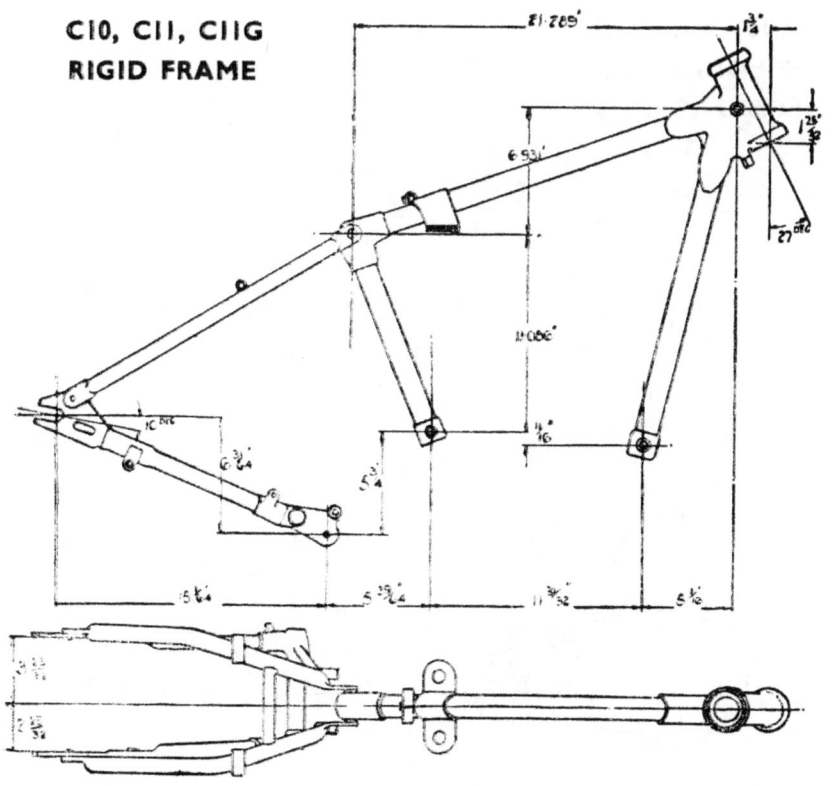

C10, C11, C11G SPRING FRAME 3 SPEED GEARBOX

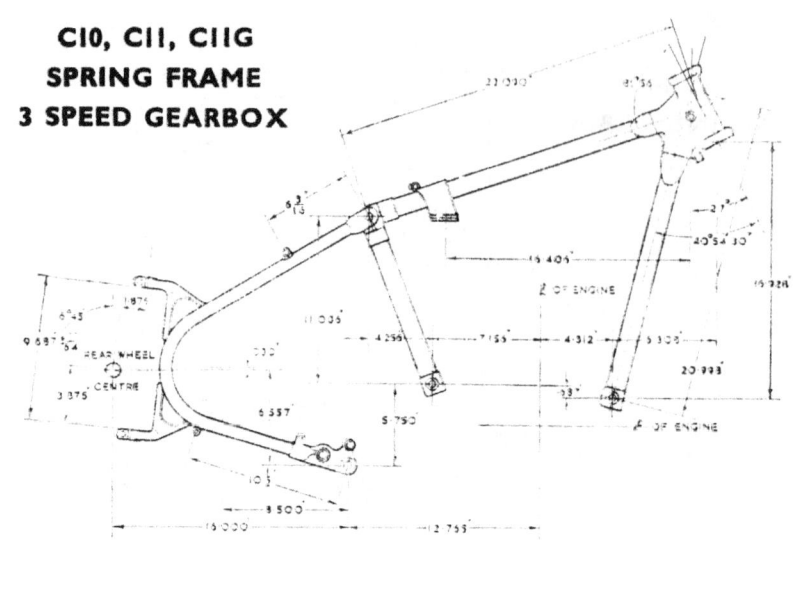

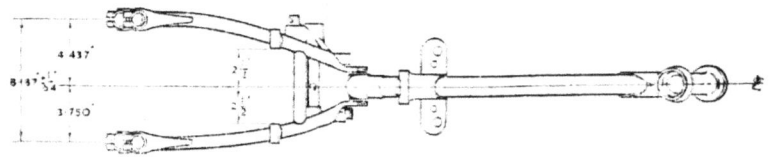

C10, C11, C11G SPRING FRAME 4 SPEED GEARBOX

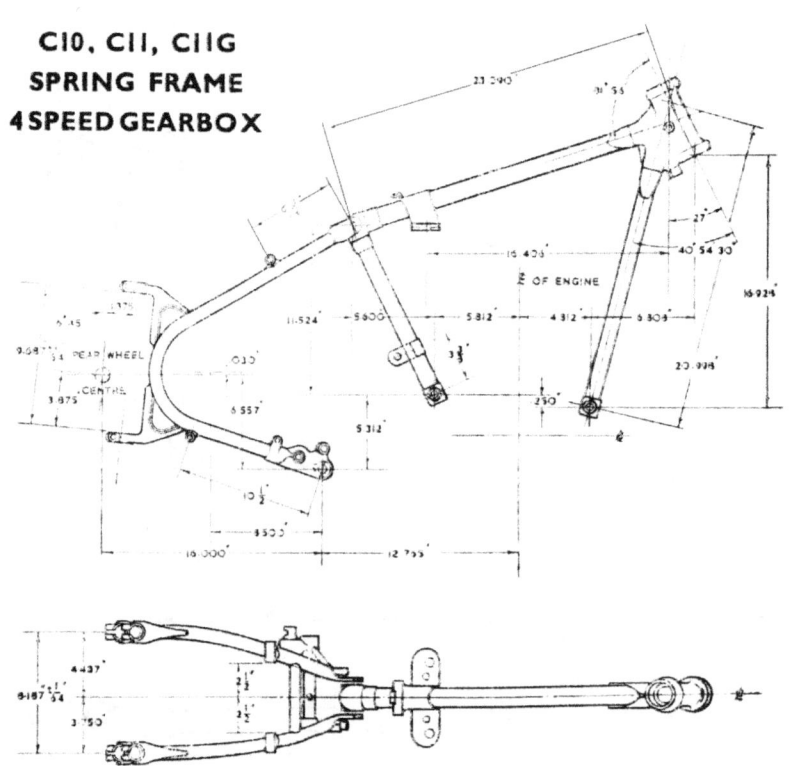

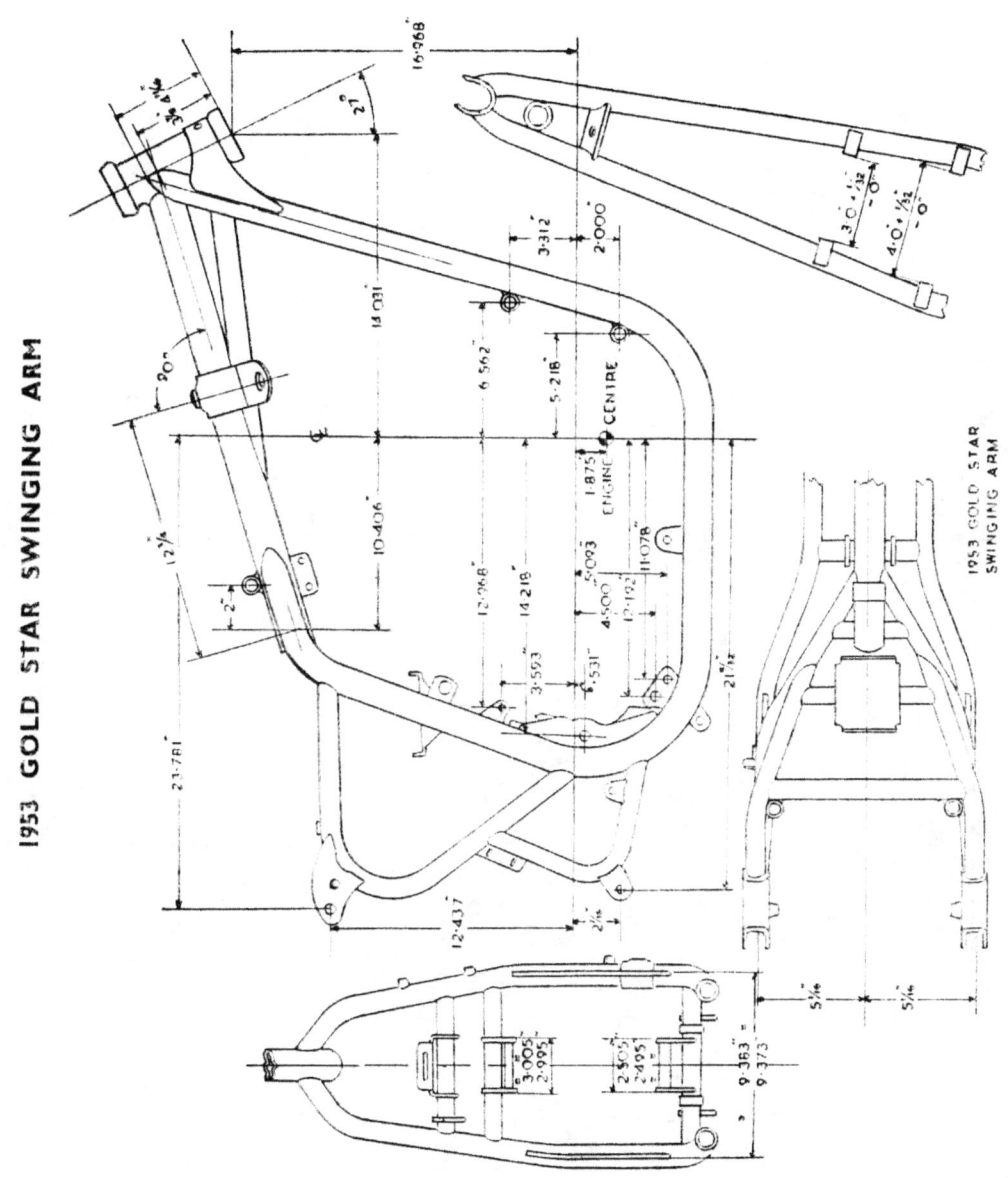

1953 GOLD STAR SWINGING ARM

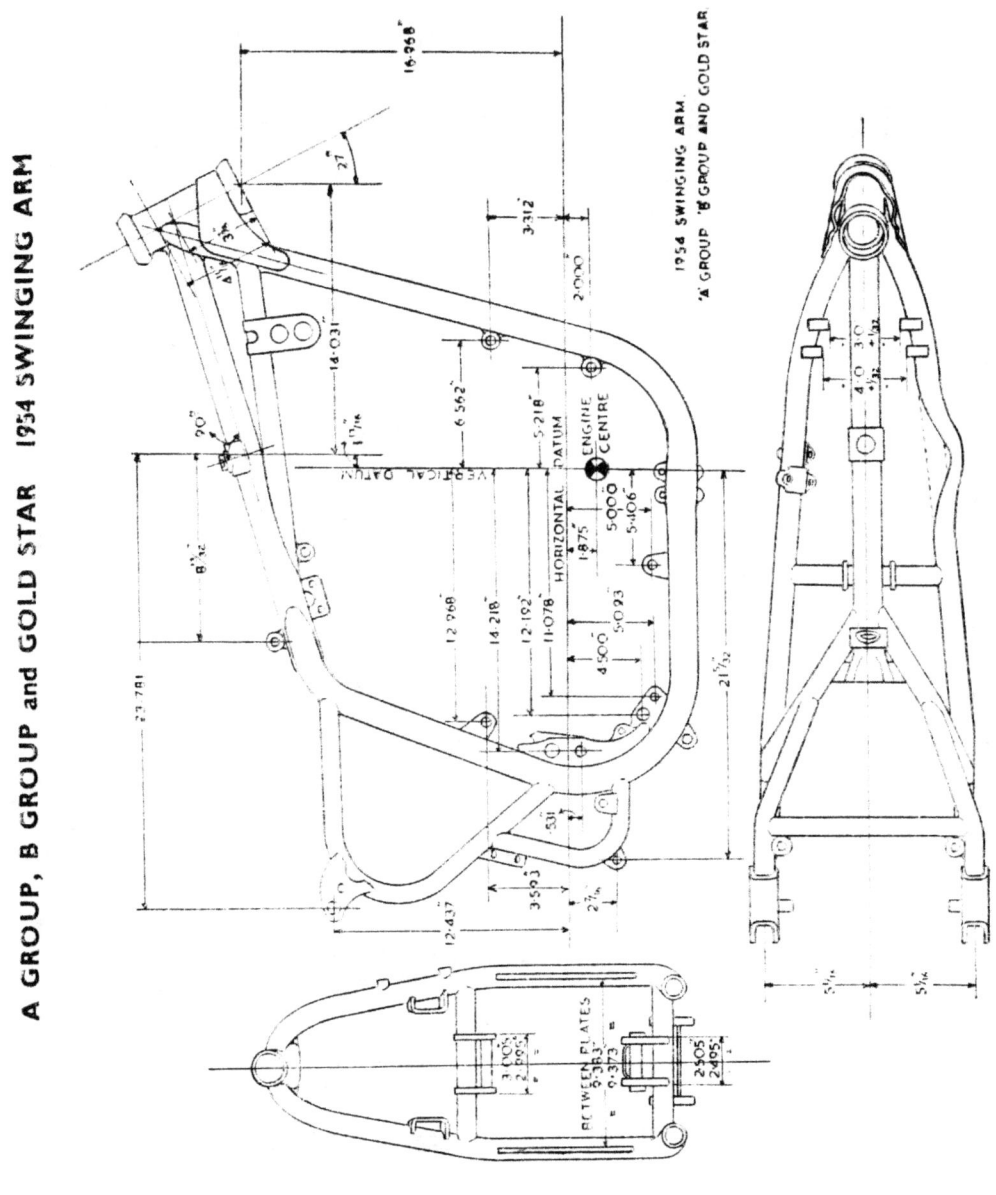

B32 and B34
1954 RIGID FRAME

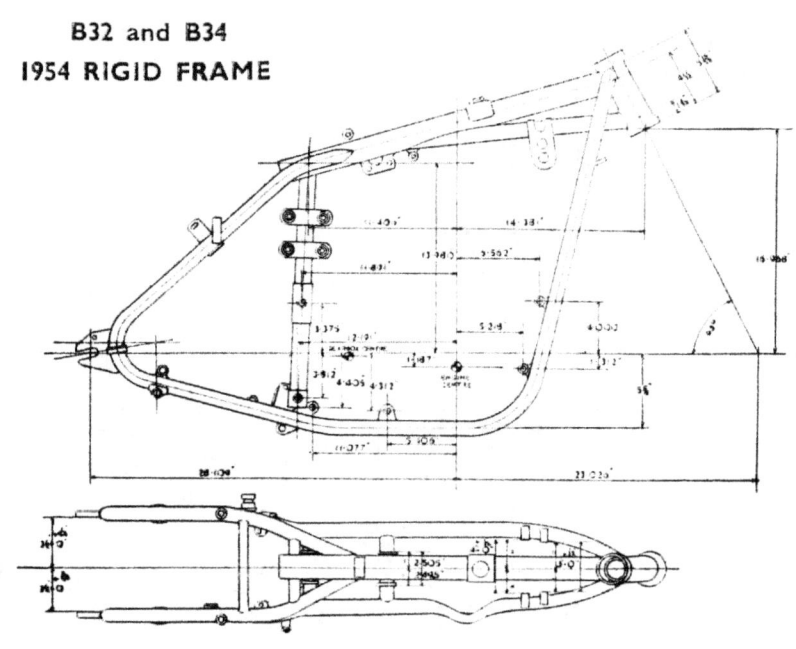

D3 SWINGING ARM

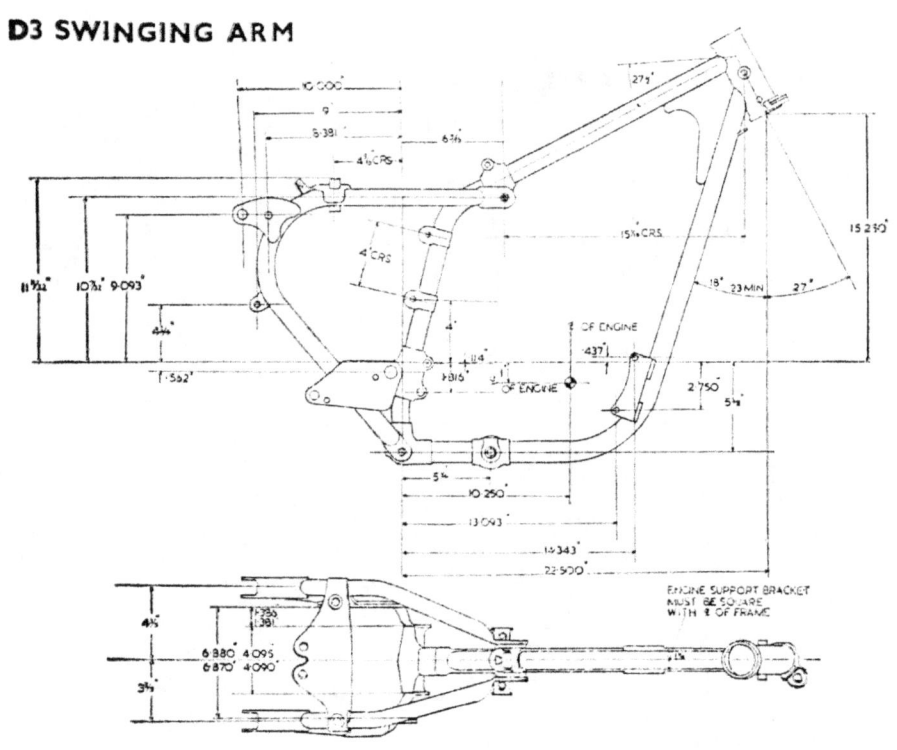

C12 SWINGING ARM

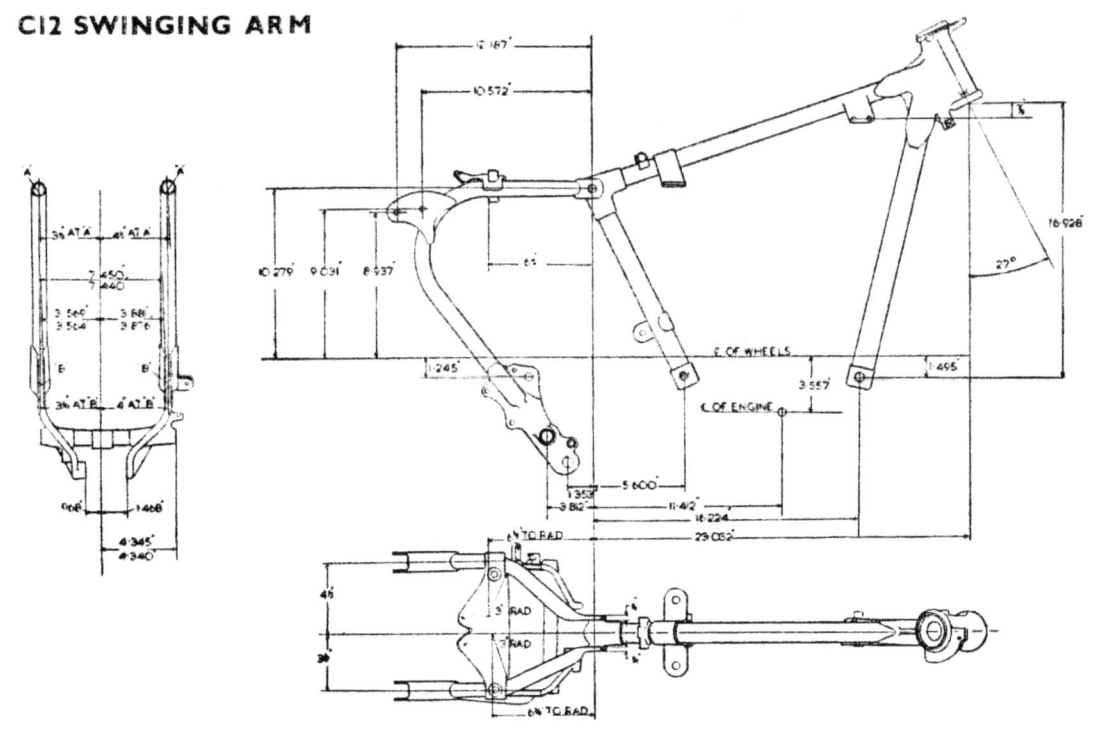

D5 SWINGING ARM

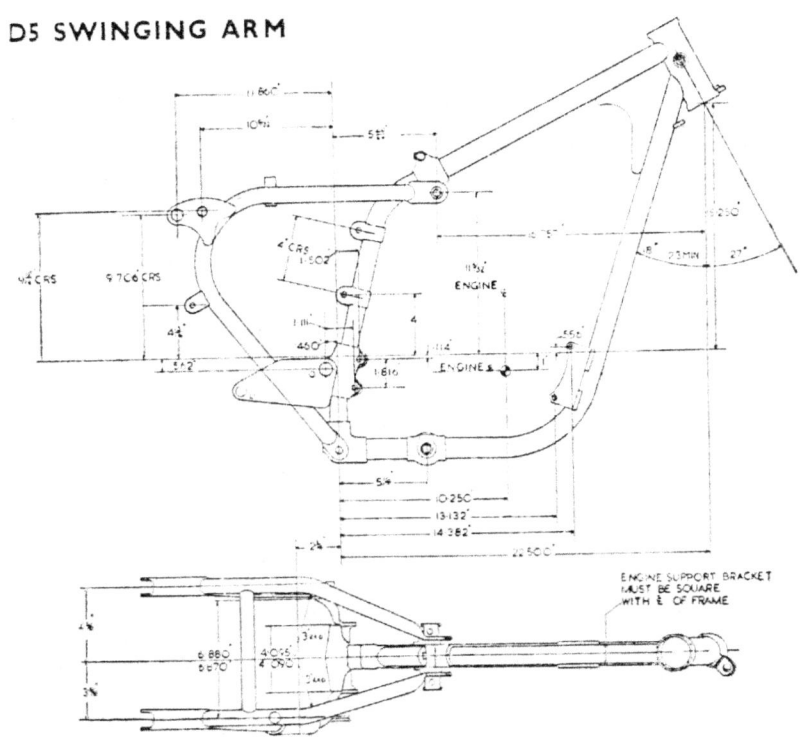

D7 SWINGING ARM

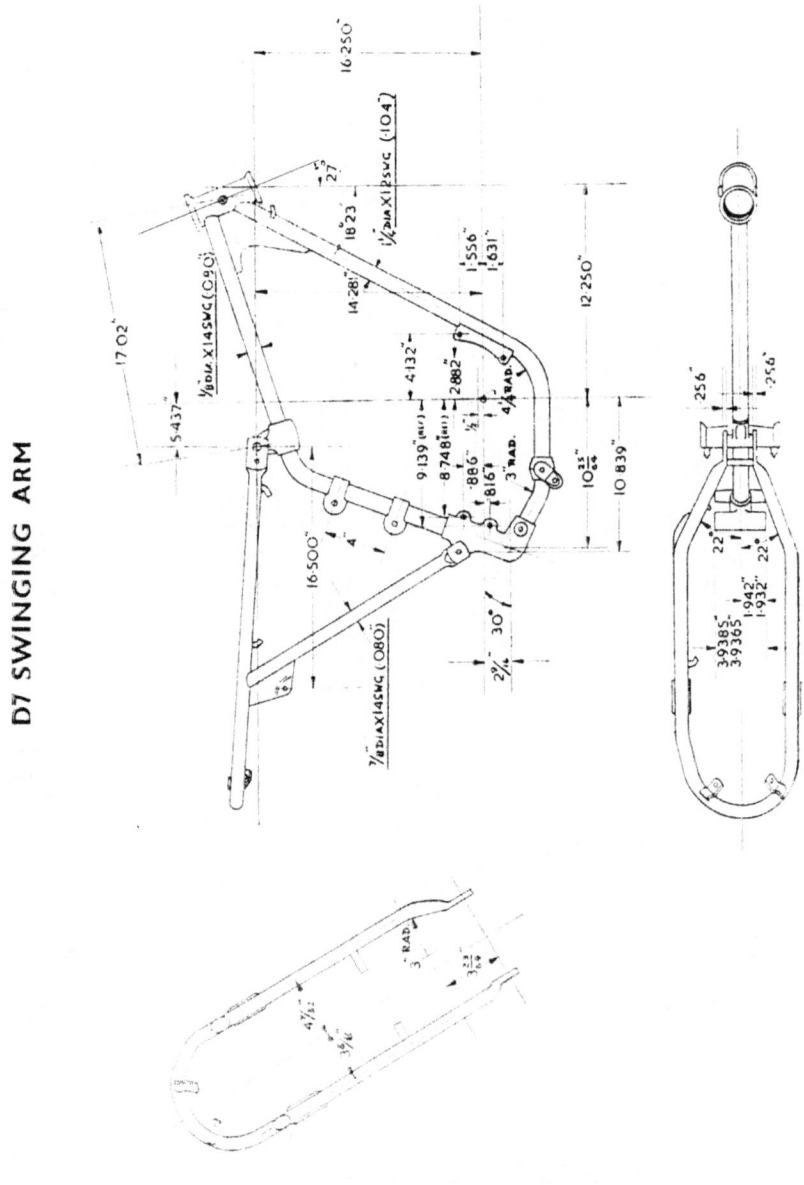

C15 STAR AND C15 SPORTS STAR

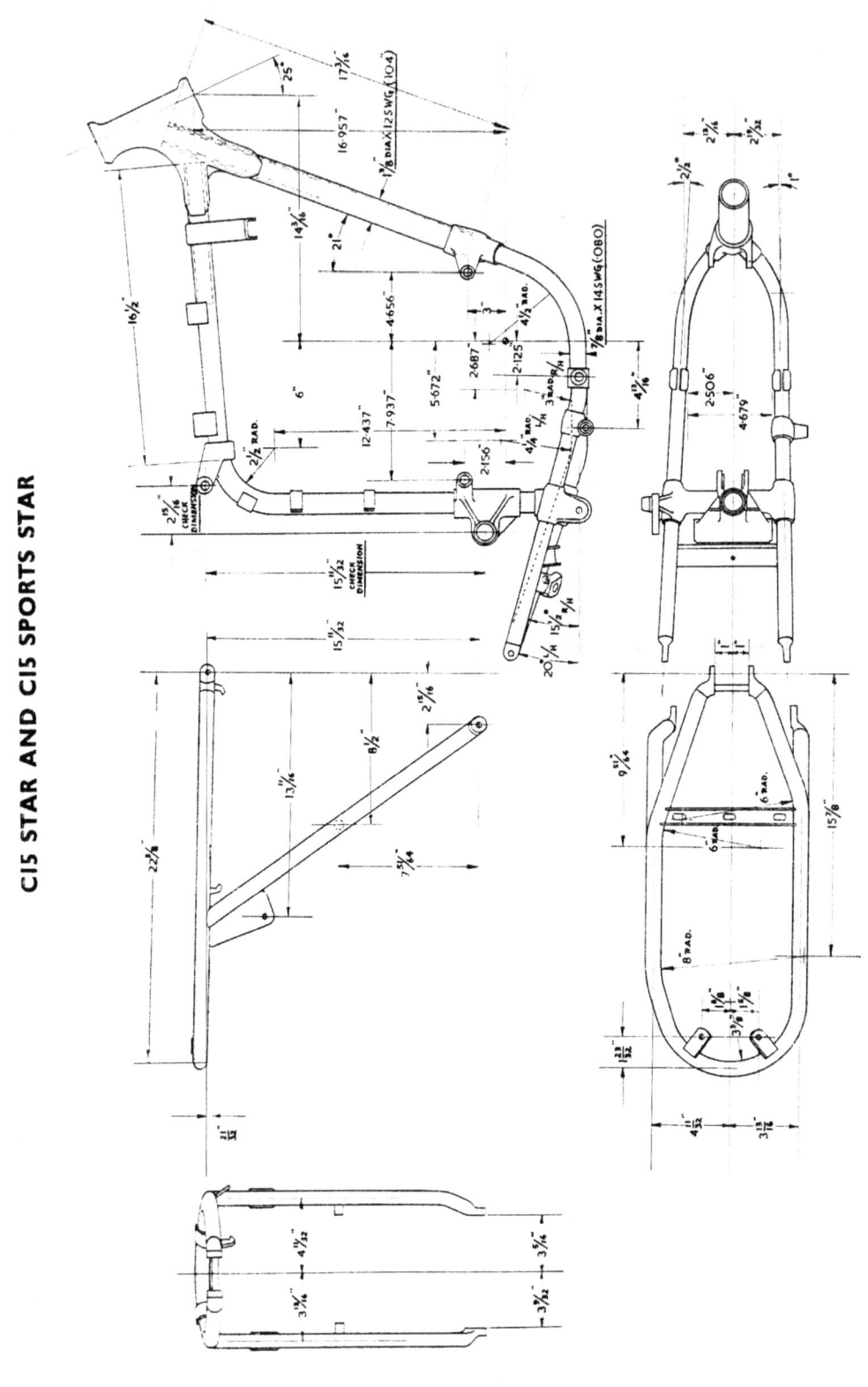

C15 TRIALS AND C15 SCRAMBLES

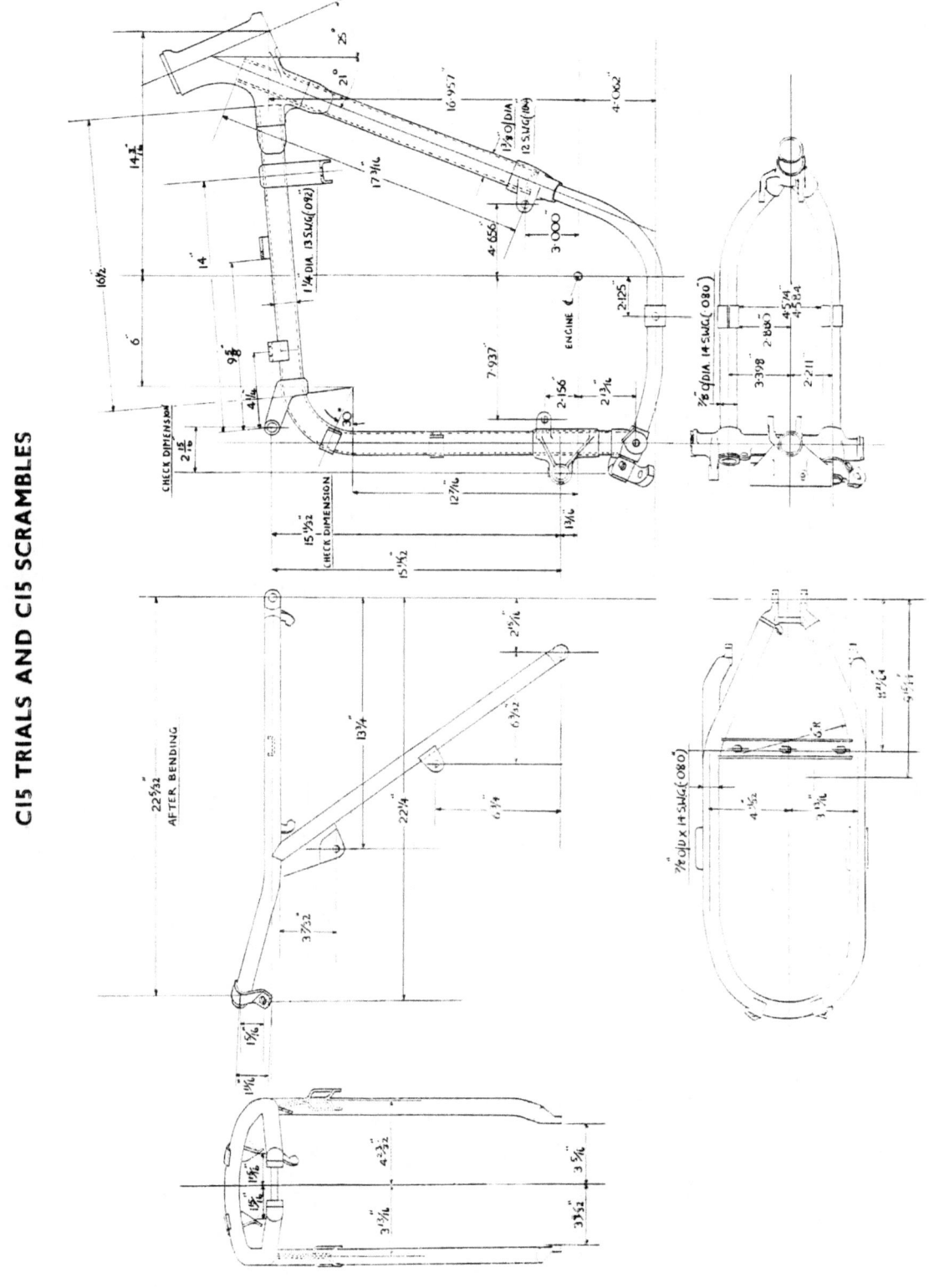

B40 STAR

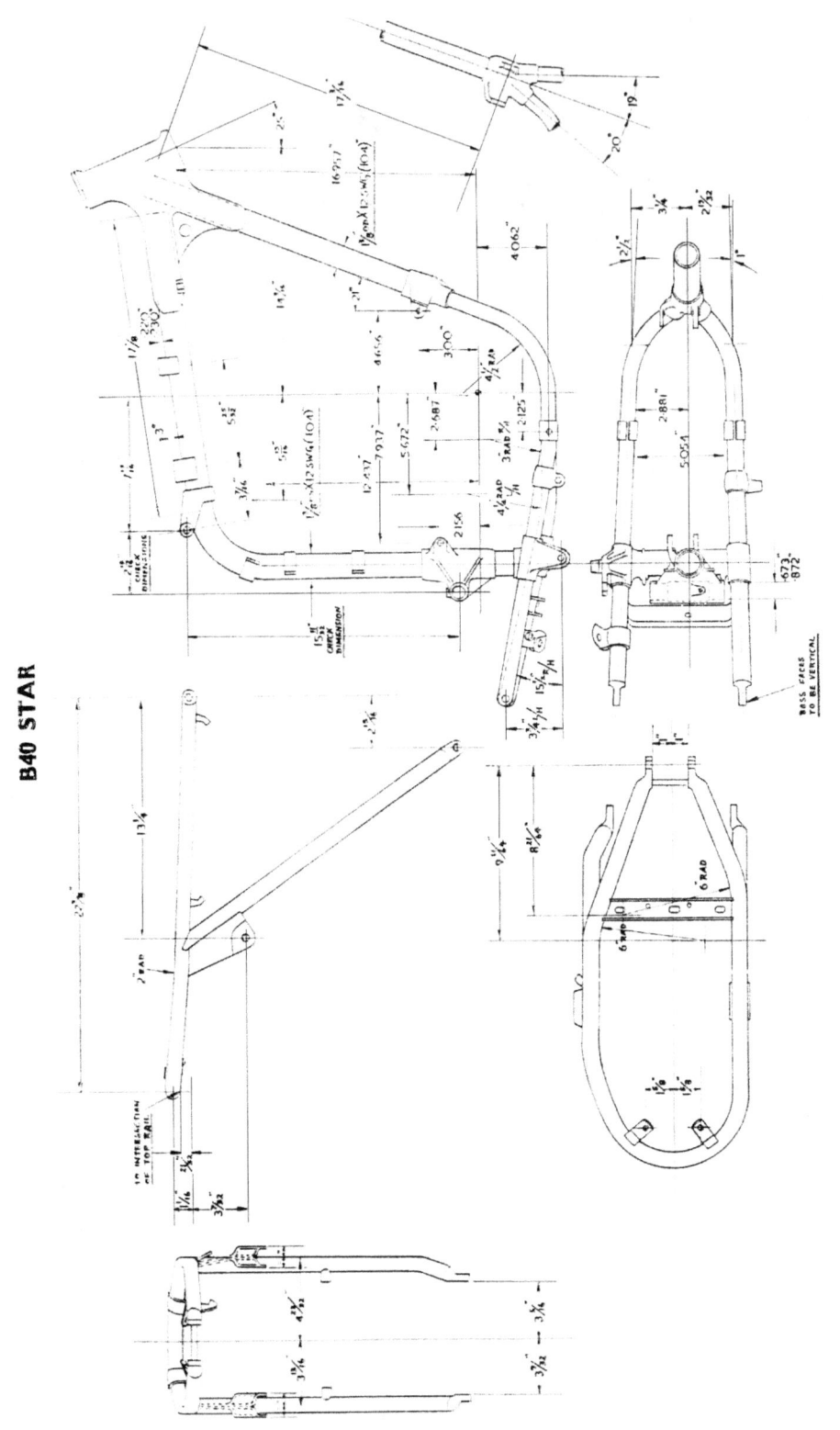

500 c.c. STAR AND 650 c.c. STAR MODELS A50 AND A65

B.S.A. Service Sheet No. 711

Revised Sept. 1958.

SERVICE TOOLS

for all

MOTOR CYCLES
1946 to 1958 Inclusive

Use in conjunction with
Service Sheet No. 711A
For Details of Models and Prices.

BSA SERVICE SHEET No. 711

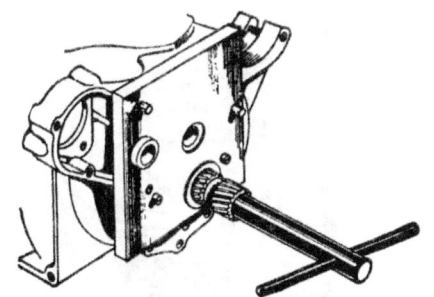

61-3281 Reaming Jig (mainshaft and camshaft gear bushes)
61-3275 Reaming Jig (mainshaft and camshaft gear bushes)

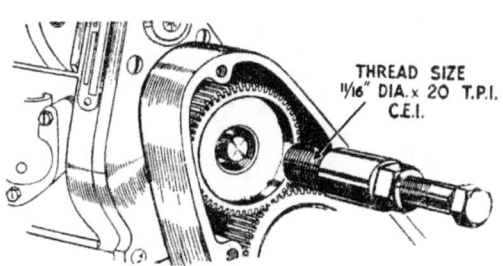

61-1903 Magdyno Driving Pinion Extractor Tool complete.
For Models fitted with Magdyno Lighting Equipment.

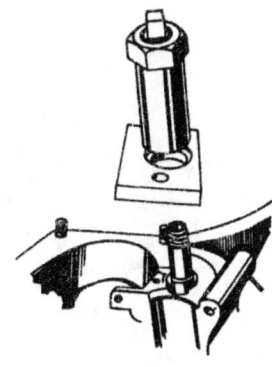

61-3069 Inlet Tappet Guide Extractor

61-3284 Mainshaft Bush Reamer
61-3285 Pilot for Jigs 61-3275
61-3286 Pilot for Jigs 61-3281
61-3287 Shell Reamer Holder
61-3288 Tommy Bar for 61-3287

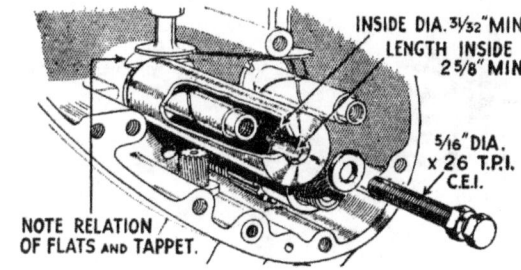

61-691 Cam Pinion Post Extractor

61-3167 Reamer for use with 61-3162 61-3281 and 61-3275

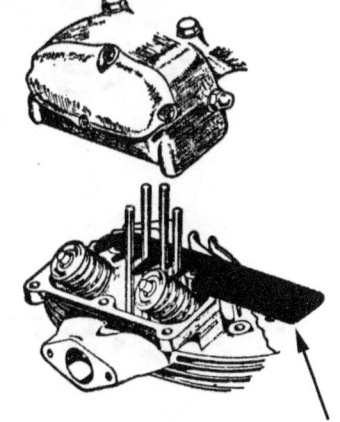

67-9114 Push Rod Assembly Tool

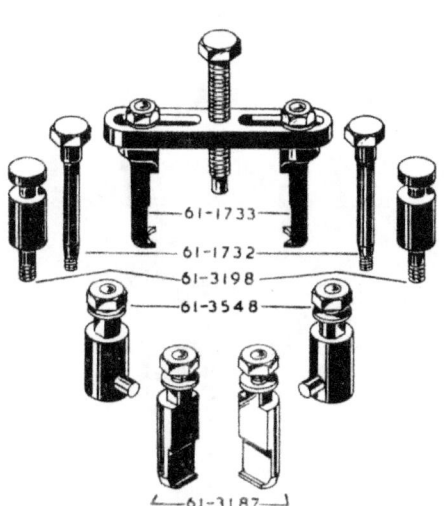

61-3256 Extractor Set Complete

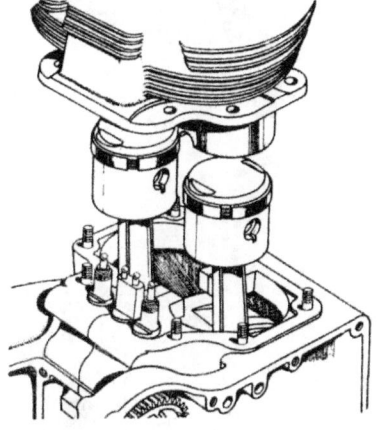

61-3061 Piston Ring Slipper
61-3334 Piston Ring Slipper,
61-3262 Piston Ring Slipper.
(2 per set)

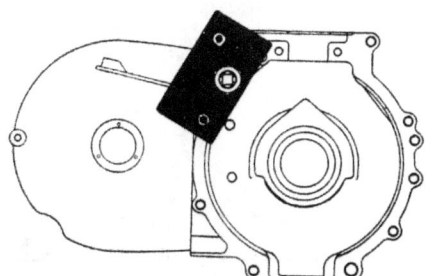

61-3159 Camshaft Bush Extractor

B.S.A. Service Sheet No. 711—continued

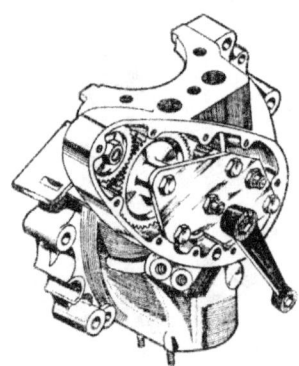

15-832 Mainshaft Nut Spanner

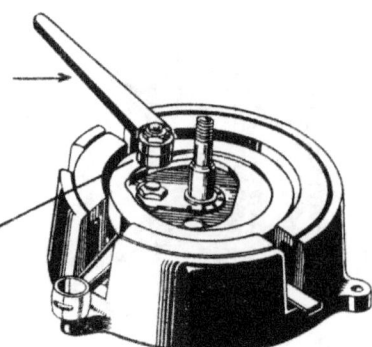

61-1817 Crankpin Nut Spanner
Tool comprises Holder, Locknut and three Sockets

Sockets for 61-1817
61-1754
61-1755
61-3228

61-1751 Flywheel Bolster
61-1750 ,, Gauge Rod
61-1747 ,, Ring
61-1749 ,, ,, ,,

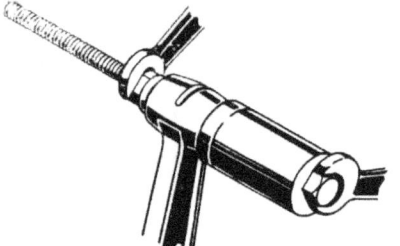

61-658 Gudgeon Pin Bush Extractor comprising Spindle with various size bushes.

65-9243 C Spanner and Fork Top Nut Spanner

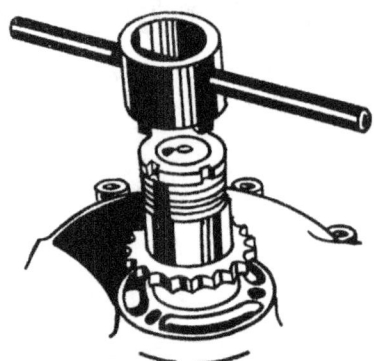

61-3220 Cush Drive Nut Tube Spanner

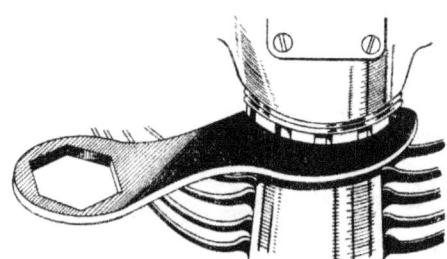

61-3305 Valve Seating Tool complete

Comprising Tommy Bar 61-3291
Holder 61-3290

Cutters
61-3298 .. 1 7/16" × 45° × 20°
61-3299 .. 1 1/2" × 45° × 20°
61-3300 .. 1 5/8" × 45° × 20°
61-3301 .. 1 3/4" × 45° × 20°
61-3302 .. 1 7/8" × 45° × 20°

Pilots
61-3293 .. 5/16"
61-3294 .. .350"
61-3295 .. 3/8"

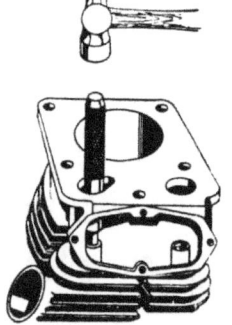

61-3263 61-3264 61-3265 61-3267 61-3268
Valve Guide fitting and extracting punches

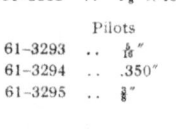

65-9240 Valve Grinding Tool

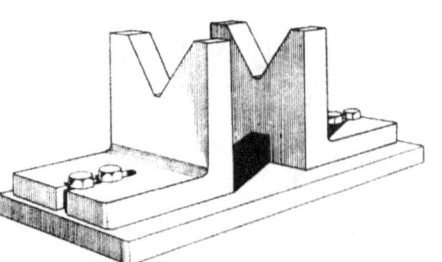

61-692 Vee Block and Base Plate

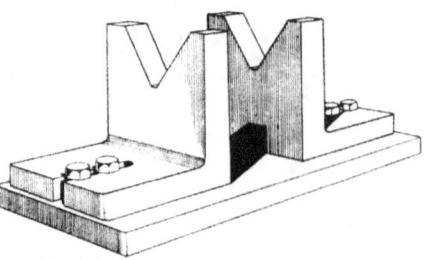

61-699 1/4" C.E.I. Stud Boxes
61-317 5/16" ,, ,,
61-545 3/8" ,, ,,

B.S.A. SERVICE SHEET No. 711—continued

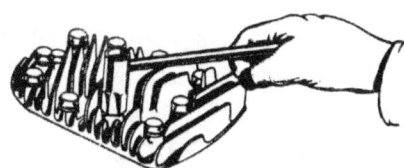

61-3049 Cylinder Head Spanner

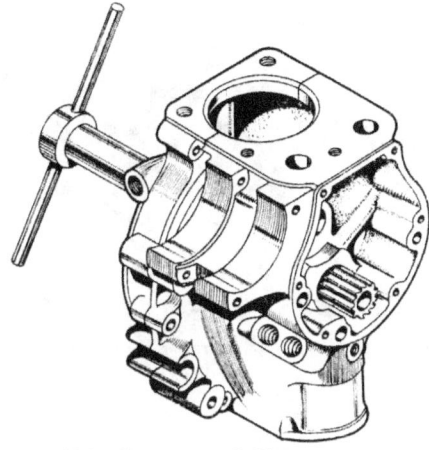

61-1932 Reamer and Holder complete
(mainshaft bush)
61-1922 Reamer for 61-1932

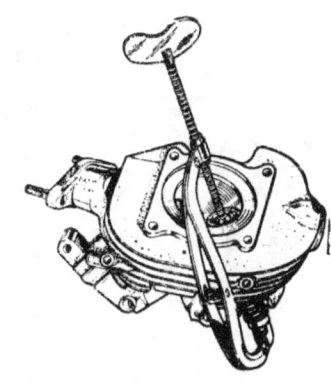

61-3340 Valve Spring Compressor with Adaptor
Models M33
"B" Group, "A" Group, and Sunbeam

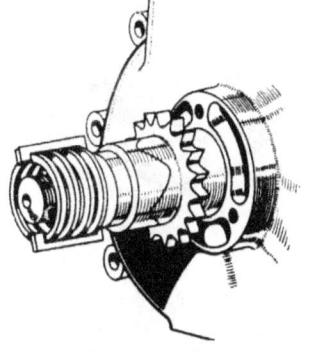

61-1822 Cush Drive Spring Assembly Tool
For holding Spring compressed whilst fitting Lockring.
(2 per set)

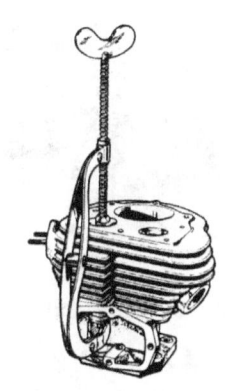

61-3340 Valve Spring Compressor
Models C10, C11, M20, M21
(Use without adaptor)

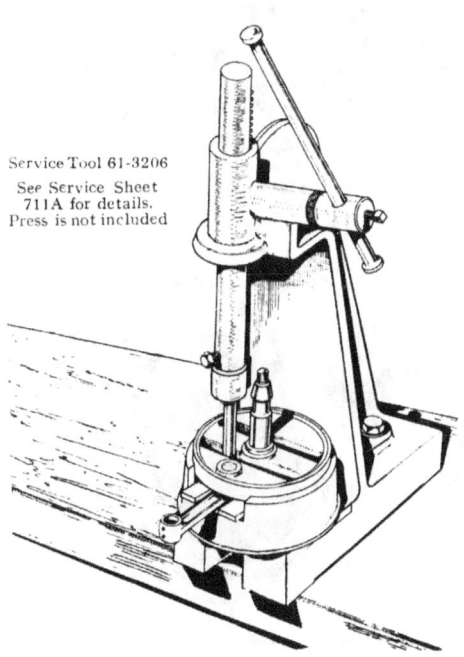

Service Tool 61-3206
See Service Sheet 711A for details.
Press is not included

61-3052 Cylinder Base Nut Spanner

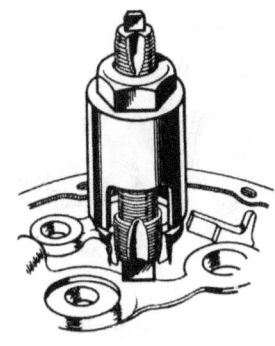

61-3185 Bush Extractor

61-3257 Gearbox Sprocket Locknut Spanner,
61-3258 Gearbox Sprocket Locknut Spanner,

61-3246 Gudgeon Pin Bush Reamer (.4687")
61-3367 Gudgeon Pin Bush Reamer (.625")
61-3556 Gudgeon Pin Bush Reamer (.6875")
61-3366 Gudgeon Pin Bush Reamer (.750")
61-3580 Gudgeon Pin Bush Reamer (.4375")
61-3581 Gudgeon Pin Bush Reamer (.5625")

B.S.A. SERVICE SHEET No. 711—continued

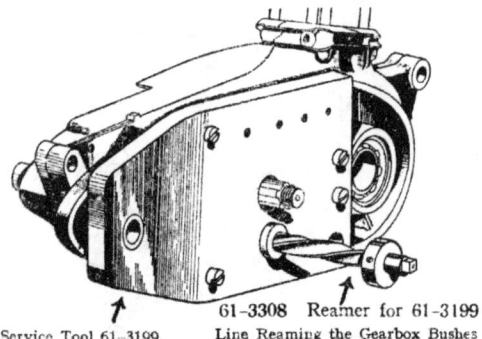

Service Tool 61-3199. 61-3308 Reamer for 61-3199
Line Reaming the Gearbox Bushes

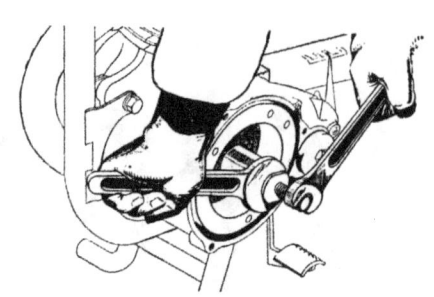

61-3188 Generator Flywheel Removal Tool (Wico Pacy)
90-297 Generator Flywheel Removal Tool (Lucas)

61-3064 Pinion Sleeve Extractor

61-3214 Ballrace Pilot (gearbox pinion bearing)
61-3215 Ballrace Pilot (gearbox mainshaft bearing)

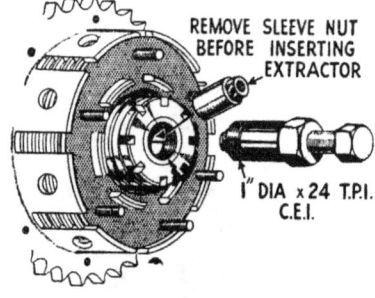
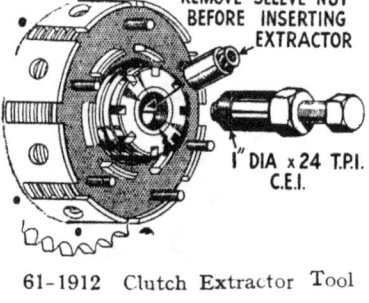

61-1912 Clutch Extractor Tool

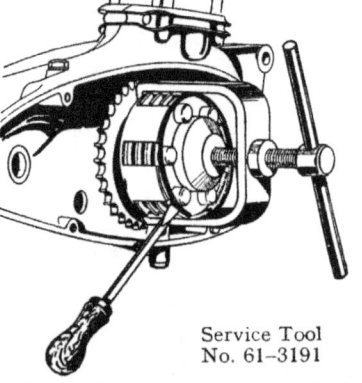

Service Tool No. 61-3191
Removing the Clutch Plate Circlip

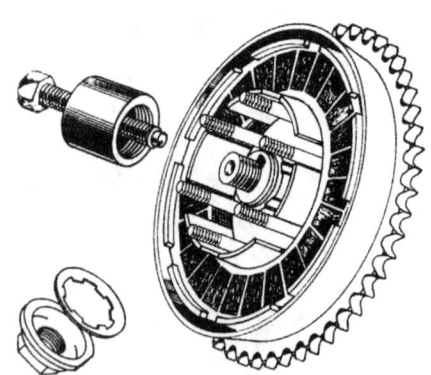

61-3362 Clutch Extractor Tool

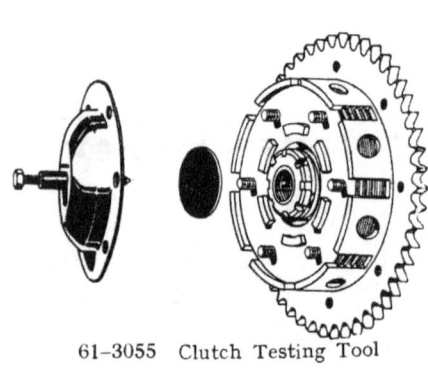

61-3055 Clutch Testing Tool

61-3212 Ballrace Pilot for large engine bearing
61-3213 Ballrace Pilot for small engine bearing

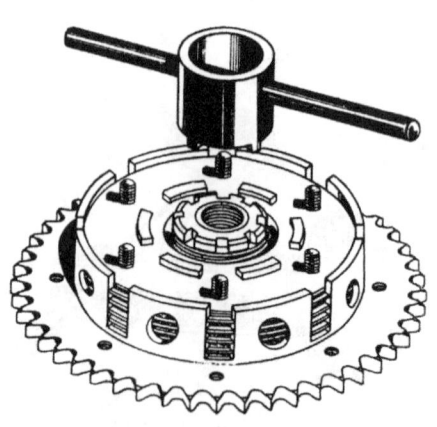

61-1915 Clutch Spring Nut Tube Spanner.

B.S.A. SERVICE SHEET No. 711—continued

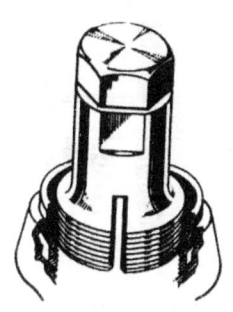

61-3060 Ballrace Extractor (steering head) for all 3/16" balls

61-3063 Ballrace Extractor (steering head) for all 1/4" balls

61-3006 Oil Seal Extractor

61-3007 Oil Seal Assembly Tool

61-3003 Spanner for Fork Plug Assembly

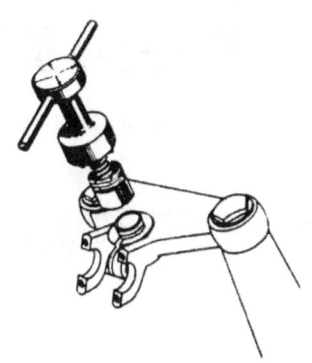

61-3002 Assembly Tool for Adjuster Sleeve
61-3008 Assembly Tool for Adjuster Sleeve

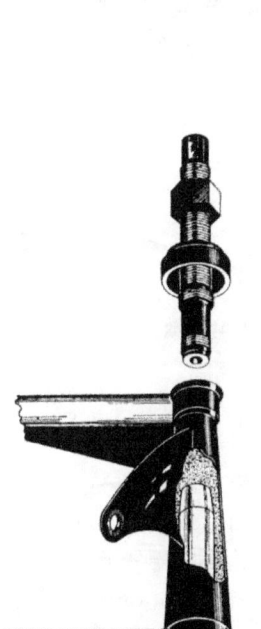

61-3350 Fork Shaft Dismantling and Assembly Tool

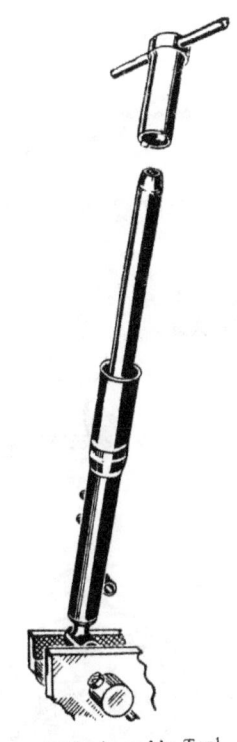

61-3005 Assembly Tool for Oil Seal Holder

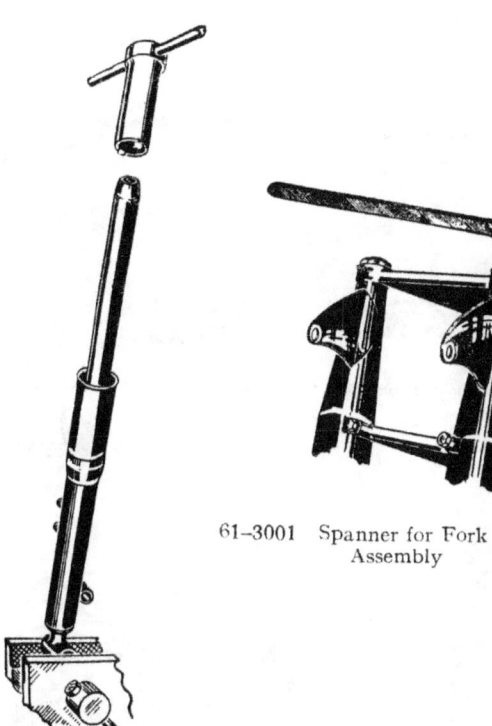

61-3001 Spanner for Fork Top Nut Assembly

61-3222 Rear Suspension Strip and Assembly Tool

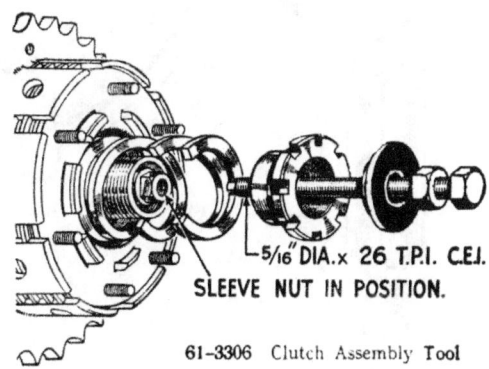

5/16" DIA. x 26 T.P.I. C.E.I. SLEEVE NUT IN POSITION.

61-3306 Clutch Assembly Tool

131

B.S.A. SERVICE SHEET No. 711—continued

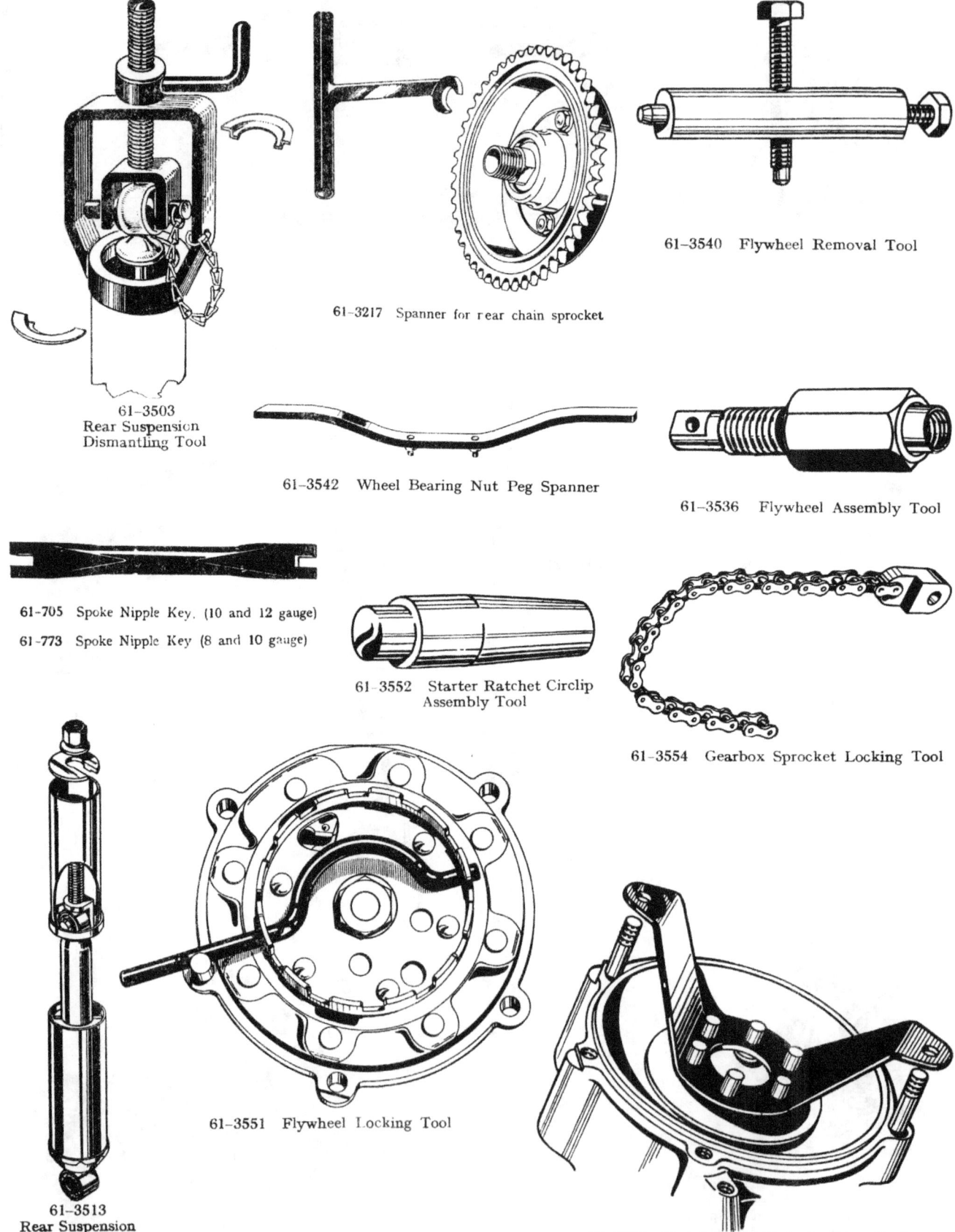

61-3503 Rear Suspension Dismantling Tool

61-3217 Spanner for rear chain sprocket

61-3540 Flywheel Removal Tool

61-3542 Wheel Bearing Nut Peg Spanner

61-3536 Flywheel Assembly Tool

61-705 Spoke Nipple Key. (10 and 12 gauge)
61-773 Spoke Nipple Key (8 and 10 gauge)

61-3552 Starter Ratchet Circlip Assembly Tool

61-3554 Gearbox Sprocket Locking Tool

61-3513 Rear Suspension Dismantling Tool

61-3551 Flywheel Locking Tool

61-3553 Clutch Back Plate Locking Tool

B.S.A. SERVICE SHEET No. 711—*continued*

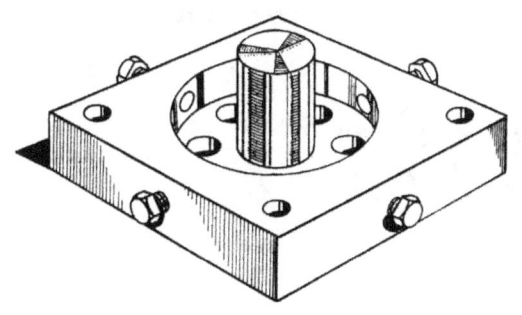

61-3499   Bench Die Holder

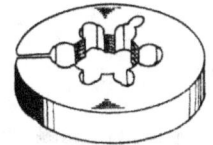

61-3483   Die

Tap

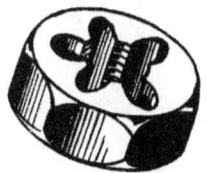

Die Nut

Part No.	Description	For
61-3574	Tap and Die Set in wooden case comprising tools listed below except 61-3483	General Workshop use
61-3575	Tap and Die Set in wooden case comprising all tools listed below	General Workshop use

TAPS.

Part No.	Taps.		For
61-3461	3/8" x 19 TPI B.S.P.	(R/H)	Petrol Tap Hole.
61-3462	3/8" x 20 TPI B.S.F.	(L/H)	Sunbeam Dynamo.
61-3463	7/16" x 20 TPI C.E.I.	(R/H)	General.
61-3464	1/2" x 20 TPI C.E.I.	(R/H)	General.
61-3502	9/16" x 20 TPI C.E.I.	(R/H)	General.
61-3465	9/16" x 20 TPI C.E.I.	(L/H)	Front Fork Spindle Hole.
61-3466	5/8" x 20 TPI C.E.I.	(R/H)	General.
61-3467	3/4" x 20 TPI C.E.I.	(R/H)	General.
65-3468	3/4" x 20 TPI B.S.W.	(R/H)	General.
61-3469	3/4" x 12 TPI B.S.F.	(L/H)	Sunbeam Rear Spindle Hole.
61-3470	7/8" x 20 TPI B.S.W.	(R/H)	Rear Suspension Shaft.
61-3471	1-1/16" x 20 TPI C.E.I.	(R/H)	Fork Shaft Top.
61-3472	1 1/8" x 28 TPI B.S.W.	(R/H)	Fork Shaft Bottom.
61-3473	1 1/2" x 20 TPI B.S.W.	(R/H)	Filler Caps.
61-3531	14 mm. x 1.25 mm.	(R/H)	14 mm. Spark Plug Hole
61-3533	1.250" x 20 TPI B.S.W.	(R/H)	Bantam Fork Tube (90-5021)

DIES.

Part No.	Dies.		For
61-3474	7/16" x 20 TPI C.E.I.	(R/H)	General.
61-3475	1/2" x 20 TPI C.E.I.	(R/H)	General.
61-3476	9/16" x 20 TPI C.E.I.	(R/H)	Gearbox Mainshaft.
61-3477	9/16" x 20 TPI C.E.I.	(L/H)	"A" Group Mainshaft.
61-3478	5/8" x 20 TPI C.E.I.	(R/H)	General.
61-3479	3/4" x 20 TPI C.E.I.	(R/H)	General.
61-3480	3/4" x 12 TPI B.S.F.	(L/H)	Sunbeam Rear Spindle.
61-3481	1" x 24 TPI C.E.I.	(R/H)	Fork Stem.
61-3482	1.120" x 24 TPI C.E.I.	(R/H)	Fork Stem.
61-3483	1 7/8" x 28 TPI WHIT.	(R/H)	Fork Sliding Tube Top.
61-3499	Bench Die Holder (for use with 61-3483)		

B.S.A. MOTOR CYCLES LTD.
Service Dept., Birmingham 11
Printed in England

B.S.A. Service Sheet No. 711A

Revised Sept., 1958

PRICE LIST
for
SERVICE TOOLS
1946 to 1958 Inclusive

Use in conjunction with Service Sheet No. 711

Part No.	Description	Used on Model	Retail Price Per Unit £ s. d.
15–832	Rear Hub Nut Spanner	A, B, C and M	4 5
61–317	Stud Box 5/16″ c.e.i.	General	3 0
61–545	Stud Box 3/8″ c.e.i.	General	3 0
61–658	Gudgeon Pin Bush Extractor	All Models	10 6
61–691	Cam Pinion Post Extractor	B and M	4 6
61–692	Flywheel "V" Blocks (used with 61–1821)	B, C and M	2 5 4
61–696	Socket Nut (used with 61–1817)	B, C and M	1 5
61–698	Crankpin Nut Spanner only (used with 61–1817)	B, C and M	1 1 0
61–699	Stud Box 1/4″ c.e.i.	General	3 0
61–705	Nipple Key (10 and 12 gauge)	General	3 10
61–773	Nipple Key (8 and 10 gauge)	General	3 10
61–1747	Flywheel Bolster Ring	C Group	4 1 3
61–1749	Flywheel Bolster Ring	B and M 500 c.c.	4 1 3
61–1750	Flywheel Bolster Gauge Rod (2 per set)	B, C and M	7 7
61–1751	Flywheel Bolster	B, C and M	3 11 9
61–1754	Crankpin Nut Socket (used with 61–1817)	C Group	8 0
61–1755	Crankpin Nut Socket (used with 61–1817)	B and M	8 0
61–1817	Crankpin Nut Spanner complete	B, C and M	2 7 6
	Comprising:—		
61–696	Socket Nut		1 5
61–698	Spanner		1 1 0
61–1754	Socket	C Group	8 0
61–1755	Socket	B and M	8 0
61–3228	Socket	Gold Star	9 1

BSA SERVICE TOOLS

Part No.	Description	Used on Model	Per Unit Retail Price £ s. d.
61-1821	"V" Block Base Plate (used with 61-692)	B, C and M	1 10 3
61-1822	Cush Drive Spring Assembly Tool (2 per set)	A, B, C and M	4 6
61-1903	Magdyno Drive Pinion Extractor	B and M	3 0
61-1912	Clutch Extractor	M to 1948	6 0
61-1915	Clutch Spring Nut Tube Spanner	M to 1948	4 6
61-1922	Reamer (used with 61-1932) (mainshaft bush)	C Group	3 5 0
61-1932	Reamer and Holder complete (used with 61-1922)	C Group	4 4 9
61-3001	Fork Top Nut Spanner (front fork)	A, B, C and M	13 6
61-3002	Adjuster Sleeve Assembly Tool (steering head)	B, C and M	12 1
61-3003	Fork Plug Spanner (front fork)	A, B, C and M	13 6
61-3005	Oil Seal Holder Assembly Tool (front fork)	A, B, C and M	1 1 2
61-3006	Oil Seal Extractor (front fork)	A, B, C and M	15 1
61-3007	Oil Seal Assembly Tool (front fork)	A, B, C and M	6 0
61-3008	Adjuster Sleeve Assembly Tool (steering head)	A7/10, S7/8	12 1
61-3049	Cylinder Head Spanner	M20/21	10 6
61-3052	Cylinder Base Nut Spanner	M20/21	1 1 2
61-3055	Clutch Testing Tool	M to 1948	15 1
61-3060	Steering Head Ballrace Extractor	For 3/16" Balls	8 3
61-3061	Piston Ring Slipper (2 per set)	A7 to 1950	7 6
61-3063	Steering Head Ballrace Extractor	For 1/4" Balls	8 3
61-3064	Pinion Sleeve Extractor	B, C and M	2 11 5
61-3069	Inlet Tappet Guide Extractor	A7 to 1950	7 7
61-3159	Camshaft Bush Extractor	A7, A10	12 8
61-3167	Camshaft Bush Reamer (used with 61-3275/81)	A Group	3 0 6
61-3185	Gearbox Bush Extractor	M Group	15 9
61-3188	Flywheel Magneto Removal Tool (Wico Pacy)	D1, D3 and D5	6 8
61-3191	Clutch Plate Circlip Removal Tool	D1, D3 and D5	1 10 3
61-3199	Gearbox Bush Line Reaming Plate (used with 61-3205)	D1, D3 and D5	2 1 6
61-3205	Layshaft Bush Reamer only (used with 61-3199)	D1, D3 and D5	2 1 11
61-3206	Flywheel Dismantling and Assembly Tool	D1, D3 and D5	3 15 6

Comprising:—
    61-3207   Jig Body
    61-3208(2) Dismantling Bar
    61-3209   Dismantling Punch
    61-3210   Assembly Bridge
(Note:—Press as illustrated is not included).

Part No.	Description	Used on Model	Per Unit Retail Price
61-3212	Ballrace Pilot for large engine bearing	D1, D3 and D5	7 7
61-3213	Ballrace Pilot for small engine bearing	D1, D3 and D5	6 8
61-3214	Ballrace Pilot for gearbox pinion bearing	D1, D3 and D5	7 7
61-3215	Ballrace Pilot for gearbox mainshaft bearing	D1, D3 and D5	6 8
61-3217	Spanner for rear wheel sprocket	A7, A10	11 3
61-3220	Tube Spanner for cush drive nut	A, B, C and M	3 6
61-3222	Rear Suspension Strip and Assembly Tool	A, B and M	13 6
61-3228	Crankpin Nut Socket (used with 61-1817)	B32/4 G/S	9 1
61-3246	Reamer Gudgeon Pin Bush	D1, D3	14 6
61-3256	Extractor Set complete	All Models	1 12 7

Comprising:—
    61-351(1)   Plate
    61-776(1)   Bolt
    61-1732(2) Extractor Leg (A Group cam pinion)
    61-1733(2) Extractor Leg (engine pinion B, C and M).
    61-3187(2) Extractor Leg (crankshaft pinion A7/10).
    61-3198(2) Extractor Leg (engine sprocket etc., D, C and A).
    61-3548(2) Extractor Leg (Dandy flywheel)

BSA SERVICE TOOLS

Part No.	Description	Used on Model	Retail Price Per Unit
			£ s. d.
61-3257	Gearbox Sprocket Locknut Spanner	A, B and M	15 1
61-3258	Gearbox Sprocket Locknut Spanner	C	15 1
61-3262	Piston Ring Slipper (2 per set)	A10	6 0
61-3263	Valve Guide Punch (used on B33/34, exhaust and G/Stars with .374 dia. valve stems).		3 0
61-3264	Valve Guide Punch (comprising 61-3265/66 and 61-3307)	C10 In. and Ex.	12 8
61-3265	Valve Guide Punch (B31/32 inlet, A7/10, C11, C12 inlet and exhaust and G/Stars with .310" dia. valve stems)		6 0
61-3267	Valve Guide Punch (comprising 61-3268/9/70)	M20, M21 In. and Ex.	8 3
61-3268	Valve Guide Punch (B31/32 exhaust, B33/34 inlet and G/Stars with .348" dia. valve stems)		6 0
61-3275	Mainshaft and Camshaft Bush Reaming Jig	A7 to 1950	2 12 11
61-3281	Mainshaft and Camshaft Bush Reaming Jig	A10, AA7 onwards	2 12 11
61-3284	Reamer (mainshaft used with 61-3275/81)	A7, A10	4 6 2
61-3285	Pilot for 61-3275	A7 to 1950	15 1
61-3286	Pilot for 61-3281	A10, AA7 onwards	15 1
61-3287	Reamer Holder (used with 61-3284)	A7, A10	9 1
61-3290	Valve Seat Cutter Holder	A, B, C and M	5 3
61-3293	Valve Seat Cutter Pilot (5/16")	A, B and C	6 8
61-3294	Valve Seat Cutter Pilot (.350")	B and M	6 8
61-3295	Valve Seat Cutter Pilot (.375")	B, and M33	6 8
61-3298	Valve Seat Cutter (1 7/16" dia. x 45° x 20°)	A7 and C	2 6 2
61-3299	Valve Seat Cutter (1 1/2" dia. x 45° x 20°)	A10 and C	2 6 2
61-3300	Valve Seat Cutter (1 5/8" dia. x 45° x 20°)	B	2 6 2
61-3301	Valve Seat Cutter (1 3/4" dia. x 45° x 20°)	B and M	2 6 2
61-3302	Valve Seat Cutter (1 7/8" dia. x 45° x 20°)	B and M	2 6 2
61-3305	Valve Seating Tool complete	A, B, C and M	12 16 2
61-3306	Clutch Assembly Tool	M to 1948	3 0
61-3308	Reamer for 61-3199 (comprising 61-3205 and 61-3309)	D1, and D3	2 8 1
61-3311	Crankshaft Balance Weight (18 ozs., 12 drms.)	A7 1951 onwards	15 1
61-3312	Crankshaft Balance Weight (16 ozs., 14 drms.)	A7 to 1951	15 1
61-3334	Piston Ring Slipper (2 per set)	A7 1951 onwards	6 0
61-3340	Valve Spring Compressor complete	A, B, C and M	1 1 2
61-3350	Front Fork Dismantling and Assembly Tool	A, B, C, M and S7/8	15 1
61-3362	Clutch Extractor Tool	A, B, C and M 1949 onwards	6 8
61-3366	Gudgeon Pin Bush Reamer (.750")	B, M and A10	1 1 10
61-3367	Gudgeon Pin Bush Reamer (.625")	C only	1 2 8
61-3487	Valve Guide Assembly Punch	S7 and S8	15 1
61-3497	Crankshaft Balance Weight (19 ozs. 8 drms.)	A10R/R and S/R	13 9
61-3499	Bench Die Holder (used with 61-3483)	A, B, C and M	2 18 6
61-3503	Rear Suspension Dismantling Tool	A and B S/A	1 17 10
61-3513	Rear Suspension Dismantling Tool	C12 and D3 S/A	1 14 4
61-3536	Flywheel Assembly Tool	Dandy	5 6
61-3540	Flywheel Removal Tool	Dandy	6 3
61-3542	Wheel Bearing Nut Peg Spanner	A and B, S/A	10 4
61-3548	Flywheel Removal Tool (2) (used with 61-3256)	Dandy	4 7
61-3551	Flywheel Locking Tool	Dandy	1 2
61-3552	Starter Ratchet Circlip Assembly Tool	Dandy	5 3
61-3553	Clutch Back Plate Locking Tool	Dandy	9 2
61-3554	Gearbox Sprocket Locking Tool	Dandy	5 5
61-3556	Gudgeon Pin Bush Reamer (11/16")	A7	1 17 10
61-3558	Locking Ring Spanner	8" Brake	11 10
61-3580	Gudgeon Pin Bush Reamer (7/16")	Dandy	1 0 0
61-3581	Gudgeon Pin Bush Reamer (9/16")	D5	1 6 10
65-9240	Valve Grinding Tool	A, B, C and M	1 10
65-9243	Combined "C" and Fork Top Nut spanner	A, B, C and M	1 10
67-9114	Push Rod Assembly Tool	A7/10 1951 onwards	1 5
90-297	Lucas Rotor Removal Tool	D1	1 3

BSA SERVICE TOOLS

Part No.	Description	Used on Models	Retail Price
			£ s. d.
61-3574	Tap and Die Set in wood case comprising taps and dies listed below except 61-3483	General	23 15 0
61-3575	Tap and Die Set in wood case comprising taps and dies listed below	General	32 7 0

TAPS

Part No.	Taps	Description	Retail Price
			£ s. d.
61-3461	$\frac{3}{8}''$ x 19 T.P.I. B.S.P. R/H	Petrol Tap Hole	7 7
61-3462	$\frac{3}{8}''$ x 20 T.P.I. B.S.F. L/H	Sunbeam Dynamo	7 7
61-3463	$\frac{7}{16}''$ x 20 T.P.I. C.E.I. R/H	General	13 1
61-3464	$\frac{1}{2}''$ x 20 T.P.I. C.E.I. R/H	General	14 6
61-3502	$\frac{9}{16}''$ x 20 T.P.I. C.E.I. R/H	General	18 7
61-3465	$\frac{9}{16}''$ x 20 T.P.I. C.E.I. L/H	Front Fork Spindle Hole ...	1 0 0
61-3466	$\frac{5}{8}''$ x 20 T.P.I. C.E.I. R/H	General	17 3
61-3467	$\frac{3}{4}''$ x 20 T.P.I. C.E.I. R/H	General	18 7
61-3468	$\frac{3}{4}''$ x 20 T.P.I. B.S.W. R/H	General	18 7
61-3469	$\frac{3}{4}''$ x 12 T.P.I. B.S.F. L/H	Sunbeam Rear Spindle Hole ...	1 0 0
61-3470	$\frac{7}{8}''$ x 20 T.P.I. B.S.W. R/H	Rear Suspension Shaft ...	1 7 6
61-3471	$1\frac{1}{16}''$ x 20 T.P.I. C.E.I. R/H	Fork Shaft Top	1 5 6
61-3472	$1\frac{1}{8}''$ x 28 T.P.I. B.S.W. R/H	Fork Shaft	1 14 4
61-3473	$1\frac{1}{2}''$ x 20 T.P.I. B.S.W. R/H	Filler Cap	2 14 7
61-3531	14 mm. x 1.25 mm. R/H	Spark Plug	1 0 7
61-3533	1.250'' x 20 T.P.I. B.S.W. R/H	D1 Fork Tube	1 11 0

DIES

Part No.	Dies	Description	Retail Price
			£ s. d.
61-3474	$\frac{7}{16}''$ x 20 T.P.I. C.E.I. R/H	General	11 0
61-3475	$\frac{1}{2}''$ x 20 T.P.I. C.E.I. R/H	General	12 4
61-3476	$\frac{9}{16}''$ x 20 T.P.I. C.E.I. R/H	Gearbox Mainshaft	13 9
61-3477	$\frac{9}{16}''$ x 20 T.P.I. C.E.I. L/H	A Group Mainshaft	17 3
61-3478	$\frac{5}{8}''$ x 20 T.P.I. C.E.I. R/H	General	13 9
61-3479	$\frac{3}{4}''$ x 20 T.P.I. C.E.I. R/H	General	18 7
61-3480	$\frac{3}{4}''$ x 12 T.P.I. B.S.F. L/H	Sunbeam Rear Spindle ...	1 2 0
61-3481	1'' x 24 T.P.I. C.E.I. R/H	Fork Stem	1 4 1
61-3482	1.120'' x 24 T.P.I. C.E.I. R/H	Fork Stem	1 13 9
61-3483	$1\frac{7}{8}''$ x 28 T.P.I. Whit. R/H ... ... (Used with holder 61-3499)	Fork Sliding Tube Top ...	9 9 1

B.S.A. Motor Cycles Ltd., Service Department, Birmingham 11

Printed in England. Sept. 1958

B.S.A. Service Sheet No. 711B

Supplement to No. 711 and 711A

July 1960

SERVICE TOOLS

for

MOTOR CYCLES

B.S.A. SERVICE SHEET No. 711B (contd.)

Removing the Clutch Centre with Extractor No. 61-3583 (Model C15).

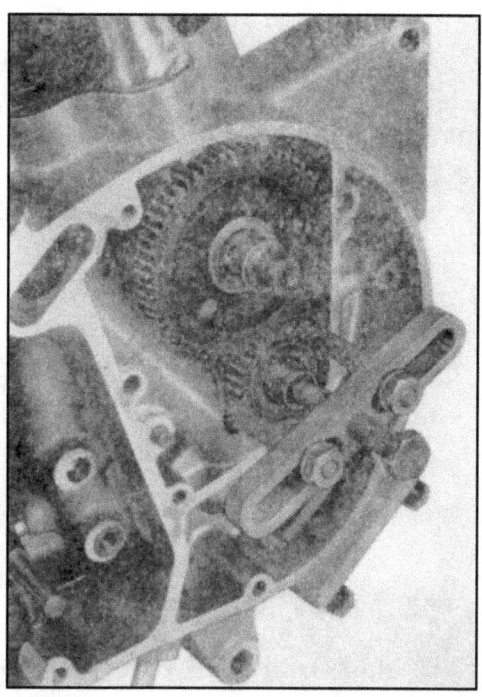

Removing the Crankshaft Pinion with Extractor No. 61-3681 using Legs No. 61-3588 (fitted with Legs 61-3585 for removing the Worm Wheel) (Model C15).

Parting the Flywheels using Bolster 61-3589, Stripping Bars 61-3590 and Punch 61-3601 (Model C15).

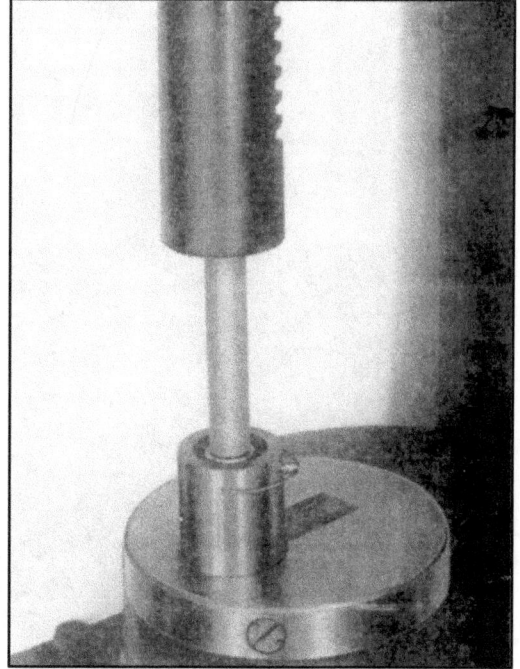

Assembling the Crankpin into the Gear Side Flywheel using Locating Gauge No. 61-3597 and Punch No. 61-3601 (Model C15).

B.S.A. SERVICE SHEET No. 711B (contd.)

Assembling the Drive Side Flywheel on to the Gear Side, using Bolster No. 61-3589, Bridge Piece No. 61-3591 and Punch No. 61-3601 (Model C15).

Flywheel Truing Sleeve No. 61-3592 used with Drive Side bearing on "V" blocks No. 61-692 (Model C15).

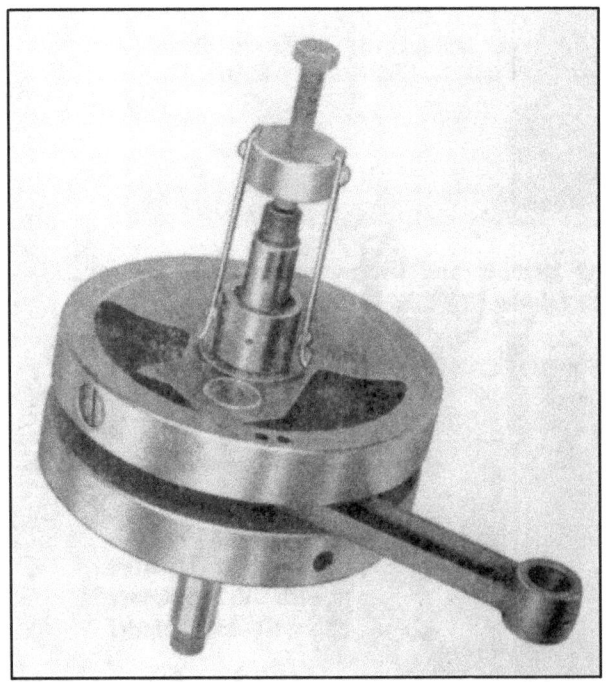

Removing the Gear Side Sleeve with Tool No. 61-3593 (Model C15).

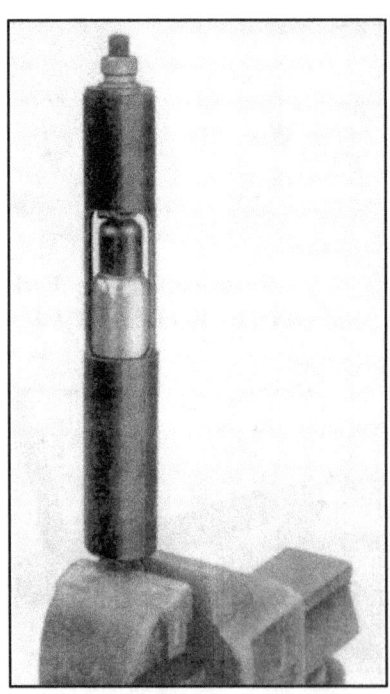

Dismantling the Rear Damper with Tool No. 61-3642 (for Models C15 and D7).

B.S.A. SERVICE SHEET No. 711B (contd.)

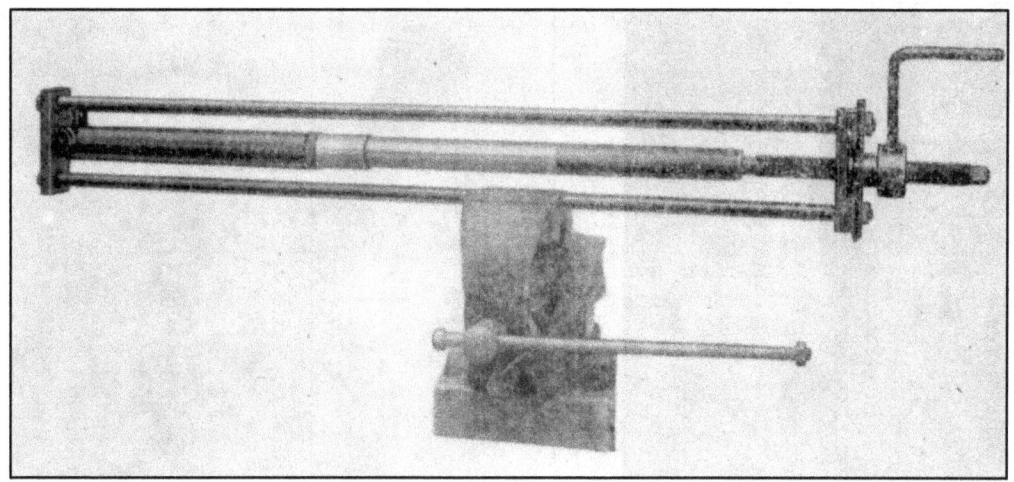

Withdrawing the Fork Main Member and Bushes from the Sliding Member using Tool No. 61-3587.

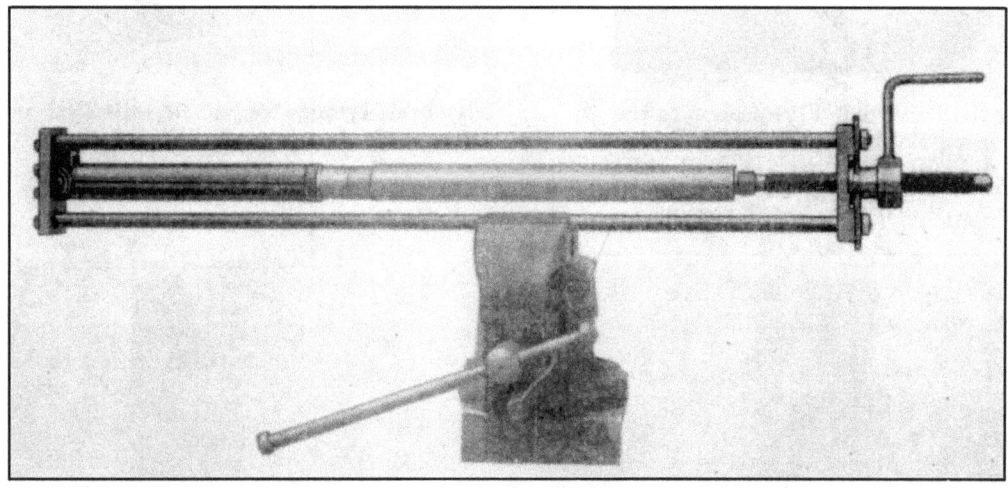

Reassembling the Fork Main Member, Sliding Member and Bushes using Tools No. 61-3587 and 61-3602 (Model C15).

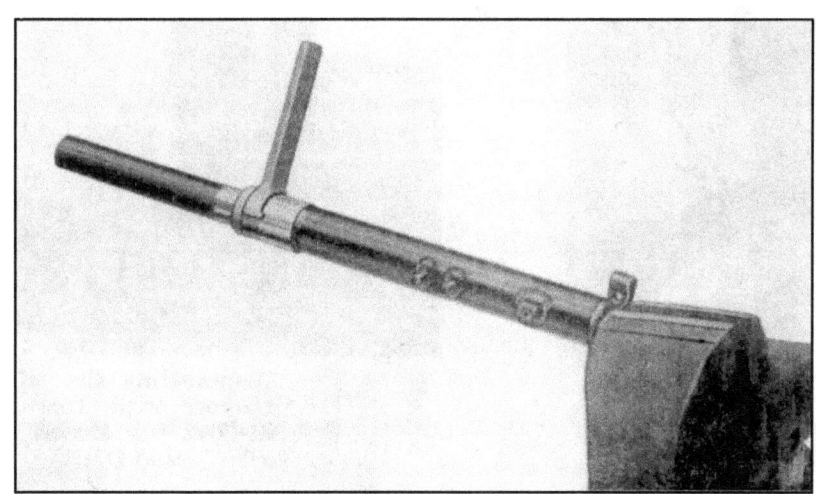

Removing the Fork Oil Seal Holder with "C" Spanner No. 61-3586 (Model C15).

B.S.A. SERVICE SHEET No. 711B (contd.)

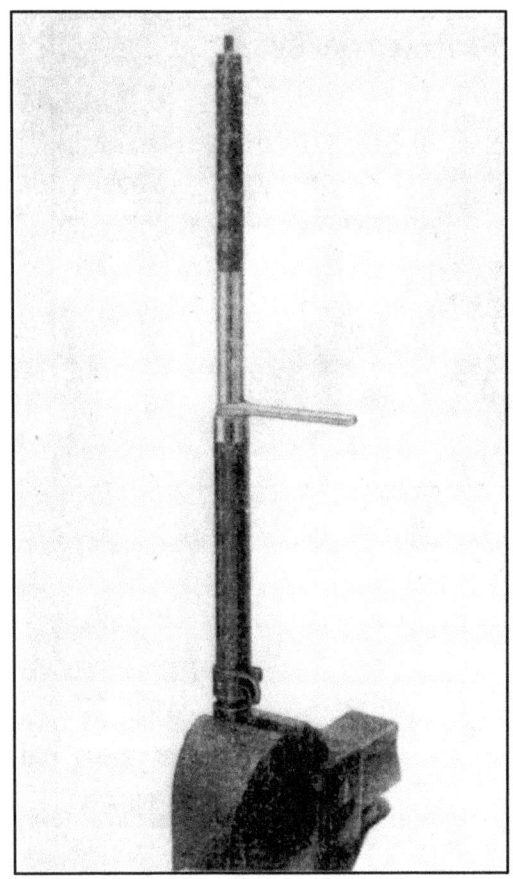

Taking off the Fork Leg Oil Seal Holder with Tool No. 3633 (Model D7).

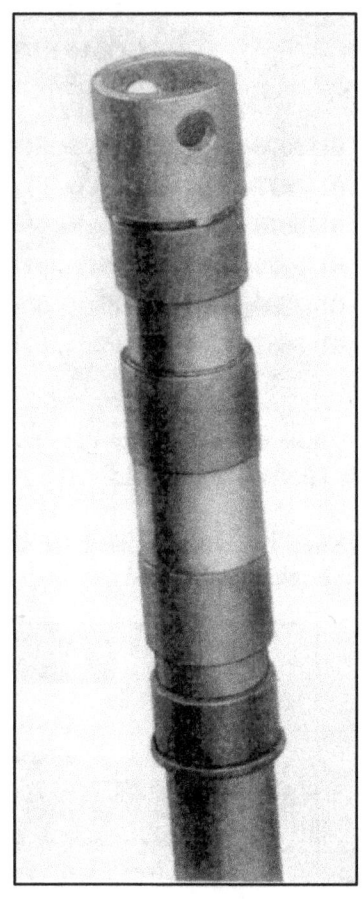

(Model C15). Removing the Fork Leg Bottom Nut with Dog Spanner No. 61-3606 (Tommy Bar not supplied).

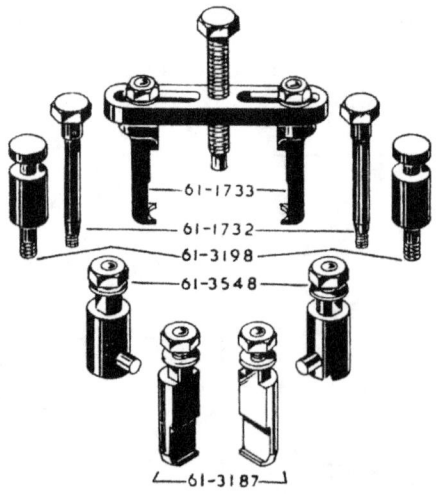

Pinion Extractor showing some of the special Legs.

PINION EXTRACTOR SETS

A Group … … …	Part No. 61-3676
B and M Groups … …	Part No. 61-3677
C Group (excepting C15)	Part No. 61-3678
C15 … … … …	Part No. 61-3681
D Group … … …	Part No. 61-3679
Dandy … … …	Part No. 61-3680
Complete Set … …	Part No. 61-3256

Details of comprising parts and applications are given overleaf.

B.S.A. SERVICE SHEET No. 711B (contd.)

COMPRISING PARTS OF EXTRACTOR SETS

61–3676 = 61–351 Plate, 61–776 Bolt, 61–1732 Leg (2), 61–3187 Leg (2), 61–3198 Leg (2).

61–3677 = 61–351 Plate, 61–776 Bolt, 61–1733 Leg (2).

61–3678 = 61–351 Plate, 61–776 Bolt, 61–1732 Leg (2), 61–1733 Leg (2), 61–3198 Leg (2).

61–3679 = 61–351 Plate, 61–776 Bolt, 61–3198 Leg (2).

61–3680 = 61–351 Plate, 61–776 Bolt, 61–3548 Leg (2).

61–3681 = 61–351 Plate, 61–776 Bolt, 61–3585 Leg (2), 61–3588 Leg (2).

These extractors are extremely useful for the removal of timing, worm or other gears, the legs being specially designed for the particular models.

They can also be used for other jobs of a like nature where a puller is required. All the legs are interchangeable and can be purchased separately if required.

61-358 GUDGEON PIN BUSH EXTRACTOR

is now cancelled and replaced by 61–3672.

This tool is now available for the individual models as detailed below:—

Tool No.	Model	Comprising
61–3651	—	Holder, Rod and Nut only.
61–3652	A7, A10	61–3651, and Bushes 61–3319/20.
61–3653	B Group	61–3651, and Bushes 61–3654/5.
61–3656	C10, C11, C12	61–3651, and Bushes 61–3657/8.
61–3659	C15, A7 (Steel Rod)	61–3651, and Bushes 61–3660/1.
61–3662	D1, D3	61–3651, and Bushes 61–3663/4.
61–3665	D5, D7	61–3651, and Bushes 61–3666/7.
61–3668	M20, M21	61–3651, and Bushes 61–654/5.
61–3669	Dandy	61–3651, and Bushes 61–3670/71.

B.S.A. SERVICE SHEET No. 711B (contd.)

Using a piston Ring Slipper makes replacement easier.

Piston Ring Slippers (Terry).

Now available for the following models:—

61–5004	55–60 mm. Bore	Models D1, D3.
61–5051	60–65 mm. Bore	Models C10L, C11, C12, D5, D7.
61–3682	65–70 mm. Bore	Models A Group, C15.

Additional Tools not illustrated

61–5035 valve grinding tool (Suction type). This tool is similar to 65–9240 shown on Service Sheet No. 711 but is suitable for valves with $\frac{3}{4}$ in. to 1 in. diameter heads.

61–3673 clutch nut screwdriver, designed specially for the moded C15.

BSA SERVICE SHEET No. 712X

ALL GROUPS
FLYWHEEL BALANCING (STATIC)

Revised and Reprinted October 1956.
Revised May 1958.

Flywheel balancing should not be undertaken except by an expert mechanic, who is fully equipped with the tools described in this Service Sheet.

Unless very great care is exercised, excessive engine vibration may result from any change of balance, and unless extreme care is practised in flywheel drilling, flywheels may be seriously weakened.

All flywheel assemblies are accurately balanced before leaving the Works and there should be no need to re-balance when fitting new big end assemblies unless the difference in weight between the old and new assembly is more than 1 to $1\frac{3}{4}$ozs.

When a fabricated crankshaft is employed as on the "C", "B" and "M" Group models, the method of flywheel truing is described in Service Sheet No. 607.

The equipment required for balancing is a drilling machine and knife edge rollers (see Fig. X10) which must be set up perfectly horizontal and sufficiently high to allow the flywheels to revolve with the Con Rod hanging.

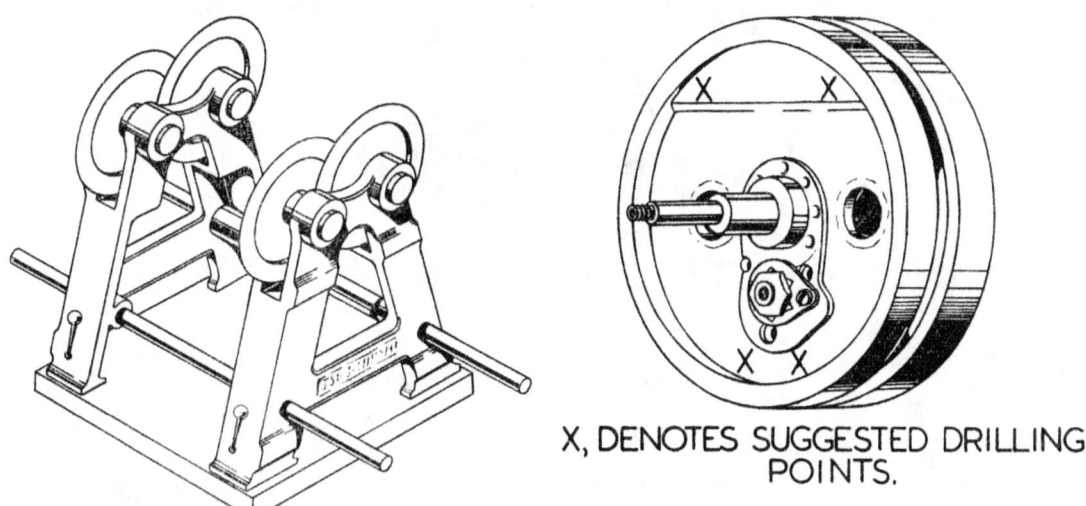

Fig. X10. Knife Edge Rollers.   Fig. X11. "B" and "M" Group Flywheels.

X, DENOTES SUGGESTED DRILLING POINTS.

For balancing purposes a small weight equivalent to part of the reciprocating weight must be attached to the small end of the Con Rod. A table of these weights is given below.

Place the assembly on the knife edges and allow to revolve till it stops, mark the lowest spot with chalk and check again two or three times.

To find the amount of the out-of-balance apply plasticine to the rim of the wheels diametrically opposite the heaviest point until the wheels remain stationary when placed in any position.

The wheels must now be drilled at the heaviest spot to remove metal equal to the weight of plasticine. Care must be taken to drill each wheel equally (see Fig. X11).

B.S.A. Service Sheet No. 712x (continued).

BALANCING "A" GROUP FLYWHEELS.

A group flywheels are treated similarly to the single cylinder models except that the Con Rods are not fitted, a balance weight being attached to each crank pin. These are available as Service Tools, 61-3310 for A7, 61-3312 for A7 after Engine No. AA7-101, 61-3311 for A10 and 61-3497 for A10 Road Rocket. New bolts and nuts must be used to secure the flywheel and the ends of the bolts peined over after locking.

Drilling is carried out on the periphery of the flywheel instead of the webs and care must be taken to keep the holes central and not too deep, the maximum depth should not be more than 3/16" (see Fig. X12). It is preferable to start with a smaller diameter hole which can be opened out if necessary, rather than a large diameter to then find that too much metal has been removed.

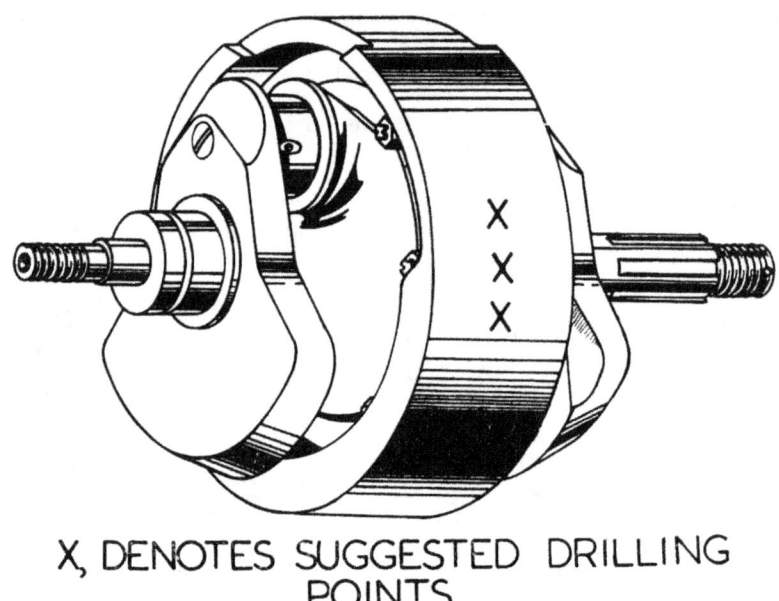

X, DENOTES SUGGESTED DRILLING POINTS.

Fig. X12. "A" Group Crankshaft.

Model	Weight attached	Model	Weight attached
A7	2 @ 19 ozs. 10 drams	B32 Competition	5 ozs. 4 drams
A7 after AA7-101	2 @ 16 ozs. 12 drams	B34 Competition	9 ozs. 9 drams
A10	2 @ 18 ozs. 10 drams	B32 Gold Star	6 ozs. 5 drams
A10 Road Rocket	2 @ 19 ozs. 8 drams	B34 Gold Star	11 ozs. 4 drams
C Group	3 ozs. 5 drams	M20	7 ozs.
B31	4 ozs. 6 drams	M21	5 ozs. 10 drams
B33 and M33	8 ozs. 8 drams		

Note:- Service Tool No. 61-3497 should be used on Crankshaft No. 67-1218 which is fitted to the Super Rocket and A10 machines after Eng. No. CA10R-4650 and DA10-101 respectively.

B.S.A. MOTOR CYCLES LIMITED, Service Dept., Birmingham, 11
(PRINTED IN ENGLAND)

BSA SERVICE SHEET No. 713

ALL MODELS EXCEPT "D" GROUP AND C15
DISMANTLING OF STEERING HEAD

Remove the headlamp from the forks after undoing the two retaining bolts, and allow it to hang in a position where it cannot be damaged. If a headlamp cowl is fitted, it should be removed complete with the headlamp.

On later models of the type shown in Fig. C31A the lamp is not removed, but it is necessary to take off the lamp front by unscrewing pin (F) and to disconnect the speedometer cable and the leads to the switch.

Detach the handlebars complete with controls, and lay them on top of the petrol tank, using a piece of rag to protect the enamel. Remove the chromium-plated top caps (A) and (B) Fig. C31. Slacken the pinch bolt (C) and remove the adjusting sleeve (D) or (E) Fig. C31A. Tap off the fork top yoke by striking it with a mallet underneath its two sides alternately.

The steering column can now be drawn downwards from the head, and the top ballrace removed. **Note.**—If the bearings are dry a means of catching the steel balls should be arranged as they will fall as the column is drawn out.

The cups which remain in the head can be withdrawn by means of extractor No. 61-3060 for "C" Group, and 61-3063 for "A", "M" and "B" Groups. This is screwed firmly into the cup, then extractor and cup are driven out from the opposite end with the aid of a suitable bar.

If the cups and cones are pitted to even a slight degree, they must be replaced, otherwise steering will be adversely affected and will rapidly become worse.

Pitting is invariably due to "hammering" of the balls in their tracks, caused by slack adjustment.

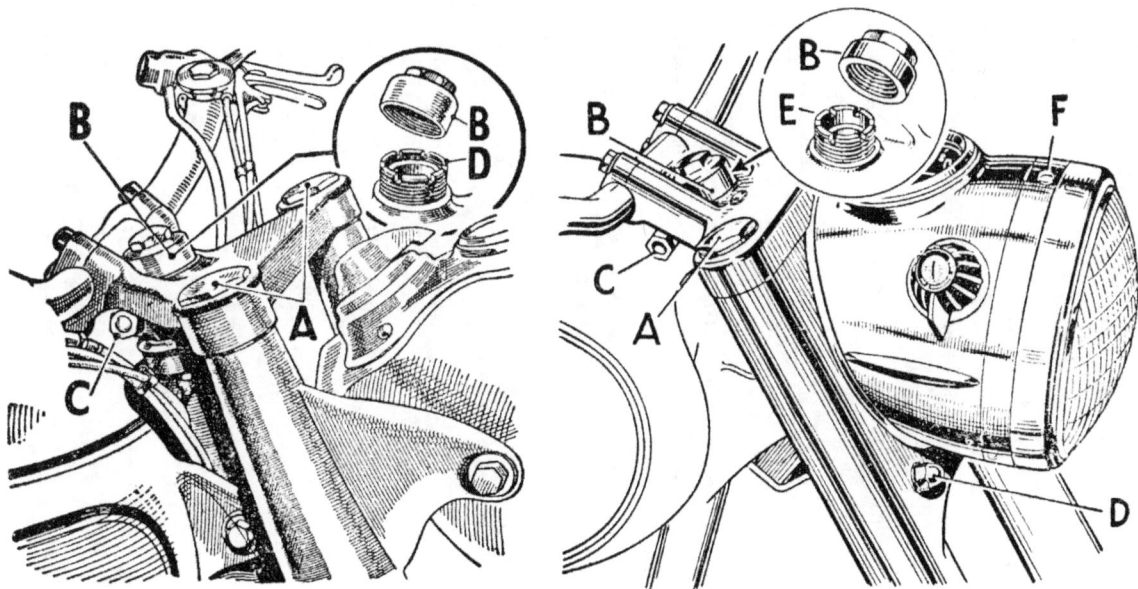

Fig. C31. The Front Fork & Steering Head.   Fig. C31A.

Reassembly of Steering Head.

When fitting new ballrace cups make sure that they are driven in squarely and that they are pressed well home. Replace the steering column balls, cone, adjusting sleeve and top-yoke. If any difficulty is experienced in retaining the balls in position, smear the tracks heavily with grease.

Adjust the column so that it turns freely without play and tighten the pinch bolt (C).

Finally replace headlamp and handlebar controls.

B.S.A. Motor Cycles Ltd., Service Dept., Armoury Road, Birmingham 11
B.S.A. Press.

BSA SERVICE SHEET No. 714

Printed September, 1956
Revised October, 1957

SPOKE SIZES.

NOTE.—All Models use Forty Spokes per Wheel except "D" Group which have Thirty-six.

YEAR	MODEL	RIM SIZE	FRONT LEFT Length	FRONT LEFT Gauge	FRONT LEFT Part Number	FRONT RIGHT Length	FRONT RIGHT Gauge	FRONT RIGHT Part Number	RIM SIZE	REAR LEFT Length	REAR LEFT Gauge	REAR LEFT Part Number	REAR RIGHT Length	REAR RIGHT Gauge	REAR RIGHT Part Number
1947	C10	WM1-19	$8\frac{3}{4}"$	10	24-7012	$8\frac{3}{4}"$	10	24-7012	WM1-19	$8\frac{1}{4}"$	10	24-7012	$6\frac{7}{8}"$	10	24-7014
	C11	WM1-20	$9\frac{1}{4}"$	10	24-6912	$9\frac{3}{16}"$	10	29-5772	WM2-20	$9\frac{1}{4}"$	10	24-6912	$7\frac{7}{8}"$	10	65-5873
	B31-B33	WM2-19	$8\frac{11}{16}"$	10	65-5872	$7\frac{1}{2}"$	10	65-5910	WM2-19	$8\frac{7}{16}"$	8/10	65-6072	$8\frac{1}{4}"$	10	24-7012
	B32-B34	WM1-21	$9\frac{11}{16}"$	10	65-5537	$8\frac{5}{8}"$	10	90-5584	WM2-19	$8\frac{5}{16}"$	8/10	65-6027	$8\frac{1}{4}"$	10	24-7012
	M20-M21 Girder Fork	WM3-19	$8\frac{3}{4}"$	10	24-7012	$6\frac{3}{4}"$	8/10	24-6899	WM3-19	$8\frac{5}{8}"$	8/10	15-7037	$8\frac{3}{4}"$	8	26-6824
	A7	WM2-19	$7\frac{22}{32}"$	10/12	67-6008	$8\frac{1}{16}"$	10/12	67-6007	WM2-19	$7\frac{22}{32}"$	10/12	67-6008	$8\frac{1}{16}"$	10/12	67-6007
1948	C10	WM1-19	$8\frac{3}{4}"$	10	24-7012	$8\frac{3}{4}"$	10	24-7012	WM1-19	$8\frac{1}{4}"$	10	24-7012	$6\frac{7}{8}"$	10	24-7014
	C11	WM1-20	$9\frac{1}{4}"$	10	24-6912	$9\frac{3}{16}"$	10	29-5772	WM1-20	$9\frac{1}{4}"$	10	24-6912	$7\frac{7}{8}"$	10	65-5873
	B31	WM2-19	$8\frac{11}{16}"$	10	65-5872	$7\frac{1}{2}"$	10	65-5910	WM2-19	$8\frac{5}{8}"$	8/10	65-6027	$8\frac{1}{4}"$	10	24-7012
	B32	WM1-21	$9\frac{11}{16}"$	10	65-5537	$8\frac{5}{8}"$	10	65-5910	WM2-19	$8\frac{5}{8}"$	8/10	65-6027	$8\frac{1}{4}"$	10	24-7012
	B33	WM2-19	$8\frac{11}{16}"$	10	65-5872	$7\frac{1}{2}"$	10	65-5537	WM2-19	$8\frac{5}{8}"$	8/10	65-6027	$8\frac{1}{4}"$	10	24-7012
	B34	WM1-21	$9\frac{11}{16}"$	10	65-5537	$8\frac{5}{8}"$	10	90-5584	WM2-19	$8\frac{5}{8}"$	8/10	65-6027	$8\frac{1}{4}"$	10	24-7012
	M20-M21 Girder Fork	WM3-19	$8\frac{3}{4}"$	10	24-7012	$6\frac{3}{4}"$	8/10	24-6899	WM3-19	$8\frac{5}{8}"$	8/10	15-7037	$8\frac{3}{4}"$	8	26-6824
	M33-G.F.	WM3-19	$8\frac{3}{4}"$	10	24-7012	$6\frac{3}{4}"$	8/10	24-6899	WM3-19	$8\frac{5}{8}"$	8/10	15-7037	$8\frac{3}{4}"$	8	26-6824
	A7	WM2-19	$7\frac{22}{32}"$	10/12	67-6008	$8\frac{1}{16}"$	10/12	67-6007	WM2-19	$7\frac{22}{32}"$	10/12	67-6008	$8\frac{1}{16}"$	10/12	67-6007
1949	D1	WM1-19	$8\frac{3}{16}"$	10	90-5584	$7\frac{7}{8}"$	10	90-5583	WM1-19	$8\frac{5}{16}"$	10	15-7072	$8\frac{3}{16}"$	10	29-5846
	D1 Comp	WM1-19	$8\frac{1}{16}"$	10	90-5584	$7\frac{7}{8}"$	10	90-5583	WM1-19	$8\frac{5}{16}"$	10	15-7072	$8\frac{5}{16}"$	10	29-5846
	C10	WM1-19	$8\frac{3}{4}"$	10	24-7012	$8\frac{3}{4}"$	10	24-7012	WM1-19	$8\frac{1}{4}"$	10	24-7012	$6\frac{7}{8}"$	10	24-7014
	C11	WM1-20	$9\frac{1}{4}"$	10	24-6912	$9\frac{3}{16}"$	10	29-5772	WM1-20	$9\frac{1}{4}"$	10	24-6912	$7\frac{7}{8}"$	10	65-5873
	B32-B34 G/S Std. & Spg. Frame	WM1-21	$9\frac{11}{16}"$	10	65-5537	$8\frac{5}{8}"$	10	90-5584	R	$8\frac{3}{16}"$	8/10	65-6027	$8\frac{3}{4}"$	10	24-7012
	B31-B32 Std. & Spg Frame	WM2-19	$8\frac{11}{16}"$	10	65-5872	$7\frac{1}{2}"$	10	65-5910	WM2-19S	$7\frac{22}{32}"$	10/12	67-6008	$7\frac{22}{32}"$	10/12	67-6008
	M20-M21-M33 Tele. Forks	WM2-19	$8\frac{11}{16}"$	10	65-5872	$7\frac{1}{2}"$	10	65-5910	R	$8\frac{5}{8}"$	10/12	65-6027	$7\frac{22}{32}"$	10/12	67-6008
	A7 Star Twin Std. & Spg. Frame	WM2-19	$8\frac{11}{16}"$	10	65-5872	$7\frac{1}{2}"$	10	65-5910	WM2-19S	$8\frac{5}{8}"$	8/10	15-7037	$8\frac{5}{8}"$	8	24-6896
		WM2-19							WM2-19	$7\frac{22}{32}"$	10/12	67-6008	$7\frac{22}{32}"$	10/12	67-6008

B.S.A. Service Sheet No. 714—continued

SPOKE SIZES—continued.

YEAR	MODEL	RIM SIZE	FRONT LEFT Gauge	FRONT LEFT Length	FRONT Part Number	FRONT RIGHT Gauge	FRONT RIGHT Length	FRONT RIGHT Part Number	RIM SIZE	REAR LEFT Length	REAR LEFT Gauge	REAR LEFT Part Number	REAR RIGHT Length	REAR RIGHT Gauge	REAR RIGHT Part Number
1950	D1 Std. & Spg. D1 Comp. Spg.	WM1-19	10	$8\frac{7}{16}''$	90-5584	10	$7\frac{1}{2}''$	90-5584	WM1-19	$8\frac{5}{16}''$	10	15-7072	$8\frac{5}{16}''$	10	90-5584
	C10	WM1-19	10	$8\frac{3}{8}''$	24-7012	10	$8\frac{3}{4}''$	24-7012	WM1-19	$8\frac{3}{4}''$	10	24-7012	$6\frac{7}{8}''$	10	24-7014
	C11	WM1-20	10	$9\frac{3}{16}''$	24-6912	10	$9\frac{3}{16}''$	29-5772	WM1-20	$9\frac{1}{4}''$	10	24-6912	$7\frac{3}{8}''$	10	65-5873
	B31-B33 Std. & Spg. Frame	WM2-19	10	$8\frac{11}{16}''$	65-5872	10	$7\frac{1}{2}''$	65-5910	R WM2-19S	$8\frac{9}{16}''$	8/10	65-6027	$8\frac{3}{4}''$	10	24-7012
	B32-B34 Comp. Models	WM1-21	10	$9\frac{11}{16}''$	65-5537	10	$8\frac{9}{16}''$	90-5584	WM2-19	$7\frac{9}{16}''$	10	65-6302	$7\frac{22}{32}''$	10	65-6302
	350 and 500 Scramble & Grass Track Models	Varies to Spec.	10	$9\frac{11}{16}''$	65-5537	10	$8\frac{9}{16}''$	90-5584	Varies to Spec.	$8\frac{9}{16}''$	8/10	65-6027	$8\frac{3}{4}''$	10	24-7012
	350 & 500 O.H.V. Gold Star, Clubmans and Road Racing	Varies to Spec.	10	$9\frac{11}{16}''$	65-5926	10	$6\frac{7}{8}''$	24-7014	Varies to Spec.	$7\frac{22}{32}''$	10	65-6302	$7\frac{22}{32}''$	10	65-6302
	M20-M21-M33	WM2-19	10	$8\frac{11}{16}''$	65-5872	10	$7\frac{1}{2}''$	65-5910	WM3-19	$8\frac{5}{8}''$	8/10	15-7037	$8\frac{5}{8}''$	8	24-6896
	A7 Star Twin Rigid & Spg. Frame	WM2-19	10	$8\frac{11}{16}''$	65-5872	10	$7\frac{1}{2}''$	65-5910	WM3-19	$7\frac{22}{32}''$	10	65-6302	$7\frac{22}{32}''$	10	65-6302
	A10	WM2-19	10	$8\frac{7}{16}''$	67-5545	10	$5\frac{11}{16}''$	67-5544	WM3-19	$7\frac{22}{32}''$	10	65-6302	$7\frac{22}{32}''$	10	65-6302
1951 and 1952 (other models as 1950)	C10 Spring Frame	WM1-19	10	$8\frac{3}{4}''$	24-7012	10	$8\frac{3}{4}''$	24-7012	WM1-19	$8\frac{3}{4}''$	10	24-7012	$6\frac{7}{8}''$	10	24-7014
	C11 Spring Frame	WM1-20	10	$9\frac{1}{4}''$	24-6912	10	$9\frac{3}{16}''$	29-5772	WM1-20	$9\frac{1}{4}''$	10	24-6912	$7\frac{3}{8}''$	10	65-5873
	M20-M21-M33 Spring Frame	WM1-19	10	$8\frac{11}{16}''$	65-5872	10	$7\frac{1}{2}''$	65-5910	WM2-19	$7\frac{22}{32}''$	10	65-6302	$7\frac{22}{32}''$	10	65-6302
1953 (other models as 1950/52)	B33-A7-A10 Rigid	WM2-19	10	$8\frac{7}{8}''$	67-5545	10	$5\frac{11}{16}''$	67-5544	WM2-19	$8\frac{3}{4}''$	10	24-7012	$8\frac{5}{16}''$	10	65-6027
	B33-A7-A10 Spring	WM2-19	10	$8\frac{7}{8}''$	67-5545	10	$5\frac{11}{16}''$	67-5544	WM2-19	$7\frac{22}{32}''$	10	65-6303	$7\frac{22}{32}''$	10	65-6302
	GOLD STAR Clubmans, Road Racing & Touring	WM1-19	10	$8\frac{3}{8}''$	67-5537	10	$8\frac{9}{16}''$	90-5584	WM2-19	$7\frac{22}{32}''$	10	65-6303	$7\frac{22}{32}''$	10	65-6302
	B32-B34 Trials	WM1-21	10	$9\frac{11}{16}''$	67-5537	10	$8\frac{5}{8}''$	90-5584	WM3-19	$7\frac{22}{32}''$	10	65-6303	$7\frac{22}{32}''$	10	65-6302
	B32-B34 Scrambles	WM1-21	8	$9\frac{11}{16}''$	42-5524	8	$8\frac{7}{16}''$	31-6015	WM3-19	$7\frac{22}{32}''$	10	65-6303	$7\frac{22}{32}''$	10	65-6302

B.S.A. Service Sheet No. 714—*continued*

SPOKE SIZES—*continued*

YEAR	MODEL	FRONT RIM SIZE	FRONT LEFT Length	FRONT LEFT Gauge	FRONT LEFT Part Number	FRONT RIGHT Length	FRONT RIGHT Gauge	FRONT RIGHT Part Number	REAR RIM SIZE	REAR LEFT Length	REAR LEFT Gauge	REAR LEFT Part Number	REAR RIGHT Length	REAR RIGHT Gauge	REAR RIGHT Part Number
1954 and 1955	D1–D3 Rigid & Spring	WM1-19	8 9/16"	10	90-5584	7 7/8"	10	90-5583	WM1-19	8 9/16"	10	90-6042	8 3/4"	10	90-5584
	D1–D3 Comp.	WM1-19	8 7/8"	10	90-5584	7"	10	29-5940	WM1-19	8 9/16"	10	90-6042	8 3/8"	10	90-5584
	C10L	WM1-19	8 3/8"	10	90-5584	7"	10	29-5940	WM1-19	8 5/16"	10	90-6042	8 5/8"	10	90-5584
	C11G	WM1-19	8 3/4"	10	24-7012	8 3/4"	10	24-7012	WM1-19	6 7/8"	10	24-7014	8 3/4"	10	24-7012
	C11G (1955) Rigid & Spring	WM1-19	8 3/4"	10	24-7012	7 1/2"	10	65-5910	WM2-19	6 7/8"	Butted 8/10	24-7014	8 3/4"	10	24-7012
	B31–B33 Rigid	WM2-19	8 11/16"	10	65-5872	7 3/4"	10	65-5910	WM2-19	8 9/16"	Butted 8/10	65-6027	8 3/4"	10	65-6302
	B31–B33 Spring	WM2-19	8 9/16"	10	65-5872	7 1/4"	10	65-5910	WM2-19	7 27/32"	10	65-6303	7 29/32"	10	65-6302
	B32–B34 Comp. Rigid	WM1-21	9 1/2"	10	65-5537	8 9/16"	10	90-5584	WM3-19	7 27/32"	10	65-6303	7 29/32"	10	65-6302
	B31 Swinging Arm	WM2-19	8 1/2"	10	65-5872	7 1/2"	10	65-5912	WM2-19	7 27/32"	10	65-6303	7 29/32"	10	65-6302
	B32–B34 Swinging Arm	WM1-21	9 1/2"	10	65-5537	8 9/16"	10	90-5584	WM2-19	7 27/32"	10	65-6303	7 29/32"	10	65-6302
	B33 1954 Swinging Arm	WM2-19	8 7/8"	10	67-5545	5 15/16"	10	67-5544	WM2-19	7 27/32"	10	65-6303	7 29/32"	10	65-6302
	B33 1955 Swinging Arm	WM2-19	8 7/8"	Butted 8/10	67-5606	5 15/16"	10	67-5544	WM2-19	7 27/32"	10	65-6303	7 29/32"	10	65-6302
	GOLD STAR Clubmans, Road Racing & Touring	WM1-19	9 1/2"	10	67-5545	5 15/16"	10	67-5544	WM2-18	7 3/16"	10	42-6011	7 7/16"	10	42-6012
	GOLD STAR Trials	WM1-21	9 1/2"	10	65-5926	6 7/8"	10	24-7014	WM3-19	7 27/32"	10	65-6303	7 29/32"	10	65-6302
	GOLD STAR Scrambles	WM1-21	9 11/16"	10	65-5537	8 9/16"	8	31-6015	WM3-19	7 27/32"	10	65-6303	7 29/32"	10	65-6302
	M20–M21–M33 Rigid	WM2-19	8 11/16"	8	42-5524	8 9/16"	10	65-5910	WM2-19	8 3/8"	Butted 8	15-7037	8 7/8"	Butted 8	24-6896
	M20–M21–M33 Spring	WM2-19	8 11/16"	10	65-5872	7 1/2"	10	65-5910	WM2-19	7 27/32"	10	65-6303	7 29/32"	10	65-6302
	"A" GROUP Plunger & Swinging Arm 1954	WM2-19	8 7/8"	10	67-5545	5 11/16"	10	67-5544	WM2-19	7 15/32"	10	65-6303	7 29/32"	10	65-6302
	"A" GROUP Plunger & Swinging Arm 1955	WM2-19	8 7/8"	Butted 8/10	67-5606	5 11/16"	10	67-5544	WM2-19	7 27/32"	10	65-6303	7 29/32"	10	65-6302

B.S.A. Service Sheet No. 714—continued

SPOKE SIZES—continued.

YEAR	MODEL	RIM SIZE	FRONT LEFT Length	FRONT LEFT Gauge	FRONT Part Number	FRONT Length	FRONT RIGHT Gauge	FRONT Part Number	RIM SIZE	REAR LEFT Length	REAR LEFT Gauge	REAR Part Number	REAR Length	REAR RIGHT Gauge	REAR Part Number
1956/7	D1 Plunger	WM1-19	8 5/16"	10	90-5584	7 1/8"	10	90-5583	WM1-19	8 1/16"	10	90-6042	8 9/16"	10	90-5584
	D3 Swinging Arm	WM1-19	8 5/16"	10	90-5584	7 1/8"	10	90-5583	WM1-19	8 5/16"	10	90-6042	8 9/16"	10	90-5584
	C10L	WM1-19	8 3/4"	10	24-7012	8 3/4"	10	24-7012	WM1-19	8 5/16"	10	90-6042	8 9/16"	10	90-5584
	C12	WM1-19	6 7/8"	10	29-5976	6 7/8"	10	29-5976	WM1-19	7"	10	29-5940	7"	10	29-5940
	B31–B33	WM2-19	6 1/4"	Butted 8/10	42-5635	6 1/4"	Butted 8/10	42-5635	WM2-19	6 1/4"	Butted 8/10	42-5635	6 1/4"	Butted 8/10	42-5635
	GOLD STAR Clubmans, Road Racing & Touring	WM1-19	5 1/4"	10	42-5552	5 1/4"	10	42-5552	WM2-19	7 27/32"	10	65-6303	7 29/32"	10	65-6302
	B32–B34 Comp.	WM1-21	9 11/16"	10	65-5537	8 5/16"	10	90-5584	WM3-19	7 27/32"	10	65-6303	7 29/32"	10	65-6302
	GOLD STAR Scrambles	WM1-21	9 11/16"	8	42-5524	8 7/16"	8	31-6015	WM3-19	7 27/32"	Butted 8	15-7037	8 5/16"	Butted 8	24-6896
	M21 Rigid	WM2-19	8 3/4"	Butted 8/10	67-5606	5 19/32"	Butted 8/10	66-5560	WM3-19	8 5/16"	10	65-6303	7 29/32"	10	65-6302
	M21–M33 Plunger	WM2-19	8 3/4"	Butted 8/10	67-5606	5 19/32"	Butted 8/10	66-5560	WM2-19	7 27/32"	Butted 8/10	42-5635	6 1/4"	Butted 8/10	42-5635
	A7 and Shooting Star	WM2-19	6 1/4"	Butted 8/10	42-5635	6 1/4"	Butted 8/10	42-5635	WM2-19	6 1/4"	Butted 8/10	42-5635	6 1/4"	Butted 8/10	42-5635
	A10 Plunger	WM2-19	8 3/4"	Butted 8/10	67-5606	5 19/32"	Butted 8/10	66-5561	WM2-19	7 27/32"	Butted 8/10	67-6017	7 29/32"	Butted 8/10	67-6016
	A10 and Road Rocket	WM2-19	6 1/4"	Butted 8/10	42-5635	6 1/4"	Butted 8/10	42-5635	WM2-19	6 1/4"	8/10	42-5635	6 1/4"	Butted 8/10	42-5635
	Dandy 70	WM0-15	5 5/8"	12	64-5505	5 5/8"	12	64-5505	WM0-15	5 5/8"	Butted 11/12	64-5507	5 5/8"	Butted 11/12	64-5507

151

BSA SERVICE SHEET No. 801

"A" Group Models

MAGNETO

These magnetos are of the rotating armature pattern. The magnet is cast into the body, so eliminating joints and improving the weatherproof properties of the magneto. The magnetos also incorporate an automatic timing control.

The automatic timing control (Fig. Y1) employs a driving gear carrying a plate fitted with two pins. A weight is pivoted on each pin and the movement of the weight is controlled by a spring connected between the pivot end of the weight and a toggle lever pivoted at approximately the centre of the weight. Holes are provided in each toggle lever, in which pegs on the underside of a driving plate secured to the magneto spindle are located. This plate is also provided with stops which limit the range of the control. When the magneto is stationary, the weights are in the closed position and the magneto retarded for starting purposes. As the speed is increased, centrifugal force acting on the weights overcomes the restraining influence of the springs and the weights move outwards, causing relative movement to take place between the driving gear and the magneto spindle, so advancing the timing. By careful design of the springs, the characteristics of the control can be arranged to conform more closely with the engine requirements than is the case with other types of control.

ROUTINE MAINTENANCE

Lubrication

To be carried out every 3,000 miles.

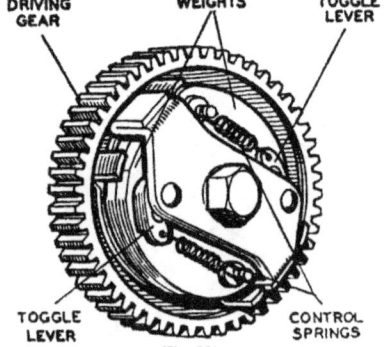
Fig. Y1.

The cam is supplied with lubricant from a felt pad contained in a pocket in the contact breaker housing. A small hole in the cam, fitted with a wick, enables the oil to find its way on to the surface of the cam. Remove the contact breaker cover and turn the engine over until the hole in the cam can be clearly seen and then carefully add a few drops of thin machine oil. Do not allow any oil to get on to the contacts. When the magneto is dismantled the felt pad should be removed, soaked in thin machine oil and after removing surplus oil, replaced.

The contact breaker rocker arm pivot also requires lubrication and the complete contact breaker must be removed for this purpose. Take out the hexagon-headed screw from the centre of the contact breaker and pull the contact breaker off the tapered shaft on which it fits. Then push aside the rocker arm retaining spring, prise the rocker arm off its bearing and lightly smear the bearing with clean engine oil. At the same time, also lightly smear the contact breaker with clean engine oil.

When replacing the contact breaker, take care to ensure that the projecting key, on the tapered portion of the contact breaker base, engages with the keyway cut in the magneto

B.S.A. Service Sheet No. 801 (contd.)

spindle, otherwise the timing of the magneto will be upset. Tighten the hexagon-headed screw with care; it must not be too slack, nor must undue force be used.

Adjustment

To be carried out every 3,000 miles.

Remove the contact breaker cover and turn the engine until the contacts are fully opened. Check the gap with a gauge having a thickness of .012 in. If the setting is correct, the gauge should be a sliding fit, but if the gap varies appreciably from the gauge it should be adjusted. Keep the engine in the position to give maximum opening of the contacts, slacken the locknut and turn the contact screw by its hexagon head until the gap is set to the gauge. Finally tighten the locknut and re-check the setting.

Cleaning

To be carried out every 6,000 miles.

Take off the contact breaker cover and examine the contact breaker. If the contacts are burned or blackened, clean them with fine carborundum stone or with very fine emery cloth, and afterwards wipe away any dust or dirt with a petrol-moistened cloth. Cleaning of the contacts is made easier if the contact breaker is removed. Procedure is given above.

Remove the high-tension pickups, wipe clean and polish with a fine dry cloth. The high-tension pickup brush must move freely in its holder. If it is dirty, clean with a cloth moistened with petrol. If the brush is worn to within $\frac{1}{8}$ in. of the shoulder it must be renewed. While the high-tension pickup is removed, clean the slip ring track and flanges by holding a soft cloth on the ring by means of a suitably shaped piece of wood, while the engine is slowly turned.

Replacement of High-Tension Cable

If, on inspection the high-tension cable shows signs of perishing or cracking it must be replaced by a suitable length of 7 mm. rubber-covered ignition cable.

To fit a new high-tension cable to a pick-up terminal, bare the end of the cable for about $\frac{1}{4}$ in., thread the knurled moulded nut over the cable, thread the bare wire through the washer removed from the end of the old cable and bend back the strands. Finally screw the nut into the pick-up.

SERVICING

Testing Magneto in position on Engine

Testing magneto in position to locate cause of misfiring or failure of ignition.

Disconnect the cable from one of the sparking plugs and hold it so that the terminal end is about $\frac{1}{8}$ in. from some part of the cylinder block while the engine is turned over.

If the spark that jumps from the cable end is strong and regular the fault lies in the sparking plug which must be removed for examination and if necessary cleaned and adjusted or replaced.

Next examine the high-tension cable. After long service it may have become cracked or perished and the magneto may be sparking through to a metal part of the engine or frame.

B.S.A. Service Sheet No. 801 (contd.)

If the magneto has been replaced recently it may be incorrectly timed. Refer to Service Sheet No. 203.

If the performance of the magneto is still not satisfactory, the contact breaker may require cleaning or adjustment. If the contacts are badly burned they should be renewed by a replacement contact set. If the contact breaker is in good order, there may be an internal fault in the magneto (see paragraph below).

To Dismantle

First remove the safety gap screw and the earthing brush otherwise the armature and slip ring may be damaged whilst dismantling. The safety gap screw is usually fitted in the underside of the magneto and the earthing brush under the name plate at the contact breaker end.

Remove the high-tension pick-ups, secured by spring clips. Take care to retain the gasket fitted under the pick-up for use when reassembling.

Take off the contact breaker cover and remove the contact breaker and cam as follows:—

Unscrew the hexagon-headed bolt from the centre of the contact breaker and draw the contact breaker off the tapered shaft on which it fits. The cam can then be pulled out of its housing. The cam is then free to be taken out.

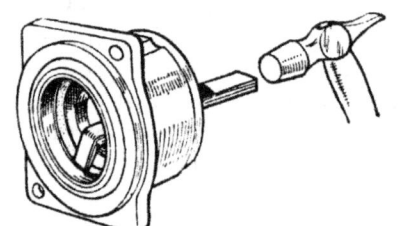

Take out the screws securing the contact breaker housing to the magneto body, and pull the contact breaker housing away from the magneto body. Retain the sealing gasket and shims for use when reassembling.

Draw the armature out of the magneto body. There is no need to put a keeper across the magnet, as it retains its properties more or less indefinitely. Although it loses a certain immaterial amount of power on the first removal of the armature, subsequent removals do not affect it.

Do not allow the magneto body to come into close contact with any iron filings as they may become attracted to the magnet and cause the armature to bind.

When the armature is removed it should be examined for mechanical faults such as a cracked or bent shaft. Any defect in the winding or condenser needs special equipment to detect, and in the event of trouble being suspected, a complete service armature should be fitted.

It is important that the two ball bearings which support the armature shaft are in good condition. If they are packed on assembly with a suitable high-melting point grease they will stand an almost unlimited amount of normal wear, but if they start to fail due to a bent shaft or other cause, they must be replaced. The balls and cages can readily be removed off the inner races which can then be pulled off the armature shaft using an extractor. The outer races can be removed with an expanding collet type extractor or by means of a tool as shown in Fig. Y2.

Carefully examine the slip ring and if it is damaged in any way it must be replaced. To do this take off the inner race of the bearing using an extractor, lift off the shims and the

B.S.A. Service Sheet No. 801 (contd.)

grease flinging plate and pull the slip ring off the shaft. (NOTE:—When removing the inner race the extractor must bear on the brass shaft extension and not on the electric contact or insulator down the centre of the shaft. A disc of appropriate diameter can be placed across the face of the shaft extension). Carefully straighten the wire coming from the armature and see that the bared end is clean, then fit the new slip ring over the shaft, taking care that the wire enters the hole in the boss in the slip ring and that it goes fully home without bending. Seal the lead-in to the slip ring boss with varnish—a special air drying varnish is used at the works but shellac varnish can be used in an emergency.

Replace the grease flinging plate, the full number of shims and inner race of the bearing.

Testing

If test apparatus is not avilable, a rough check of the armature windings can be made by means of a two-volt battery (a tapping across one cell of the motor cycle battery) and an ammeter.

To check the Primary Winding of the Armature

Screw the contact breaker retaining screw into the end of the armature shaft.

Connect one terminal of the battery to one terminal of the ammeter.

Connect the second terminal of the ammeter to the screw in the armature shaft.

Connect the second terminal of the battery to the metal body of the armature.

The ammeter will record the current taken by the armature primary winding and should be approximately 4 amperes.

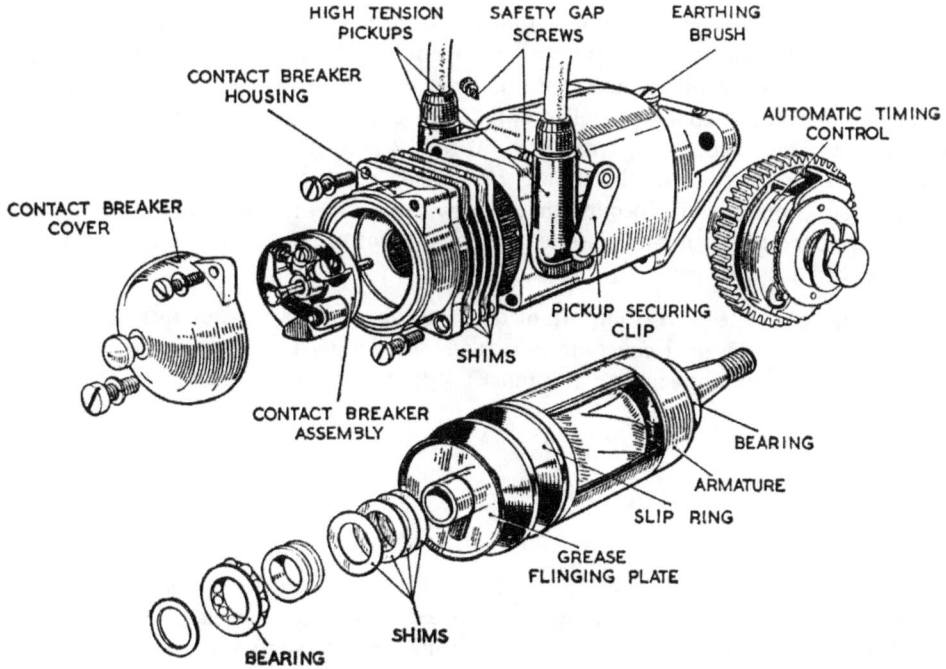

Fig. Y3.

B.S.A. Service Sheet No. 801 (contd.)

To check the Secondary Winding of the Armature

Leave the connections as detailed for the primary winding check.

Take a piece of high-tension cable about 15 in. long and bare one end back about ½ in. and the other end about 4 in. Wrap the longer bared end round the brass insert of the slip ring and hold the other end about ⅛ in. from the body of the armature.

If the lead from the battery which was connected to the armature body to test the primary winding is then flashed quickly on and off the body a spark should occur between the high-tension wire and the armature body.

Failure to spark indicates a fault in the armature windings or the condenser and a replacement armature must be fitted.

An armature test can be carried out by connecting in series an 8-volt accumulator, a four lobe cam and contact breaker (having 45° closed period) and the armature under test, the contact breaker to coil connection being at earth potential. A 0.2 mfd. condenser must be connected across the contacts. Run the contact breaker at 750 r.p.m. giving 3,000 operations of the contacts per minute, and connect the high-tension cable from the coil to either a 3-point spark gap or rotary gap set to 13 kv. Regular sparking should occur under these conditions. Explore the surface of the winding with an earthed pointer—no flashover must occur.

It should be noted that in the above test, sparking will occur, provided that the armature winding is in order, even if the condenser in-built with the armature is open-circuited. Disconnect the 0.2 mfd. condenser from the supply circuit above when regular sparking should continue. Failure to do so indicates that the armature condenser is faulty and a replacement armature must be fitted.

If satisfactory performance is not obtained during the above test, measurement should be made of the maximum primary running current. To do this, include also in the above series circuit a moving coil ammeter (of not more than 5 amperes full scale deflection) and a variable resistance of approximately 5 ohms (of adequate current rating for cool running). Connect the high-tension cable from the coil to a 3-point spark gap set to 5.5 mm. or a rotary gap set to 9.5 kv. Run the contact breaker as before, and adjust the variable resistance until occasional missing occurs, that is, when the coil is just failing to spark regularly. Under these conditions, the permissible primary current as read on the ammeter should be not more than 1.2 amperes.

In both the above tests, it is important that the supply voltage be maintained at 8-volts, that the cam speed be kept constant, and that the winding under test is not subjected to any external magnetic influence (e.g. it must not be tested on an iron bed-plate).

Reassembly

See that the bearings are clean and if necessary wash them in petrol and dry thoroughly. Lightly pack them with high-melting point grease. Fit the inner races on the armature shaft using a hand press and a length of tube fitting over the shaft and locating on the race. Fit the balls and cages in position over the inner races. Place a new oil seal in the bearing housing at the driving end of the magneto body and press the outer races into their housings

B.S.A. Service Sheet No. 801 (contd.)

with a mandrel of the type shown in Fig. Y4, taking care that a suitable serrated insulating washer is positioned between each race and its housing, to ensure that the race is a tight fit in its housing.

See that the slip ring and metal insert are clean; if necessary carefully wipe it clean with a petrol-moistened cloth. See that the inside of the magneto body is clean and free from swarf and insert the armature in the body, drive end first.

Refit the contact breaker end plate taking care that the end plate shims and gasket are in position, and replace and tighten the end plate fixing screws.

Check the armature for end play. It should revolve freely when turned by hand, but no end play should be felt. If necessary adjust by adding or removing shims behind the contact breaker plate until adjustment is correct.

Replace the cam and contact breaker as follows:—

First add a few drops of thin machine oil to the felt contained in the contact breaker housing.

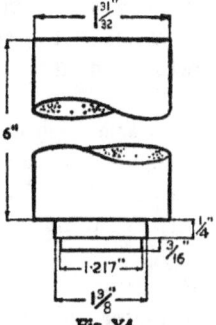

Fig. Y4.

Insert the cam in the housing so that the broad slot locates over the two pegs in the contact breaker housing. Fit the contact breaker in position, ensuring that the projecting key on the tapered portion of the contact breaker base engages with the keyway cut in the magneto spindle otherwise the magneto timing will be upset. Tighten the hexagon-headed screw with care; it must not be too slack, not must undue force be used.

Adjust the contacts to the correct setting and replace the contact breaker cover.

See that the pick-ups are clean and the brushes move freely. Place the cork washers in position on the magneto body, followed by the pick-ups and secure by means of the spring arms.

B.S.A. MOTOR CYCLES LTD., Service Department, Armoury Road, Birmingham 11.
Printed in England   B.S.A. PRESS

BSA SERVICE SHEET No. 804

C10, C11, "A", "B" AND "M" GROUP MODELS
REGULATOR UNIT–Models MCR1 and MCR2

This unit houses the generator voltage regulator unit and the cut-out. Although combined structurally, the regulator and cut-out are electrically separate.

On machines fitted with an E3L dynamo the regulator unit is type MCR2, this unit is slightly different in construction to the MCR1. The procedure for testing and adjusting is, however, unaltered.

Positive Earth Lighting System
Some machines have the battery positive terminal connected to the frame instead of the negative terminal. This does not affect the regulator adjustment except that the voltmeter connections should be reversed.

The Regulator
The regulator unit is arranged to work in conjunction with the shunt-wound generators described in Service Sheet No. 809. The regulator is set to maintain a pre-determined generator voltage at all speeds, the field strength being controlled by the automatic insertion of a resistance in the generator field circuit, and a current or series winding on the same regulator compensates this voltage figure in accordance with the output current, to ensure that the battery does no receive an excessive charging current when in a discharged condition. Hence the charging current depends upon the difference between the controlled generator voltage and the battery terminal voltage and is therefore at a maximum when the battery is discharged, automatically tapering off to a minimum as the battery becomes charged and its voltage rises. In addition, a form of temperature compensation ensures that the voltage characteristics of the regulator are matched to those of the battery for large variations in working temperature.

Normally, during day-time running, when the battery is in good condition, the generator gives only a trickle charge, so that the ammeter reading will seldom exceed 1—2 amperes.

The Cut-out
The cut-out is an automatic switch which is connected between the dynamo and battery. It consists of a pair of contacts held open by a spring and closed magnetically. When the engine is running fast enough to cause the voltage of the generator to exceed that of the battery, the contacts close and the battery is charged by the generator. On the other hand, when the speed is low or the engine is stationary, the contacts open, thus disconnecting the generator from the battery and preventing current flowing from the battery through the windings.

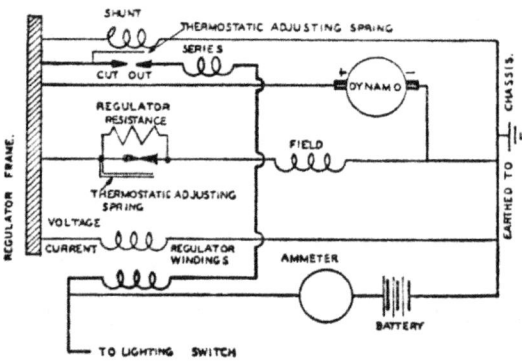

Fig. Y15. *Circuit diagram of Charging System.*

B.S.A. Service Sheet No. 804 (contd.)

Test Data

Cut-out	MCR.1	MCR.2
Cut-in voltage	6.2—6.6 volts	6.3—6.7 volts
Drop-off voltage	3.5—5.3 volts	4.5—5.0 volts
Reverse current	0.7—2.5 amperes	3.0—5.0 amperes

Regulator

SETTING IN OPEN CIRCUIT

10°C.	50°F.	8.0—8.4 volts	7.7—8.1 volts
20°C.	68°F.	7.8—8.2 volts	7.6—8.0 volts
30°C.	86°F.	7.6—8.0 volts	7.5—7.9 volts
40°C.	104°F.	7.4—7.9 volts	7.4—7.8 volts

Servicing

TESTING IN POSITION TO LOCATE FAULT IN CHARGING CIRCUIT

If the procedure given in Service Sheet No. 809 shows the generator to be in order, proceed to check further as follows:—

First ensure that the wiring between regulator and battery is in order. To do this disconnect the wire from the (A) terminal of the regulator (Fig. Y16). It may be necessary in some cases to remove the regulator from the motorcycle.

Connect the end of the wire removed to the positive terminal of a voltmeter, and connect the negative voltmeter terminal to an earthing point on the machine.

If a voltmeter reading is given, the wiring is in order and the regulator must be examined If there is no reading, examine the wiring for broken wires or loose connections.

Regulator Adjustment

Remove the cover of the regulator unit, insert a piece of paper between the cut-out contacts, and proceed as follows:—

Connect the positive terminal of the moving coil voltmeter (0—10 volts) to the (D) terminal on the regulator and connect the other lead of the voltmeter to an earthing point on the engine.

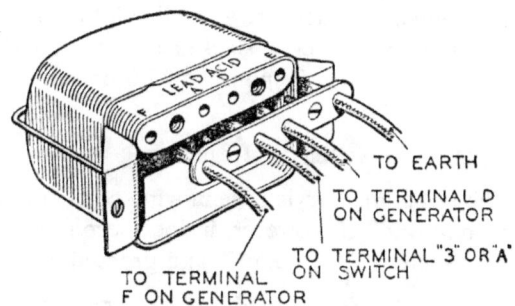

Fig. Y16. *Connections to Regulator Unit.*

Start the engine and slowly increase the speed until the voltmeter needle "flicks" and then steadies; this should occur at a voltmeter reading between the limits for the particular atmospheric temperature.

If the voltage at which the reading becomes steady is outside these limits, the regulator must be adjusted.

Shut off the engine, release the locknut (A) Fig. Y17, on the regulator adjusting screw (B) and turn the screw in a clockwise direction to raise the setting, or in an anti-clockwise direction to lower the setting. Turn the screw a fraction of a turn at a time and then tighten the locknut.

B.S.A. Service Sheet No. 804 (contd.)

When adjusting, do not run the engine up to more than half-throttle, as while the dynamo is on open circuit, it will build up to a high voltage if run at a high speed and so a false voltmeter reading would be obtained.

Remove paper from between cut-out contacts.

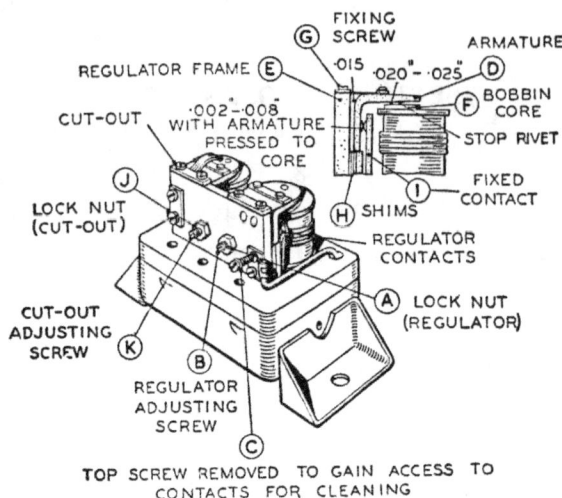

Fig. Y17. *Regulator and Cut-out Adjustment and Setting.*

Cleaning the Regulator Contacts

After long periods of service it may be found necessary to clean the vibrating contacts of the regulator. These are accessible if the top screw (C) securing the fixed contact is removed and the bottom screw slackened to permit the fixed contact to be swung outwards. The contacts can then be polished with fine emery cloth.

Mechanical Setting of Regulator

The armature carrying the moving contact of the regulator is accurately set and should not be removed. If, however, it does become necessary to re-set the contacts, slacken the two fixing screws (G) Fig. Y17, and proceed as follows:—

Insert a .015 in. (0.20 in.) feeler gauge between the back of the armature (D) and the regulator frame (E).

Press back the armature against the frame and down on to the top of the bobbin core with the gauge in position, and lock the armature by tightening the two fixing screws (G). Check the air gap between the top of the bobbin core (F) and the underside of the armature (D)—not under the stop rivet. Adjust if necessary to .025 in. (.012—.020 in.), by removing shims (H) at the back of the fixed contact on an MCR1 regulator or by bending the fixed contact breaker on an MCR2 regulator. The gap between the regulator contacts when the armature is pressed down should now be .002—.008 in. (.006—.017 in.). Finally check, and if necessary re-set, the electrical adjustment of the regulator.

The figures in brackets refer to the MCR2 regulator.

B.S.A. Service Sheet No. 804 (contd.)

Electrical Setting of Cut-out

If the regulator setting is within the correct limits, but the battery is still not receiving current from the dynamo, the cut-out may be out of adjustment or there may be an open circuit in the wiring of the cut-out and regulator unit.

Remove the cable from the terminal on the regulator marked (A). Remove the voltmeter lead from the (D) terminal of the regulator unit and connect it to terminal (A). Run the engine as before: at a fairly low engine speed, the cut-out should operate, when a voltmeter reading should be given of the same value as that when the voltmeter was connected to terminal (D). If there is no reading, the setting of the cut-out may be badly out of adjustment and the contacts not closing.

To check the voltage at which the cut-out operates, the voltmeter must be connected between the (D) terminal and earth. Start the engine and slowly increase its speed until the cut-out contacts are seen to close, noting the voltage at which this occurs. This should be 6.2—6.6 volts.

If operation of the cut-out is outside these limits, it will be necessary to adjust. To do this slacken the locknut (J) Fig. Y17, on the cut-out adjustment screw (K) and turn the screw in a clockwise direction to raise the voltage setting or in an anti-clockwise direction to reduce the setting, testing after each adjustment by increasing the engine speed until the cut-out is seen to operate, and noting the corresponding reading.

Tighten the locknut after making the adjustment. If the cut-out contacts appear burnt or dirty, place a strip of fine glasspaper between the contacts then, with the contacts closed by hand, draw the paper through. This should be done two or three times with the rough side towards each contact.

Mechanical Setting of Cut-out

If, for any reason, the armature has to be removed from the cut-out frame, care must be taken to obtain the correct air-gap settings on reassembly. These can be obtained as follows:—

Slacken the two armature fixing screws, adjusting screw (K) and the screw securing the fixed contact. Insert a .014 in. gauge between the back of the armature and the cut-out frame. (The air-gap between the core face and the armature shim should now measure .011—.015 in. If it does not, fit a armature assembly). Press the armature back against the gauge and tighten the fixing screws. With the gauge still in position, set the gap between the armature and the stop plate arm to .030—.034 in. be carefully bending the arm. Remove the gauge and tighten the screw securing the fixed contact.

Insert a .025 in. gauge between the core face and the armature. Press the armature down on to the gauge. The gap between the contacts should now measure .002—.006 in, and the drop-off voltage should be between the limits given in the test data. If necessary, adjust the gap by carefully bending the fixed contact breaker.

B.S.A. MOTOR CYCLES LTD., Service Department, Armoury Road, Birmingham 11.

BSA SERVICE SHEET No. 804A

"A", "B" AND "M" GROUP MODELS
CONTROL BOX - MODEL BR107

General

The regulator and cut-out contacts are positioned, for ease of access, above their respective armatures. It will be noticed that some of the internal electrical joints are resistance brazed.

SETTING DATA
Cut-out

Cut-in voltage	... 6.3—6.7 volts
Drop-off voltage	... 4.8—5.3 volts
Reverse current	... 3.0—5.0 volts

Regulator

Setting on open circuit relative to ambient temperature.

10°C.	50°F.	...	7.7—8.1 volts
20°C.	68°F.	...	7.6—87.0 volts
30°C.	86°F.	...	7.5— .9 volts
40°C.	104°F.	...	7.4— .8 volts

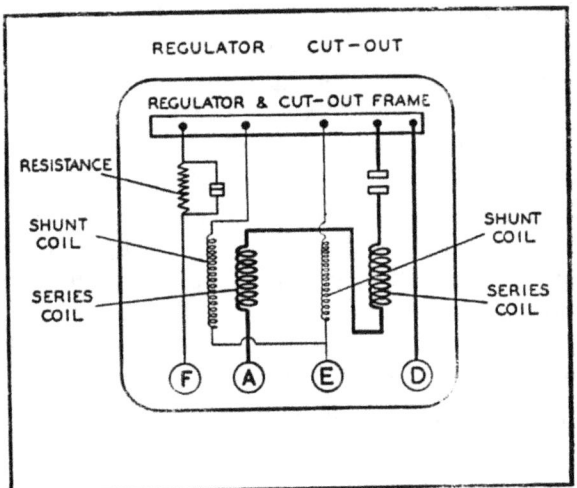

Fig. Y15a. *Internal Connections of Control Box.*

Servicing

Before making any adjustment to the regulator, ensure that the dynamo, dynamo drive and battery are in order.

If the machine is used regularly and a sound battery does not keep in a charged condition, or if the dynamo output does not fall when the battery is fully charged, the following procedure should be adopted:—

Withdraw the cable from terminal (A) Fig. Y16a, and connect it to the negative terminal of a voltmeter. Connect the positive voltmeter terminal to an earthing point on the machine. If a voltmeter reading is given, the circuit from the battery to terminal (A) is in order.

If there is no reading, examine the wiring for defective cables or loose connections. Reconnect the cable to terminal (A).

Check that the wiring between dynamo terminal (D) and control box terminal (D), and between dynamo terminal (F) and control box terminal (F), is in good condition.

B.S.A. Service Sheet No. 804A (contd.)

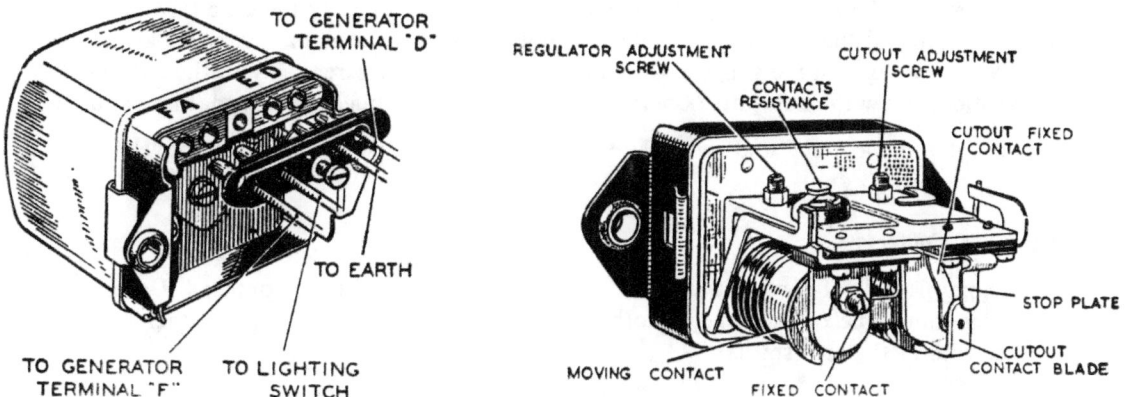

Fig. Y16a. *Control Box Connections and Internal Layout*

Electrical Setting of Regulator

The regulator is carefully set during manufacture and it should not be necessary to make further adjustment. If the charging system is suspect, it is important that only a good quality moving coil voltmeter (0—20 volts) is used for checking.

Connect the negative voltmeter lead to terminal (D) and the positive lead to terminal (E) on the control box. Remove the negative cable from the battery.

Start the engine and slowly increase the speed until the voltmeter needle "flicks" and then steadies. Note the reading and stop the engine.

If the voltage lies outside the limits given in the setting data, the regulator must be adjusted.

Remove the control box from the machine and take off the cover. It is importan that adjustments are carried out with the control box supported in a similar position to that in which it is mounted on the machine. Re-start the engine.

Slacken the locknut of the adjusting screw, Fig. Y17a, and turn the screw clockwise to raise, or anti-clockwise to lower the setting. Turn the screw only a fraction of a turn at a time and then tighten the locknut. Repeat until the correct setting is obtained. Then stop the engine.

Adjustment should be completed within 30 seconds, otherwise heating of the shunt-winding will cause false settings to be made. A dynamo run at high speed on open circuit will build up a high voltage; therefore, do not run the engine up to more than half full speed.

Mechanical Setting of Regulator

If the armature has been removed, the air-gap settings will have to be re-adjusted. Otherwise they should not be altered. To adjust, proceed as follows:—

Slacken the locknut on the voltage adjusting screw and unscrew the adjuster until it is well clear of the armature tension spring. Also slacken the two armature securing screws, Fig. Y17a.

B.S.A. Service Sheet No. 804A (contd.)

Insert a .015 in. feeler gauge wide enough to cover completely the core face between the armature and the core shim, taking care not to damage the shim. Press the armature squarely down against the gauge and tighten the two securing screws. With the gauge still in position, screw the adjustable contact down until it just touches the armature contact.

Tighten the locknut, and re-set the voltage adjusting screw as described above.

Cleaning Contacts

After long periods of service it may be found necessary to clean the contacts. Use a fine carborundum stone or fine emery cloth. Wipe away all traces of dust or other foreign matter with methylated spirits.

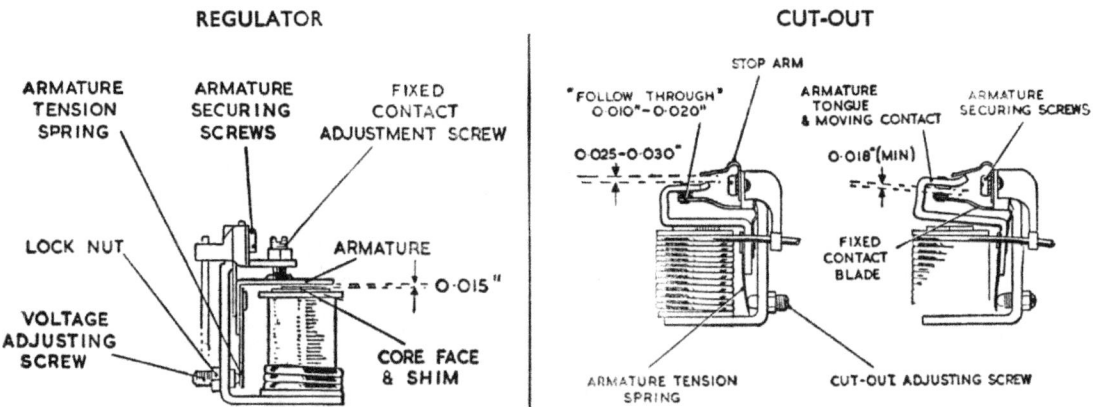

Fig. Y17a. *Regulator and Cut-out Adjustment and Setting.*

Electrical Setting of Cut-out

If the regulator is correctly set but the battery is still not being charged, the cut-out may be out of adjustment.

Connect a voltmeter between terminals (D) and (E) on the control box, start the engine and slowly increase the speed until the contacts close. Note the reading, and stop the engine. If outside the limits of 6.3—6.7 volts, it will be necessary to adjust the cut-out.

Re-start the engine, and slacken the locknut securing the cut-out adjusting screw, Fig. Y17a. Turn the screw clockwise to raise, or anti-clockwise to lower the setting. Move the screw only a fraction of a turn at a time and then retighten the locknut. Test after each adjustment by increasing engine speed and noting the voltmeter reading at the instant of contact closure. Stop the engine.

Setting of the cut-out, like that of the regulator, must be made as quickly as possible because of temperature rise effects.

If the cut-out fails to operate, there may be an open circuit in the wiring of the control box, in which case the unit should be replaced.

B.S.A. Service Sheet No. 804A (contd.)

Mechanical Setting of Cut-out

If, for any reason, the armature has been removed from the frame, the correct air-gap settings must be obtained on reassembly.

Slacken the adjusting screw locknut and unscrew the adjuster until it is well clear of the tension spring. Press the armature squarely down on the core face and tighten the securing screws. Adjust the gap between the armature tongue and the stop arm by carefully bending the arm. The gap must be .025—.030 in. when the armature is pressed down, Fig. Y17a. Similarly, the fixed contact blade must be bent so that, when the armature is pressed down, there is a minimum "follow-through" or blade deflection of .010 in. To prevent contact chatter, the "follow-through" must not exceed .020 in.

With the armature in the free position, the contact gap must be .018 in. minimum.

Finally, re-set the cut-out adjusting screw.

Cleaning Contacts

If the cut-out contacts appear rough or burnt, place a strip of fine glasspaper between them, close the contacts by hand and draw the paper through two or three times with the rough side towards each contact in turn. Wipe away dust or other foreign matter with methylated spirits.

Do not use emery cloth or carborundum stone for cleaning cut-out contacts.

B.S.A. MOTOR CYCLES LTD., Service Department, Armoury Road, Birmingham 11.

Printed in England

B.S.A. Press.

BSA SERVICE SHEET No. 805

Reprinted June, 1960

All Models

BATTERY — LEAD-ACID TYPES

The range of Lucas batteries listed here covers those models fitted to B.S.A. motor cycles in recent years.

PU5E and LVW5E Small capacity batteries for lightweight machines.

PU7E .. .. Standard battery for cradle mountting.

GU11E .. .. Larger capacity battery for sidecar machines.

SC7E .. .. Large capacity lightweight battery for machines fitted with starting motors or two-way radio equipment, e.g. police machines.

All current Lucas motor cycle batteries are 'dry charged', and do not require initial charging. Except that these batteries have porous rubber separators, they are identical with earlier models supplied wet or uncharged and require the same routine maintenance when in service.

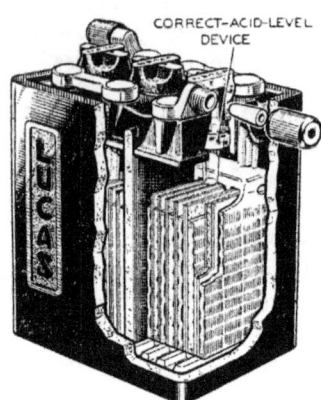

Fig. Y18. Sectioned battery, model PU7E/9

STORAGE

Used batteries must be fully charged before storing. In temperate climates they should be examined fortnightly, or weekly in the case of model LVW5E and all models when stored in the tropics. If necessary, give them a short refreshing charge.

After a long period of storage, the condition of the battery will often improve if it is put through a 'cycle', as described on page 4.

MAINTENANCE

Every fortnight, or more frequently in hot climates, examine the condition of the battery. Examine five-plate batteries every week.

Never use a naked light when examining the condition of the cells, as there is a **danger** of igniting the gas coming from the active materials.

Cleaning

Remove the battery cover and clean the cell tops. Examine the connections. If they are loose or dirty, remove them and scrape the contact surfaces clean. Coat them with petroleum jelly before replacing.

Remove the filler plugs and check that the vent holes are clear and that the rubber washer fitted under some plugs is in good condition.

Topping-up

During charging, water is lost by gassing and evaporation. Examine the electrolyte level in each cell and, if necessary, add distilled water to raise the electrolyte level with the top edges of the separators.

SC7E batteries have a woven glass pad fitted in each cell to reduce splashing when the battery is gassing during charging. When 'topping-up' this type of battery it is useful to note that the correct electrolyte level is reached when moisture appears through the porous glass pad.

B.S.A. Service Sheet No. 805 (continued)

The Lucas Battery Filler

The use of a Lucas motor cycle Battery Filler will be found helpful in this 'topping-up' process, as it ensures that the correct electrolyte level is automatically attained and also prevents distilled water from being spilled over the battery top.

Correct-Acid-Level-Devices

The correct-acid-level-device fitted to some Lucas batteries consists of a central tube with a perforated flange which rests on a ledge in the filling orifice.

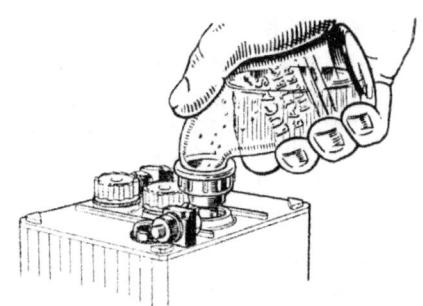

Fig Y19. The Lucas battery filler

When 'topping-up' a battery fitted with these devices, pour distilled water round the flange (not down the tube) until no more drains through into the cell. This will happen when the electrolyte level reaches the bottom of the central tube and prevents further escape of air displaced by the 'topping-up' water. Lift the tube slightly to allow the small amount of water in the flange to drain into the cell. The electrolyte level will then be correct.

If a battery requires 'topping-up' too frequently, the voltage regulator (on machines fitted with d.c. generators) may be out of adjustment, i.e. set too high, and should be checked. Conversely, a persistently low state of charge may be due to a regulator being set too low.

If one cell in particular needs 'topping-up' more than another, it is likely the container is cracked, in which event replace the battery and clean the carrier, using a solution of ammonia or bi-carbonate of soda in water. After cleaning and drying, paint the battery carrier and other surfaces affected by the electrolyte with anti-sulphuric paint.

TABLES OF SPECIFIC GRAVITIES AND CHARGING RATES

Battery	Plates per cell	Amp. Hr. Capacity		Electrolyte to fill one two-volt cell		Home Trade and Climates Ordinarily below 90°F. (32°C.) Specific Gravity of Acid (corrected to 60°F.)		Climates frequently over 90°F. (32°C.) Specific Gravity of Acid (corrected to 60°F.)		Initial Charge Current	Re-charge Current
		At 10 hour rate	At 20 hour rate	Pint	c.c.	Filling	Fully Charged	Filling	Fully Charged	Amp.	Amp.
1	2	3		4		5	6	7	8	9	10
LVW5E	5	5	5.7	1/8	71	1.270	1.270–1.290	1.210	1.210–1.230	0.3	0.5
PU5E	5	8	9	1/6	94	1.270	1.270–1.290	1.210	1.210–1.230	0.6	1.0
PU7E	7	12	13.5	1/5	113	1.270	1.270–1.290	1.210	1.210–1.230	0.8	1.5
GU11E	11	20	22.8	1/3	189	1.270	1.270–1.290	1.210	1.210–1.230	1.3	2.2
SC7E	7	22.5	26	—	250	1.270	1.270–1.290	1.210	1.210–1.230	1.5	2.5

The maximum permissible electrolyte temperature during charging is given below. Should the temperature of the electrolyte exceed this value interrupt the charge and allow the battery temperature to fall at least 10°F. (5.5°C.) before charging is resumed.

Climates normally below 80°F. (27°C.)	Climates between 80°–100°F. (27°–38°C.)	Climates frequently above 100°F. (38°C.)
100°F. (38°C.)	110°F. (43°C.)	120°F. (49°C.)

The specific gravity of the electrolyte varies with temperature. For convenience in comparing specific gravities, they are always corrected to 60°F., which is adopted as the reference temperature. The method of correction is as follows:

For every 5°F. *below* 60°F., *deduct* 0.002 from the observed reading to obtain the true specific gravity at 60°F. For every 5°F. *above* 60°F., *add* 0.002 to the observed reading to obtain the true specific gravity at 60°F.

The temperature must be that indicated by a thermometer having its bulb actually immersed in the electrolyte, and not the ambient temperature.

B.S.A. Service Sheet No. 805 (continued)

SERVICING

Battery Persists in Low State of Charge

First consider the conditions under which the battery is used. If the battery is subject to continuous discharge, e.g. long periods of night parking with lights on without suitable opportunities for recharging, a low state of charge is inevitable.

A fault in the dynamo or regulator, or neglect during a period out of commission, may also be responsible.

Vent Plugs

See that the ventilating holes in each vent plug are clear, and that the rubber washer fitted under the plug is in good condition.

Level of Electrolyte

The surface of the electrolyte should be level with the tops of the separators. If necessary, top-up with distilled water. Any loss of acid from spilling or spraying (as opposed to normal loss of *water* by evaporation) should be made good by dilute acid of the same specific gravity as that already in the cell.

Cleanliness

See that the top of the battery is free from dirt or moisture which might provide a discharge path. Check that the battery connections are clean and tight.

Hydrometer Tests

The space between each separator is not wide enough to permit the nozzle of an hydrometer to be inserted. Before taking a sample, tilt the battery to bring sufficient electrolyte above the separators. If the level of the electrolyte is so low that an hydrometer reading cannot be taken, no attempt should be made to take a reading after adding distilled water until the battery has been on charge for at least 30 minutes.

Measure the specific gravity of the acid in each cell in turn. The reading given by each cell should be approximately the same; if one cell differs appreciably from the others, an internal fault in that cell is indicated.

Specific gravity readings and their indications are as follows:

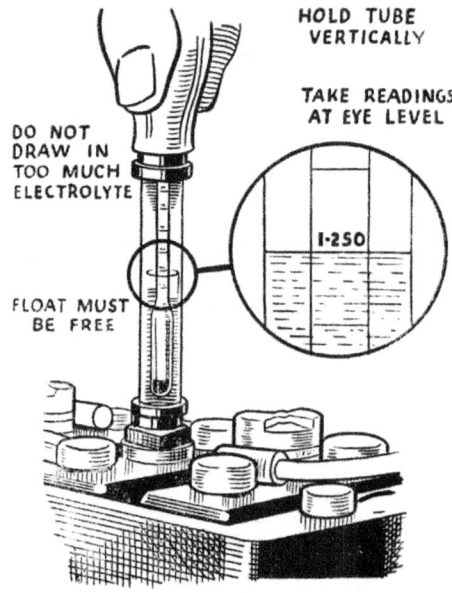

Fig Y20. Taking hydrometer readings

Climates under 90°F.		Climates over 90°F.
1.270—1.290	Cell fully charged	1.210—1.230
1.190—1.210	Cell about half discharged	1.130—1.150
1.110—1.130	Cell fully discharged	1.050—1.070

The appearance of the electrolyte drawn into the hydrometer when taking a reading gives a useful indication of the state of the plates: if it is very dirty, or contains small particles in suspension, it is possible that the plates are in a bad condition.

Discharge Test

Motor-cycle batteries must *not* be subjected to the heavy discharge test, as recommended for motor-car and commercial vehicle batteries.

RECHARGING FROM AN EXTERNAL SUPPLY

If the hydrometer test indicates that the battery is merely discharged, and is otherwise in a good condition, it should be recharged, either on the motor-cycle by a period of daytime running, or on the bench from an external supply.

B.S.A. Service Sheet No. 805 (continued)

If the latter, the battery should be charged at the rate given in the table until the specific gravity and voltage show no increase over three successive hourly readings. During the charge the electrolyte must be kept level with the tops of the separators by the addition of distilled water.

A battery that shows a general falling-off in efficiency, common to all cells, will often respond to the process known as 'cycling'. This process consists of fully charging the battery by passing through it from an external source the appropriate re-charge current given in the table. The battery is then discharged by connecting to a lamp board, or other load, taking a current equal to the normal re-charge current. The battery should be capable of providing this current for at least 7 hours before it is fully discharged, as indicated by the voltage of each cell falling to 1.8. If the battery discharges in a shorter time, repeat the 'cycle' of charge and discharge.

PREPARING BATTERIES FOR SERVICE

All new batteries are supplied without electrolyte but with the plates in a charged condition. When they are required for service it is only necessary to fill each cell with sulphuric acid of the correct specific gravity. No initial charging is required.

Preparation of Electrolyte

The electrolyte is prepared by mixing together distilled water and concentrated sulphuric acid. The mixing must be carried out either in a lead-lined tank or in suitable glass or earthenware vessels. Slowly add the acid to the water, stirring with a glass rod. *Never add water to acid*, as the resulting chemical reaction causes violent and dangerous spurting of the concentrated acid. The specific gravity of the filling electrolyte depends on the climate in which the battery is to be used.

The approximate proportions of acid and water are indicated in the following table:

To obtain Specific Gravity (corrected to 60°F.) of	Add 1 vol. of acid 1.835 S.G. (corrected to 60°F.) to
1.270	2.8 vols. of water
1.210	4.0 vols. of water

Heat is produced by the mixture of acid and water, and the electrolyte should be allowed to cool before pouring it into the battery.

The total volume of electrolyte required can be estimated from the figures quoted in the table on page 2.

Filling the Battery

Carefully break the seals in the cell filling holes and fill each cell with electrolyte to the top of the separators, *in one operation*. The temperature of the filling room, battery and electrolyte should be maintained between 60°F. and 100°F. If the battery has been stored in a cool place, it should be allowed to warm up to room temperature before filling.

Putting into Use

Batteries filled in this way are 90 per cent charged. If time permits, however, a freshening charge of four hours at the normal recharge rate given in the table would be beneficial.

During the charge the electrolyte must be kept level with the top edge of the separators by the addition of distilled water. Check the specific gravity of the acid at the end of the charge; if 1.270 acid was used to fill the battery, the specific gravity should now be between 1.270 and 1.290; if 1.210, between 1.210 and 1.230.

Maintenance in Service

After filling, the battery needs only the recommended attention.

B.S.A. MOTOR CYCLES LTD.
Service Dept., Waverley Works,
Birmingham, 10.
Printed in England.

JU/B5029

BSA SERVICE SHEET No. 806

Reprinted April, 1960

All Models

LAMPS

LUCAS LIGHTING

Headlamps

Although the headlamps fitted to individual models may vary in detail, they remain similar with regard to the general features described below. All headlamps are fitted with a double filament main bulb and a pilot bulb. One of the double filaments provides the main riding beam while the second, brought into operation by means of the dipper switch, provides the dipped beam.

On some models the headlamp incorporates a panel containing the ammeter and lighting switch but if a cowl is fitted then it carries these components externally to the headlamp shell.

Other headlamps contain wire wound resistances for the purpose of reducing the charging rates under certain conditions and these are described under the appropriate lighting circuit.

Setting and Focusing

The best way of checking the setting of the lamp is to park the motor cycle in front of a light coloured wall at a distance of about 25 feet. If necessary, slacken the bolts securing the headlamp and move the lamp until, with the main driving light switched on, the beam is projected straight ahead and parallel with the ground. With the lamp in this position, the height of the beam centre from the ground should be the same as the height of the centre of the headlamp from the ground.

Fig. Y.22 Headlamp Focusing.

The headlamp must be focused so that, when the main driving light is switched on, a uniform beam without any dark centre is given. If the bulb needs adjusting, remove the lamp front and reflector, as described below, and slacken the bulb holder clamping clip at the back of the reflector. Move the bulb holder backwards and forwards until the correct position is obtained, and then tighten the clamping clip.

More sealed beam light units are fitted with the pre-focus type of bulb and therefore no focusing is necessary.

Removal of Front and Reflector, pre-1948 models

Press back the fixing clip at the bottom of the lamp. The front and reflector can now be taken off. The bulb holder is secured to the reflector by means of two fixing springs. When replacing the front, locate the top of the rim first, then press on at the bottom and secure with the fixing clip.

B.S.A. Service Sheet No. 806 (cont.)

1948 Models (Fig. Y.23)

Press back the fixing clip at the bottom of the lamp, and remove the lamp front. The reflector is secured to the lamp body by means of a rubber bead. When refitting the rubber bead, locate its thinner lip between the reflector rim and the edge of the lamp body. To replace the front, locate the metal tongue in the slot at the top of the lamp, press the front on, and secure by means of the fixing catch.

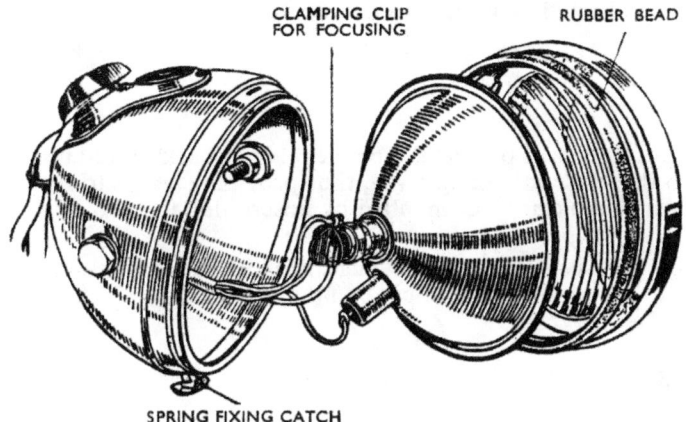

Fig. Y.23.

Sealed Beam Headlamps

Later models are fitted with a sealed light unit having the reflector and glass sealed together. After slackening the securing screw on the top of the headlamp, the rim, complete with light unit, may be removed. To replace, locate the rim on the lip at the bottom of the lamp body, press the light unit assembly and rim into position and tighten the securing screw. The main headlamp bulb in some of these headlamps is of the pre-focus type and is held in position by a cap with bayonet type fitting. In all cases access to the main or pilot bulbs is obtained by removal of the light unit assembly.

Breakage of the headlamp glass with this type of unit involves replacement of the glass and reflector complete. The light unit may be removed from the headlamp rim after prising out the retaining clips.

Replacement of Bulbs

When the replacement of a bulb is necessary, it is important not only that the same size bulb is fitted, but that it has a high efficiency and will focus in the reflector. Cheap and inferior replacement bulbs often have the filament of such a shape that it is impossible to focus correctly; for example, the filament may be to the one side of the axis of the bulb resulting in loss of range and light efficiency.

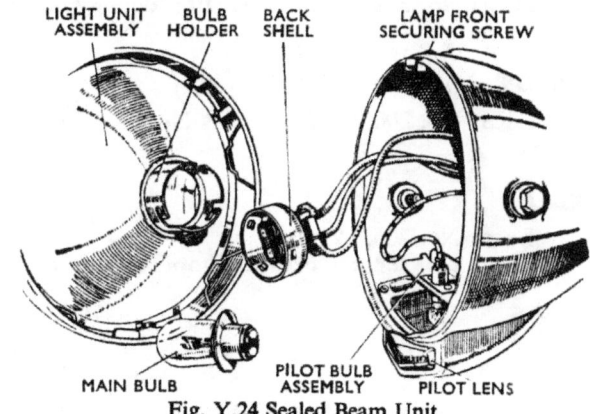

Fig. Y.24 Sealed Beam Unit.

Lucas Genuine Spare Bulbs are specially tested to check that the filament is in the correct position to give the best results with Lucas lamps. To assist in identification, Lucas bulbs are marked on the metal cap with a number. When fitting a replacement, see that it has the same number as the original bulb.

B.S.A. Service Sheet No. 806 (cont.)

When fitting a main headlamp bulb, care must be taken to insert it the correct way round, i.e. with the dipped beam filament above the centre filament.

The pre-focus type bulb is located by a flange and there is a notch which engages on a raised portion of the bulb holder to ensure correct positioning.

Where the pilot bulb is contained in an underslung cowl, the metal strip on which the bulb is mounted should be pushed to the rear and lifted away in order to provide access to the bulb.

Tail Lamps

Where the tail lamp is of the metal type the body or back should be removed by pushing it in, rotating to the left, and pulling away, thus providing access to the bulb. The moulded plastic type of rear lamp can be dismantled by unscrewing the two screws in the cover.

When a stop lamp is fitted, a two-filament type of bulb is employed with offset bayonet type fixing pins to ensure that it can only be fitted correctly.

MAIN BULBS

Models A7, A10, B31, 32, 33, 34, C12, C15 and M20, M21.

Lucas No. 168, 6v. 24/24w. (with E3H Dynamo). Lucas No. 169, 6v. 30/30w. (with E3L Dynamo). Lucas No. 312, 6v. 30/24w. (Pre-focus type Bulb).

Models C10 and C11.

Lucas No. 180, 6v., 18/18w. (with E3H Dynamo). Lucas No. 168, 6v. 24/24w. (with E3L Dynamo).

Models C11G and D1 (early) Lucas

Lucas No. 312, 6v. 30/24w. (Pre-focus type Bulb).

PILOT

Lucas No. 200, 6v. 3w. Lucas No. 988, 6v. 3w. (with Sealed Beam Light Unit).

TAIL

Lucas No. 205, 6v. 6w.
Lucas No. 384, 6v. 6/18w. (Stop/Tail Lamp).

B.S.A. MOTOR CYCLES LTD.
Service Dept., Waverley Works,
Birmingham, 10
Printed in England.

JU/B4780

BSA SERVICE SHEET No. 807

Reprinted June 1960

All Models

ELECTRIC HORN—HIGH FREQUENCY MODELS

General

Electric horns are adjusted to give their best performance before leaving the Works, and will give long periods of service without any attention.

Servicing

If the horn becomes uncertain in action or does not vibrate, it does not follow that the horn has broken down. The trouble may be due to a discharged battery or a loose or broken connection in the horn wiring.

The performance of the horn may be upset by the fixing bolt working loose, or by the vibration of some part adjacent to the horn. To check this, remove the horn from its mounting, hold it firmly in the hand by its bracket and press the push. If the note is still unsatisfactory, the horn may require adjustment, but this should only be necessary after a very long period of service.

Method of Adjusting

The adjustment of a horn does not alter the characteristics of the note but merely takes up wear of vibrating parts.

If the horn is used repeatedly when badly out of adjustment, due usually to unsuccessful attempts at adjustment, the horn may become damaged, due to the excessive current which it will take. When testing, do not continue to operate the push if the horn does not sound. If, when the push is operated, the horn does not take any current (indicated by an ammeter connected in series with the horn) it is possible that the horn has been adjusted so that its contact breaker is permanently open.

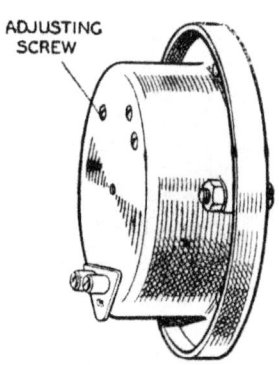

Fig. Y26.
Typical electric horn, showing adjustment screw.

After adjusting, note the current consumption, which must not exceed 3—4 amperes. A horn may give a good note, yet be out of adjustment and taking an excessive current. When adjusting do not attempt to unscrew the nut securing the tone disc or any other screw in the horn.

The adjustment is made by turning the adjustment screw, usually in a clockwise direction. The underside of the screw is serrated, and the screw must not be turned for more than 2 or 3 notches before re-testing. If the adjustment screw is turned too far in a clockwise direction, a point will occur at which the armature pulls in but does not separate the contacts.

B.S.A. Service Sheet No. 807 (contd.)

Some models have no adjustment screw at the back of the horn. Adjustment is carried out by means of the grub screw and locking collar which are revealed upon removal of the large domed nut on the front of the horn. Take care that the large nut securing the sounding disc is not disturbed. The locking collar requires a special tool, or a large screwdriver with the blade ground so as to leave two projecting prongs, in order that it may be undone. No attempt should be made to loosen the collar without a proper tool as it is very tight and may become damaged so that it cannot be removed. The adjustment should be carried out in a similar manner to that described for the other type of horn, but the locking collar should be firmly tightened after each adjustment as this affects the note.

B.S.A. MOTOR CYCLES LTD.,
Service Dept., Waverley Works,
Birmingham, 10.
Printed in England.

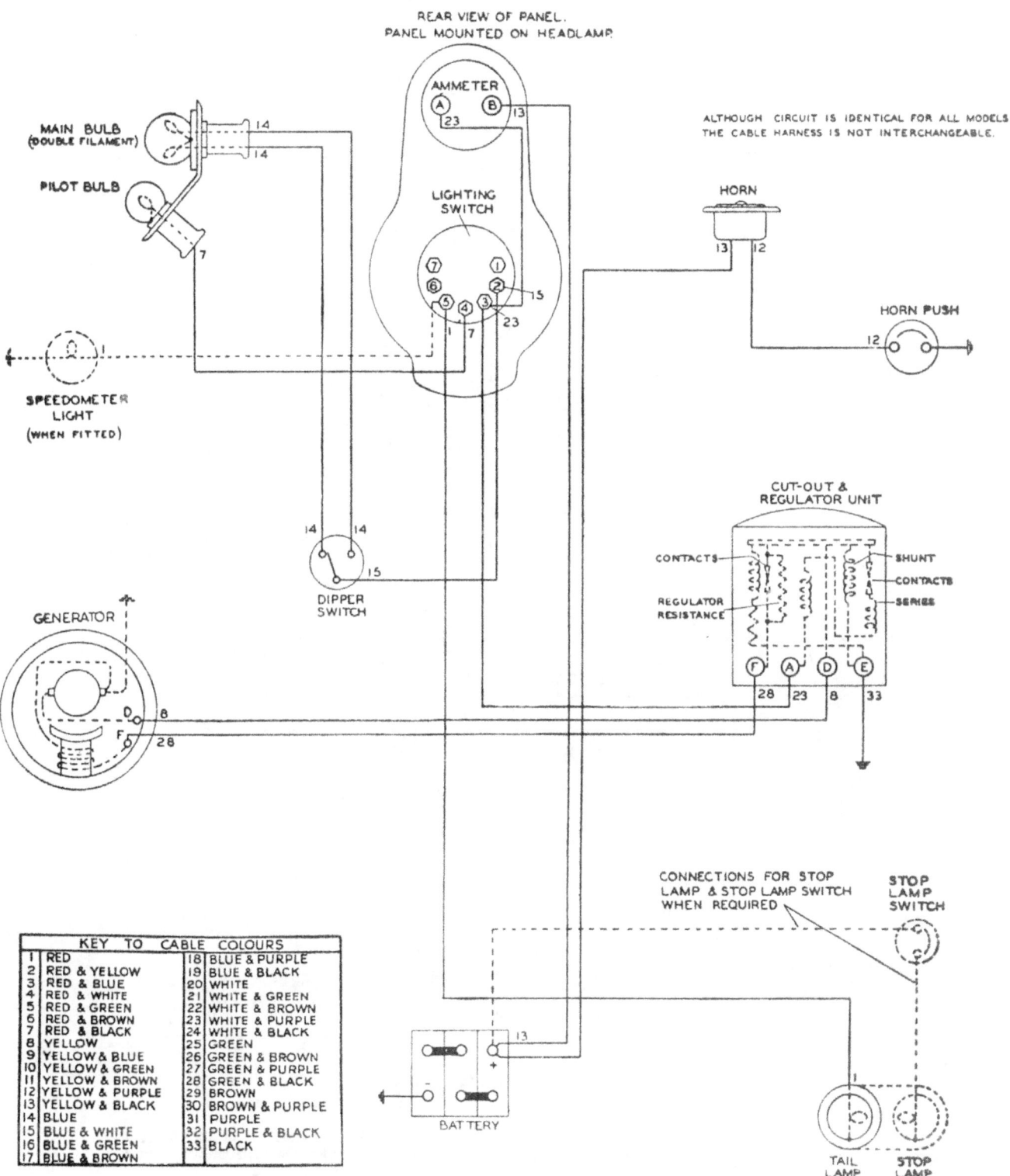

B.S.A. Service Sheet No. 808 (cont.)

C10 and C11 Models
WIRING DIAGRAM
(NEGATIVE EARTH)

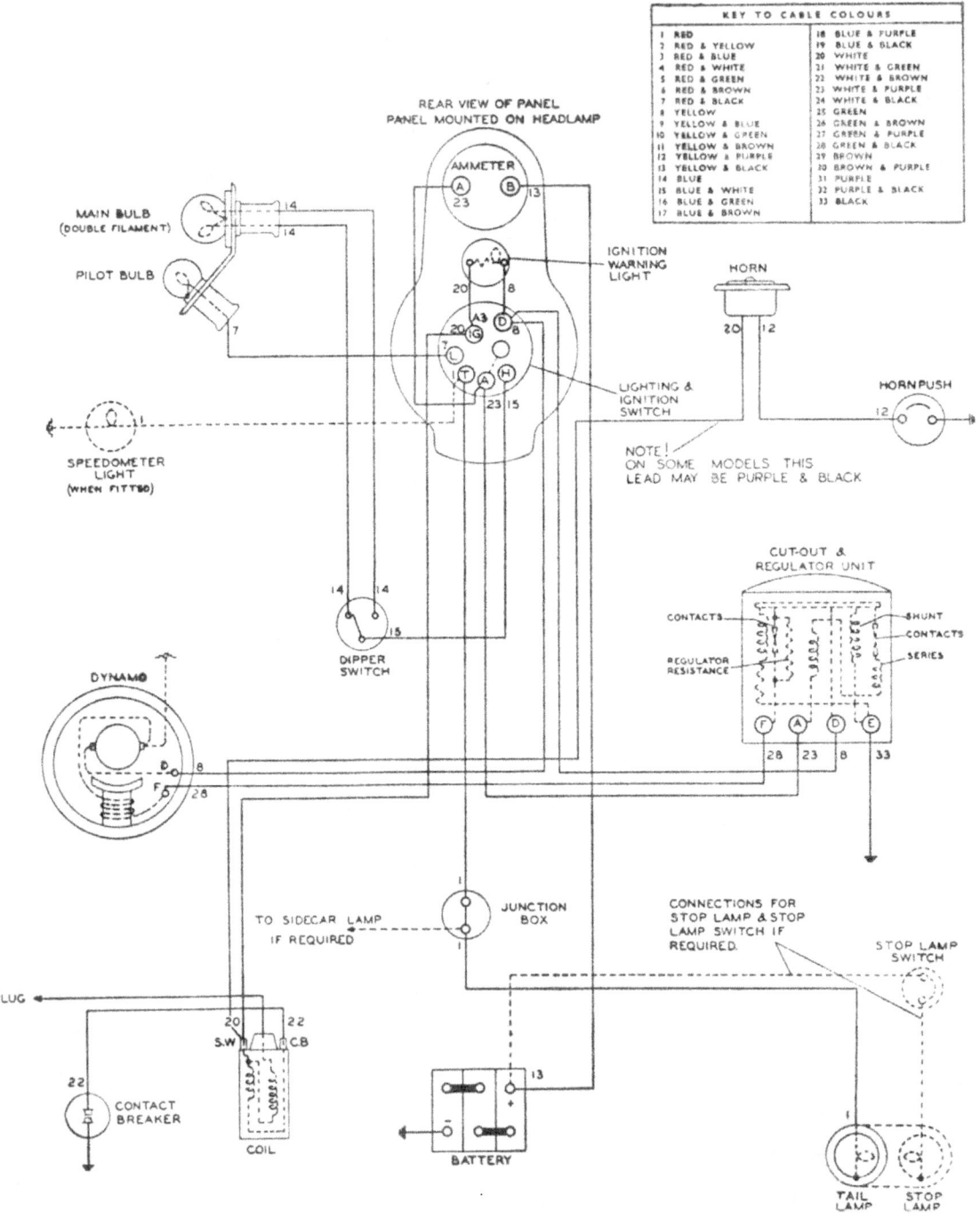

Numbers indicate cable identification colours. See key.

B.S.A. MOTOR CYCLES LTD.
Service Dept., Armoury Road,
Birmingham, 11

Printed in England.

BSA SERVICE SHEET No. 808A
A, (except A50/A65) B and M Group Models
WIRING DIAGRAM
(Positive Earth System)

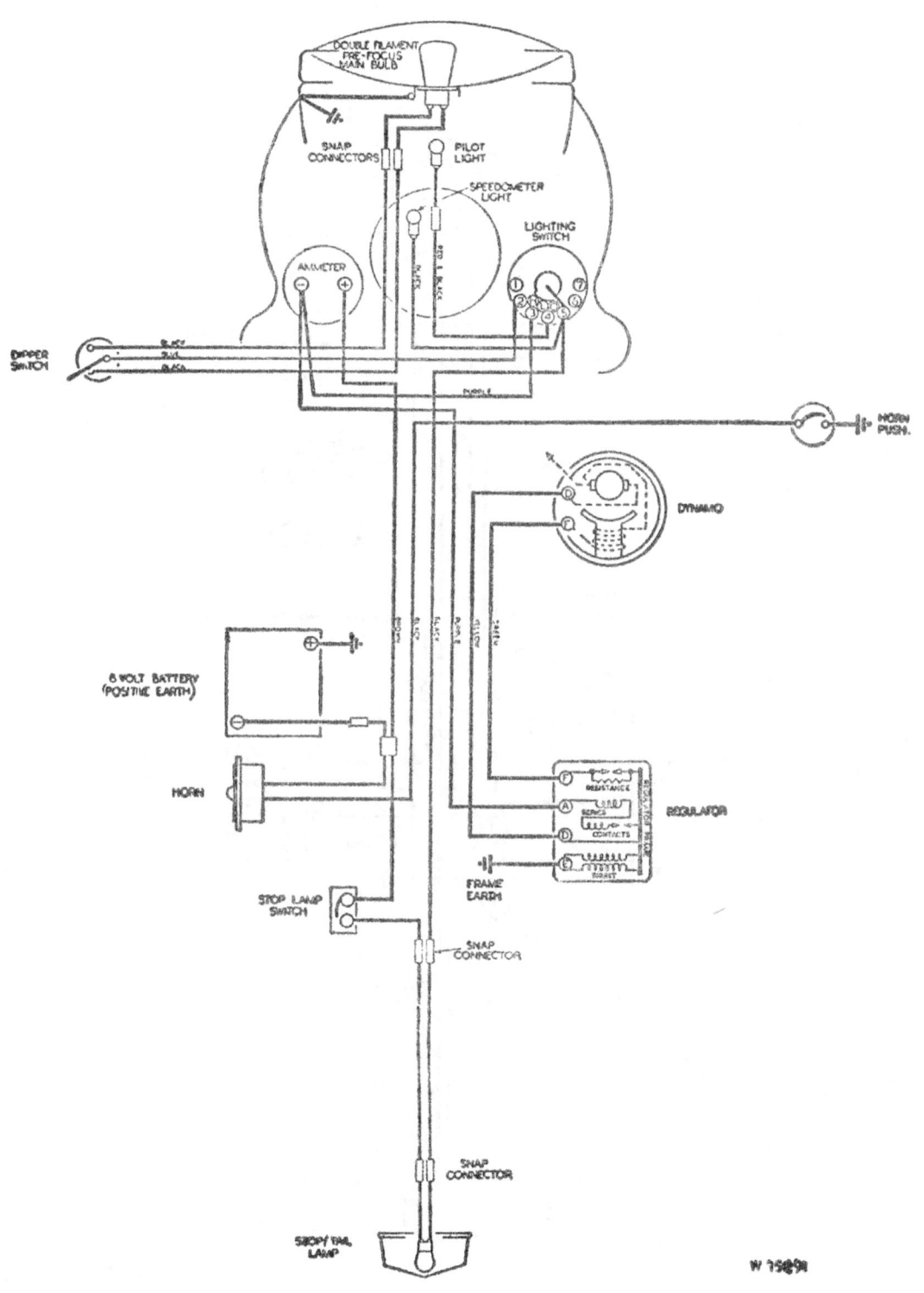

B.S.A. Service Sheet No. 808A (contd.)

C Group Models
WIRING DIAGRAM
(Positive Earth System)

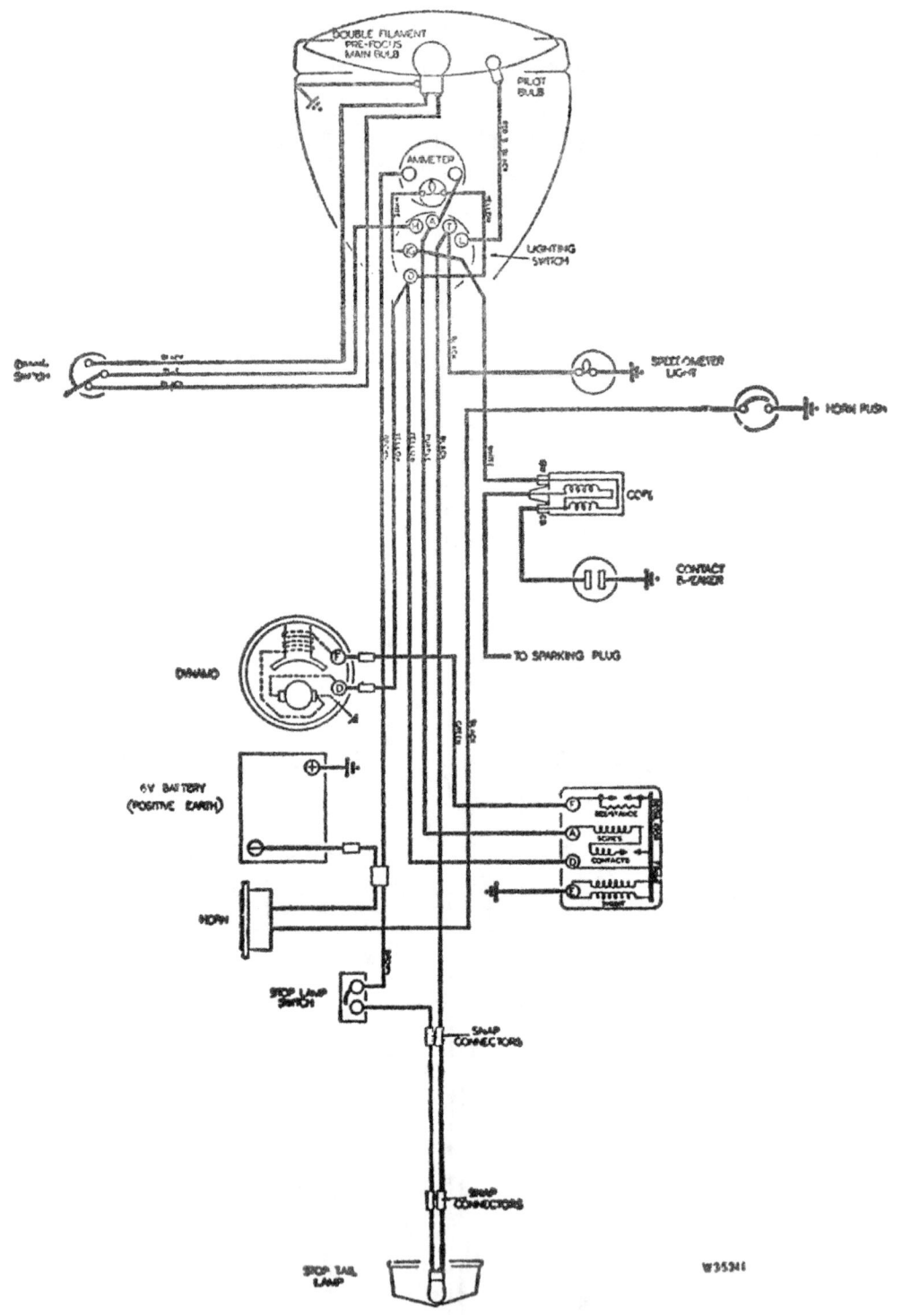

B.S.A. MOTOR CYCLES LTD.,
Service Dept., Armoury Road, Birmingham 11,

BSA SERVICE SHEET No. 808F

M Group Models

WIRING DIAGRAM (Positive Earth System)

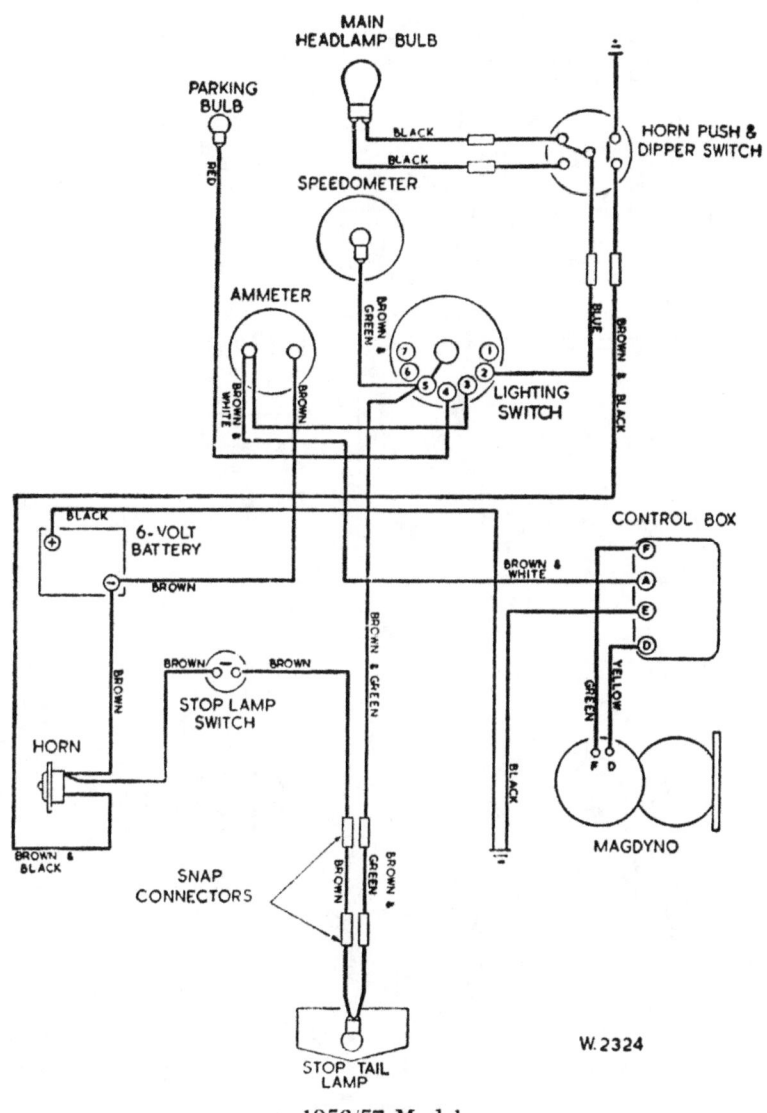

1956/57 Models

B.S.A. Service Sheet No. 808F—*continued*

A and B Group Models   Wiring Diagrams

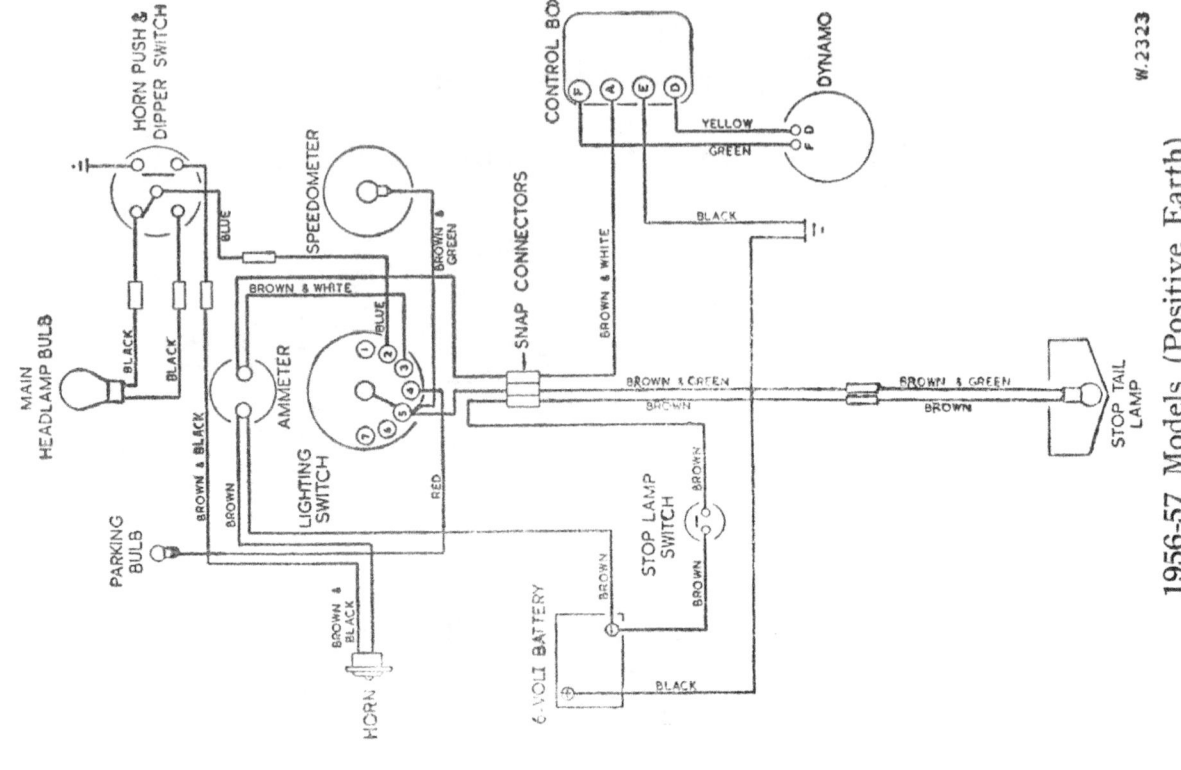

1956-57 Models (Positive Earth)

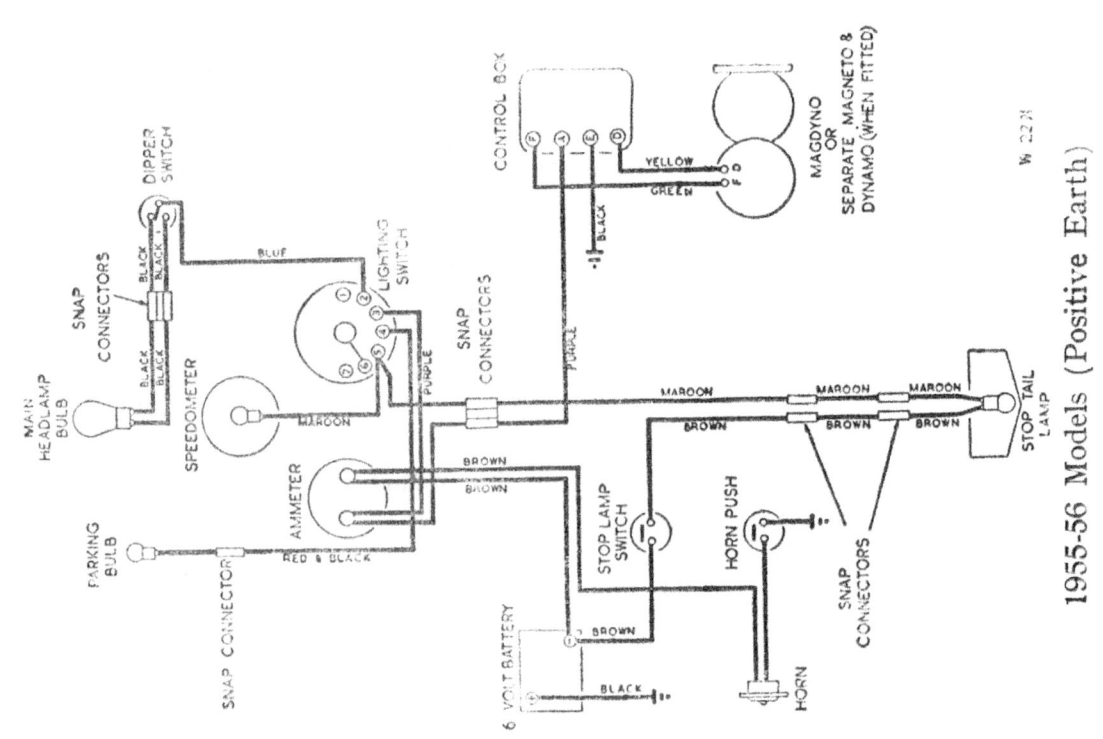

1955-56 Models (Positive Earth)

B.S.A. Press.

B.S.A. MOTOR CYCLES LTD
Service Dept., Armoury Road,
Birmingham 11

BSA SERVICE SHEET No. 809

All Models except D1, C10L, C11G, C12, C15 and "B" Group fitted with Alternators

GENERATORS–MODELS E3H and E3HM

The generator is a shunt-wound two pole machine, arranged to work in conjunction with a regulator unit to give an output which is dependent on the state of charge of the battery and the loading of the electrical equipment in use. When the battery is in a low state of charge, the generator gives a high output, whereas if the battery is fully charged the generator gives only a trickle charge to keep the battery in a good condition without overcharging. In addition, an increase of output is given to balance the current taken by the lamps when in use.

Models E3H and E3HM are similar in construction. The former will be found on motor cycles having separate magneto or coil ignition, while model E3HM is the generator portion of the combined unit known as the "magdyno".

ROUTINE MAINTENANCE

Lubrication
The lubricator at the commutator end bracket must be given a few drops of good grade thin machine oil every 1,000—2,000 miles. The bearing at the driving end is packed with H.M.P. grease and will last until the machine is taken down for a general overhaul, when the bearing should be repacked.

Inspection of Commutator and Brush Gear
About once every six months remove the cover band for inspection of commutator and brushes. The brushes are held in contact with the commutator by means of springs. Move each brush to see that it is free to slide in its holder; if it sticks, remove it and clean with a

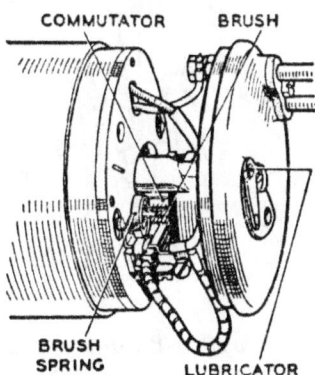

Fig. Y30. *Commutator and Bracket Assembly.*

cloth moistened with petrol. Care must be taken to replace the brushes in their original positions, otherwise they will not "bed" properly on the commutator. If, after long service, the brushes have become worn to such an extent that the brush flexible is exposed on the

B.S.A. Service Sheet No. 809 (contd.)

running face, or if the brushes do not make good contact with the commutator, they must be replaced by genuine Lucas brushes. The commutator should be free from any trace of oil or dirt and should have a highly polished appearance. Clean a dirty or blackened commutator by pressing a fine dry cloth against it while the engine is slowly turned over by means of the kickstarter crank. (It is an advantage to remove the sparking plug before doing this). If the commutator is very dirty, moisten the cloth with petrol.

Test Data
Cutting-in speed: 1,250—1,500 r.p.m. at 7 generator volts.
  Output: 6.5 amps at 1,900—2,200 r.p.m. at 7 generator volts, taken on 1.1 ohm resistance load. Resistance to be capable of carrying 10 amps without overheating.
  Field resistance: 3.2 ohms.

SERVICING

Testing in position to locate fault in Charging Circuit

In the event of a fault in the charging circuit, adopt the following procedure to locate the cause of trouble.

Check that the generator and regulator unit are connected correctly. The generator terminal (D) should be connected to the regulator unit terminal (D) and generator terminal (F) to regulator unit terminal (F).

Remove the cables from the generator terminals (D) and (F) and connect the two terminals with a short length of wire. Start the engine and set to run at normal idling speed.

Connect the positive lead of a moving coil voltmeter, calibrated 0—10 volts, to one of the generator terminals and connect the negative lead to a good earthing point on the generator yoke or engine.

Fig. Y31. *Testing Brush Spring Tension.*

Gradually increase the engine speed, when the voltmeter reading should rise rapidly and without fluctuation. Do not allow the voltmeter reading to rise above 10 volts, and do not race the engine in an attempt to increase the voltage. It is sufficient to run the generator up to a speed of 1,000 r.p.m. If there is no reading, check the brush gear as

B.S.A. Service Sheet No. 809 (contd.)

described below. If there is a low reading of approximately ½ volt, the field winding may be at fault. If there is a reading of approximately 1½ to 2 volts, the armature winding may be at fault.

Remove the cover band and examine the brushes and commutator. Hold back each of the brush springs and move the brush by pulling gently on its flexible connector. If the movement is sluggish, remove the brush from its holder and ease the sides by lightly polishing on a smooth file. Always replace brushes in their original positions. If the brushes are worn so that they do not bear on the commutator, or if the brush flexible is exposed on the running face, new brushes must be fitted.

Test the brush spring tension with a spring scale. The correct tension is 10—15 oz. and new springs must be fitted if the tension is low.

If the commutator is blackened or dirty, clean it by holding a petrol-moistened cloth against it while the engine is turned slowly by means of the kickstart (with sparking plug removed).

Re-test the generator as above. If there is still no reading on the voltmeter, there is an internal fault and the complete unit, if a spare is available, should be replaced. Otherwise the unit must be dismantled for internal examination.

If the generator is in good order, restore the original connections. Connect regulator unit terminal (D) to generator terminal (D) and regulator terminal (F) to generator terminal (F). Proceed to test the regulator unit as described in Service Sheet No. 804.

To Dismantle

Remove the generator from the motor cycle. To remove the generator from the magdynos unscrew the hexagon-headed nut from the driving end cover and slacken the two screws securing the band clip. Proceed to dismantle, as follows:—

On E3HM machines, bend back the tag on the washer (B) Fig. Y33, locking the screw (A) securing the driving gear (C) and remove the screw. On E3H machines, withdraw the cotter pin (A) and remove the nut (B) from the armature shaft. Withdraw the gear from

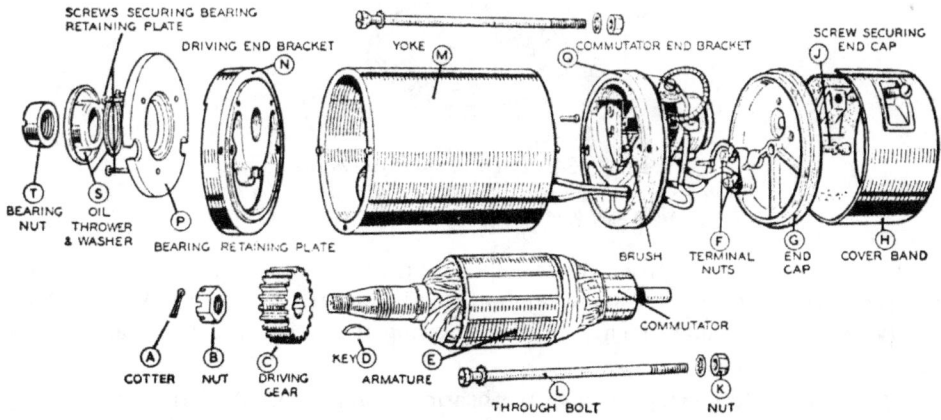

Fig. Y32. *Generator, model E3H (with oil seal).*

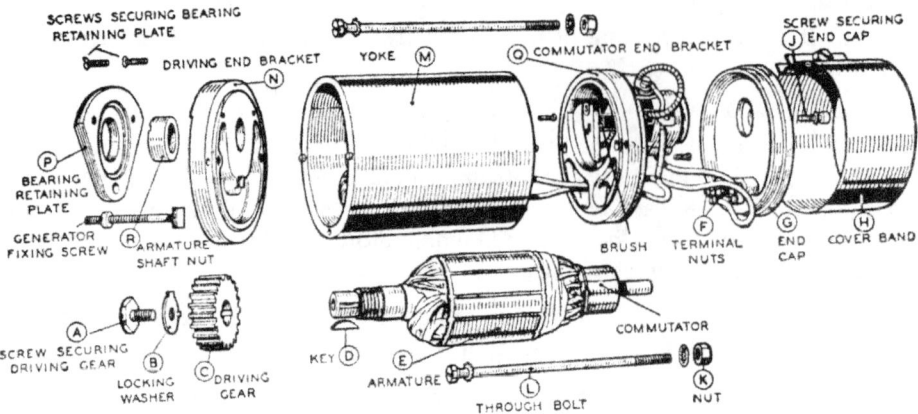

Fig. Y33. *Generator, model E3HM.*

the shaft by carefully levering it off or by means of an extractor. Remove the key(s) (D), from the shaft.

Remove the cover band (H), hold back the brush springs and lift the brushes from their holders.

Take out the screw (J), with spring washer, from the centre of the black moulded end cap (G). Draw the cap away from the end bracket, take off terminal nuts (F), and spring washers, and lift the connections off the terminals.

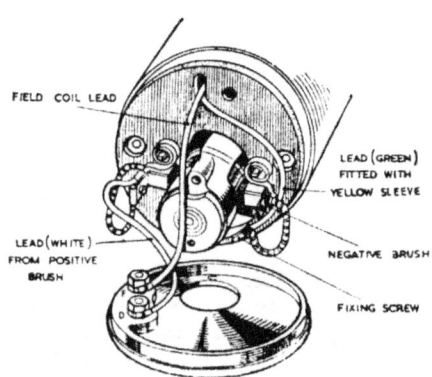

Fig. Y34. *Generator Connections.*
Note:- *On later machines, the white lead is omitted, the brush flexible lead being connected direct to terminal "D"*

Unscrew and remove from the driving end bracket the two through bolts (L) securing the driving end bracket (N) and commutator end bracket (Q) to the yoke (M). Hold the nuts (K) at the commutator end while unscrewing the bolts, and take care not to lose the nuts.

On E3HM Machines.—Remove the bearing retaining plate (P) from the driving end bracket secured by two screws and a long threaded bolt. Unscrew the nut (R) from the end of the armature shaft and the armature can then be removed from the driving end bracket (N) by means of a hand press.

B.S.A. Service Sheet No. 809 (contd.)

On E3H Machines.—Remove the bearing nut (T) and the oil thrower and washer (S). Withdraw the three screws securing the retaining plate (P). The armature can then be removed from the driving end bracket (N) by means of a hand press.

Take out the screw securing the green field coil lead with the yellow sleeve to commutator end bracket and remove the end bracket (Q), withdrawing the connectors through the slot in the insulating plate.

Unscrew the three screws securing the insulating plate to the commutator end bracket and remove the plate complete with brush gear.

Commutator

Examine the commutator. If it is in good condition, it will be smooth and free from pits or burned spots. Clean with a petrol-moistened cloth. If this is ineffective, carefully polish with a strip of very fine glasspaper while rotating the armature. To remedy a badly worn commutator, mount the armature with or without the drive end bracket in a lathe, rotate at high speed and take a light cut with a very sharp tool. Do not remove more metal than is necessary. Polish the commutator with very fine glasspaper.

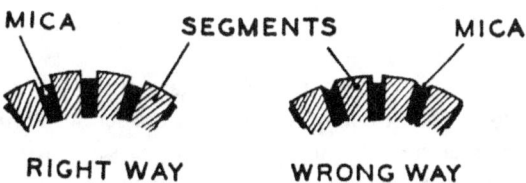

Fig. Y35. *Method of Undercutting Commutator Insulation.*

Undercut the mica insulation between the segments to a depth of $\frac{1}{32}$ in. with a hacksaw blade ground down until it is only slightly thicker than the mica.

Field Coil

Measure the resistance of the field winding by means of an ohm meter. If this is not available, connect a 6-volt D.C. supply with an ammeter in series across the coil. The ammeter reading should be approximately 1.9 amperes. No reading on the ammeter indicates an open circuit in the field winding.

To check for earthed coil, connect a mains test lamp between one end of the coil and the yoke. If the bulb lights, there is an earth between coil and yoke.

In either case, unless a replacement generator is available, the field coil must be replaced but this should only be attempted if a wheel-operated screwdriver and pole shoe expander are at hand, the latter being especially necessary to ensure that there will not be any air-gap between the pole shoe and the inner face of the yoke.

To replace the field coil, proceed as follows:—

Unscrew the pole shoe retaining screw (Fig. Y36) by means of the wheel-operated screwdriver.

Draw the pole shoe and field coil out of the yoke and lift off the coil.

B.S.A. Service Sheet No. 809 (contd.)

Fit the new field coil over the pole shoe and place it in position inside the yoke. Take care to ensure that the taping of the field coil is not trapped between the pole shoe and the yoke.

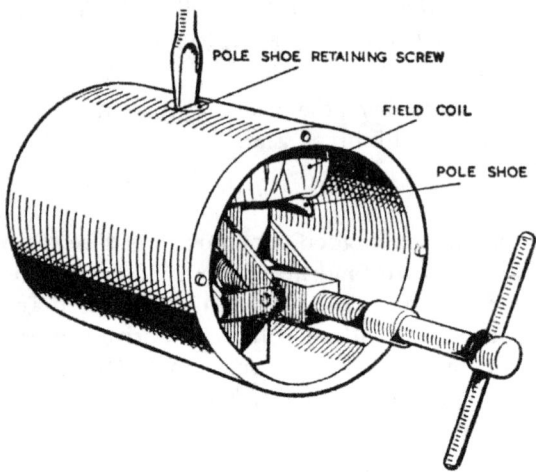

Fig. Y36. *Pole Shoe and Field Coil Assembly.*

Locate the pole shoe and field coil by lightly tightening the fixing screw. Insert the pole shoe expander, open to its fullest extent and tighten the screw. Remove the expander and give the screw a final tightening with the wheel-operated screwdriver. Lock the screw in position by caulking, that is, by tapping some of the metal of the yoke into the slot in the head of the screw.

Armature
The testing of the armature winding requires the use of a voltdrop test or growler. If these are not avilable, the armature should be checked by substitution. No attempt should be made to machine the armature core or to true a distorted armature shaft.

Bearings
A ball bearing is fitted at the driving end and a plain porous bronze bearing bush at the commutator end.

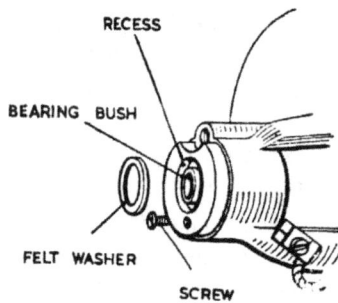

Fig. Y37. *Commutator End Bracket with Bearing Bush.*

Bearings which are worn to such an extent that they will allow side movement of the armature shaft must be replaced. To replace the bearing bush at the commutator end, proceed as follows:—

B.S.A. Service Sheet No. 809 (contd.)

Remove the screw, press the bearing bush out of the commutator end bracket and remove the felt washer (see Fig. Y37).

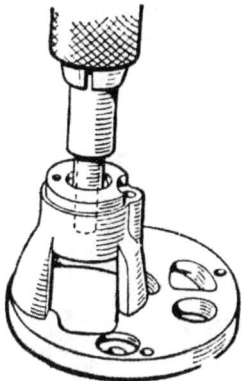

Fig. Y38. *Fitting Bearing Bush using a shouldered Mandrel.*

Press the new bearing bush into the end bracket using a shouldered mandrel (Fig. Y38) of the same diameter as the shaft which is to fit in the bearing. (NOTE:—Before use, new bearing bushes should be stored in a covered container and fully covered with oil of a grade equivalent to Mobiloil Arctic, or other good thin mineral oil. The minimum time of soaking should normally be 24 hours, but in cases of extreme urgency this period may be shortened by heating the oil to 100°C., when the time of immersion may be reduced to 2 hours). The bush should be pressed in until it is flush with the face of the end bracket. Fit the felt washer in the space between the bearing and the wall of the bearing housing.

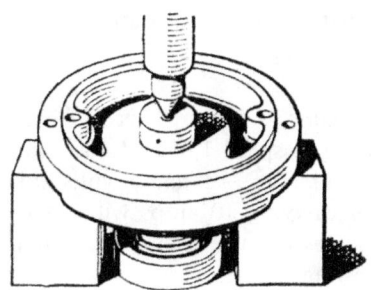

Fig. Y39. *Removing the Ball Race.*

The ball bearing at the driving end is replaced as follows:—

Remove bearing retaining plate from driving end bracket as previously described.

Press the bearing out of the end bracket, using a metal drift locating on the inner journal of the bearing (Fig. Y39).

Wipe out the bearing housing and pack the new bearing with H.M.P. grease.

Position the bearing in its housing and press it squarely home, applying pressure on the outer journal of the bearing (Fig. Y40).

B.S.A. Service Sheet No. 809 (contd.)

Reassembly

In the main, the reassembly of the generator is a reversal of the operations described in the paragraph on dismantling, bearing in mind the following points.

The field coil lead fitted with the short length of yellow tubing must be connected together with eyelet of the negative brush to the commutator end bracket by means of the screw provided.

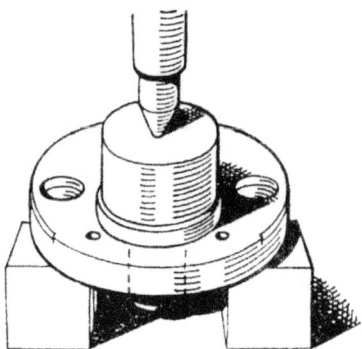

Fig. Y40. *Fitting the Ball Race.*

The second field coil lead must be connected to terminal (F) on the mouled end cap

The lead (coloured white) from the terminal on the positive brush box must be connected to terminal (D) on the mouled end cap.

(NOTE:—On later machines, the brush flexible lead is connected direct to terminal (D) and the white lead is omitted).

Take care to refit cover band in original position and make sure that the securing screw, when of flush-fitting pattern, does not short on brush gear.

E3L Dynamo

On some models an E3L dynamo is fitted. This is a higher output machine and the test figures are as follows. Cutting in speed 1,050—1,200 r.p.m. at 6.5 dynamo volts. Output 8.5 amps at 1,850—2,000 r.p.m. at 7 dynamo volts taken on .8 ohm resistance load. Resistance to be capable of carrying 10 amps without overheating. Field resistance 2.8 ohms. The dismantling and testing instructions are similar to those given for the E3H dynamo except for the following:—

1. Ball bearing fitted at commutator end.
2. Brush spring tension, 13—20 ozs.
3. Testing field coils, the ammeter reading will be 2.1 amperes.

B.S.A. MOTOR CYCLES LTD., Service Department, Armoury Road, Birmingham 11

BSA SERVICE SHEET No. 813A

C12, A Group and M21 Models

ADJUSTING THE CHARGING RATE OF LUCAS ALTERNATORS ON RADIO EQUIPPED MACHINES

GENERAL

The running conditions of radio equipped machines vary from long distance daylight patrol work with occasional use of the radio, to slow running convoy or short distance local work involving considerable use of the radio and possibly of the lights as well. There is a heavy load on the battery while transmitting, and the receiver may be left switched on for long periods representing a constant drain on the battery.

Obviously, the charging rates necessary to balance these varying loads must differ widely. Lucas alternators are designed to provide three alternative charge-rates which are selected by inter-changing the wiring connections.

The adjustments are simple to perform but the responsibility for making them should rest with the Maintenance Personnel who, being familiar with the running conditions and the state of charge of the batteries, are best placed to judge when any alteration is necessary. In the event of doubt, advice should be sought from Lucas Service Organisation.

It must be emphasised that battery charging from an external source may become necessary if a large proportion of night riding with the radio in use, or transmitting for long periods with the engine stopped is involved.

The C12 is fitted with a model RM13/15 Alternator in conjunction with a PRS8 Lighting and Ignition Switch.

By connecting or removing a wire link between switch terminals 5 and 6, two intermediate charge-rates can be obtained in addition to the three already mentioned.

B.S.A. Service Sheet No. 813A—*continued*

With the link in place the switch automatically increases the alternator output in the "Pilot" and "Head" positions. When the link is removed, the output increases only in the "Head" position.

If the alternator wiring is connected as in stage 3, maximum output is developed in all switch positions.

"A" GROUP AND M21 MODELS

These machines are fitted with a model RM15 Alternator as well as the normal 60 watt, E3L dynamo, and have a model U39 Lighting Switch. This is similar to the switch fitted to standard models, but it is provided with two toggle arms to control the alternator output in the various switch positions.

As on C12, stage 3, connections give maximum alternator output in all switch positions.

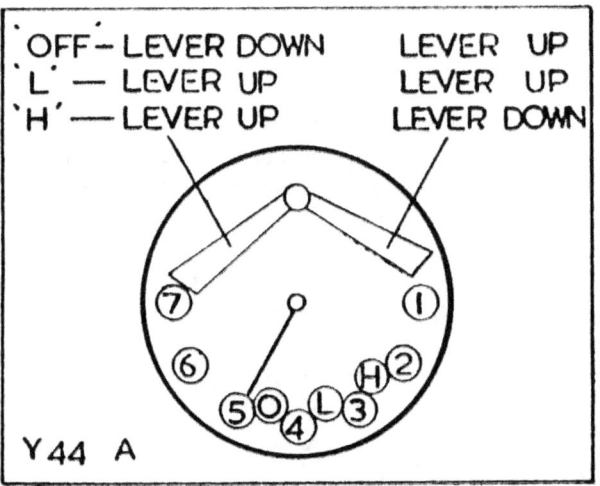

Current for all normal purposes is supplied by the alternator. This is supplemented by the dynamo as necessary when a heavy load is placed on the system. For servicing and testing purposes the two instruments should be dealt with separately, one being disconnected while testing the other.

When the radio is out of use for a prolonged period, it is important that the light green wire from the alternator is disconnected and the end taped up, otherwise the battery will become over-charged.

TESTING

As the radio is connected directly across the battery, the current taken will not be shown on the ammeter. To check whether the charging output is sufficient to balance the load, a second ammeter must be inserted in the cable between battery and radio. The reading on this ammeter must then be deducted from the charge shown on the ammeter fitted to the machine.

B.S.A. Service Sheet No. 813A—*continued*

DAYTIME CHARGING RATES

Alternator Cable Connections—Stage 1

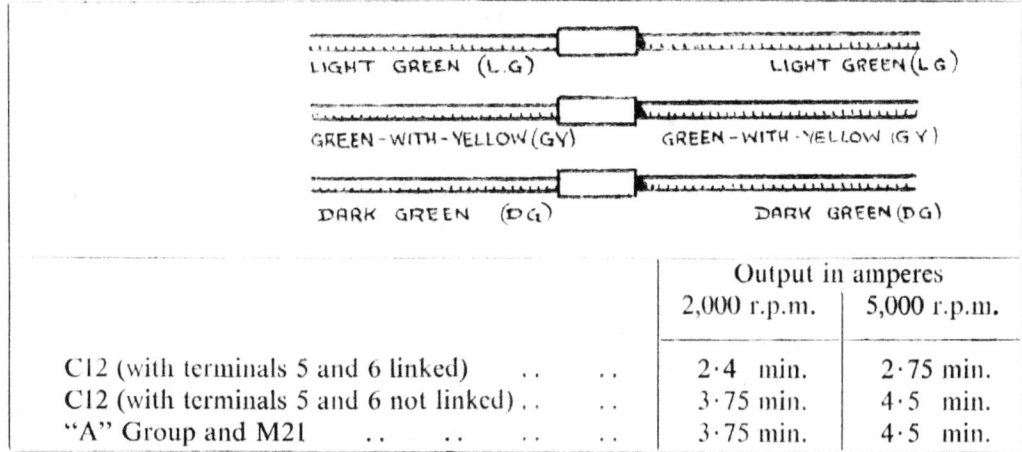

	Output in amperes	
	2,000 r.p.m.	5,000 r.p.m.
C12 (with terminals 5 and 6 linked)	2·4 min.	2·75 min.
C12 (with terminals 5 and 6 not linked)	3·75 min.	4·5 min.
"A" Group and M21	3·75 min.	4·5 min.

Alternator Cable Connections—Stage 2

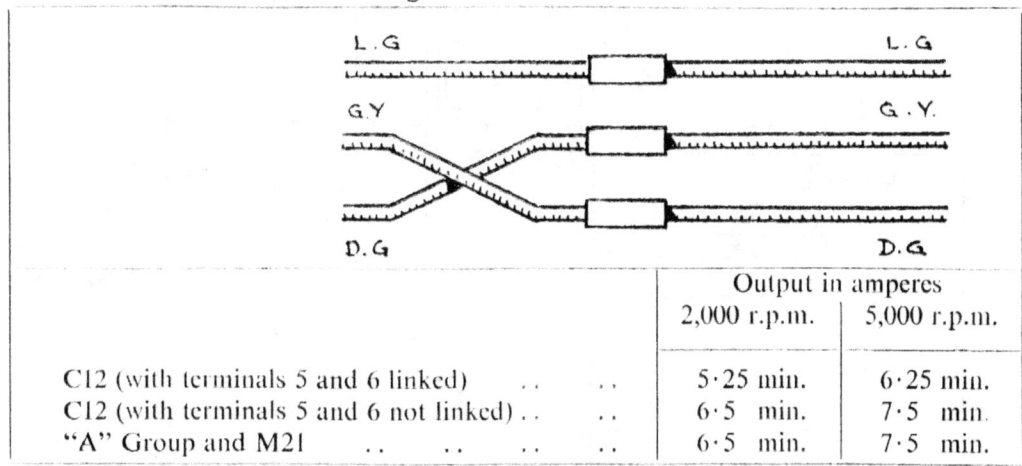

	Output in amperes	
	2,000 r.p.m.	5,000 r.p.m.
C12 (with terminals 5 and 6 linked)	5·25 min.	6·25 min.
C12 (with terminals 5 and 6 not linked)	6·5 min.	7·5 min.
"A" Group and M21	6·5 min.	7·5 min.

Alternator Cable Connections—Stage 3

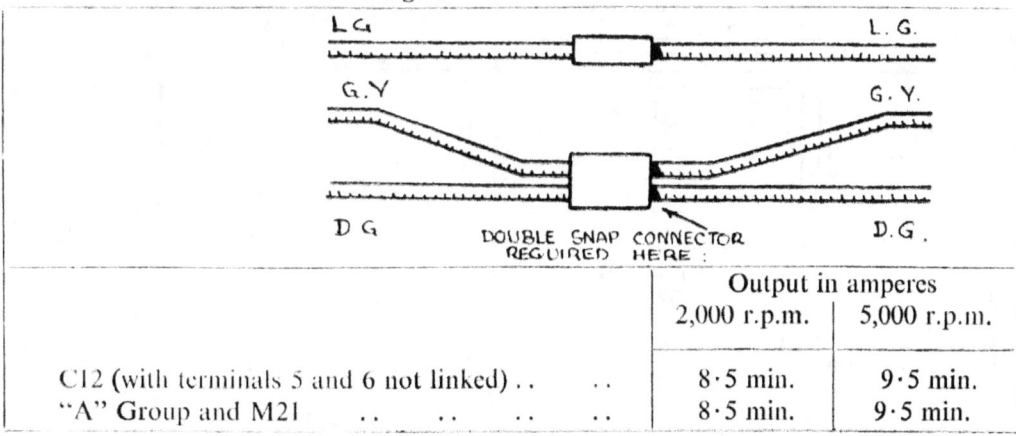

	Output in amperes	
	2,000 r.p.m.	5,000 r.p.m.
C12 (with terminals 5 and 6 not linked)	8·5 min.	9·5 min.
"A" Group and M21	8·5 min.	9·5 min.

B.S.A. Service Sheet No. 813A
continued

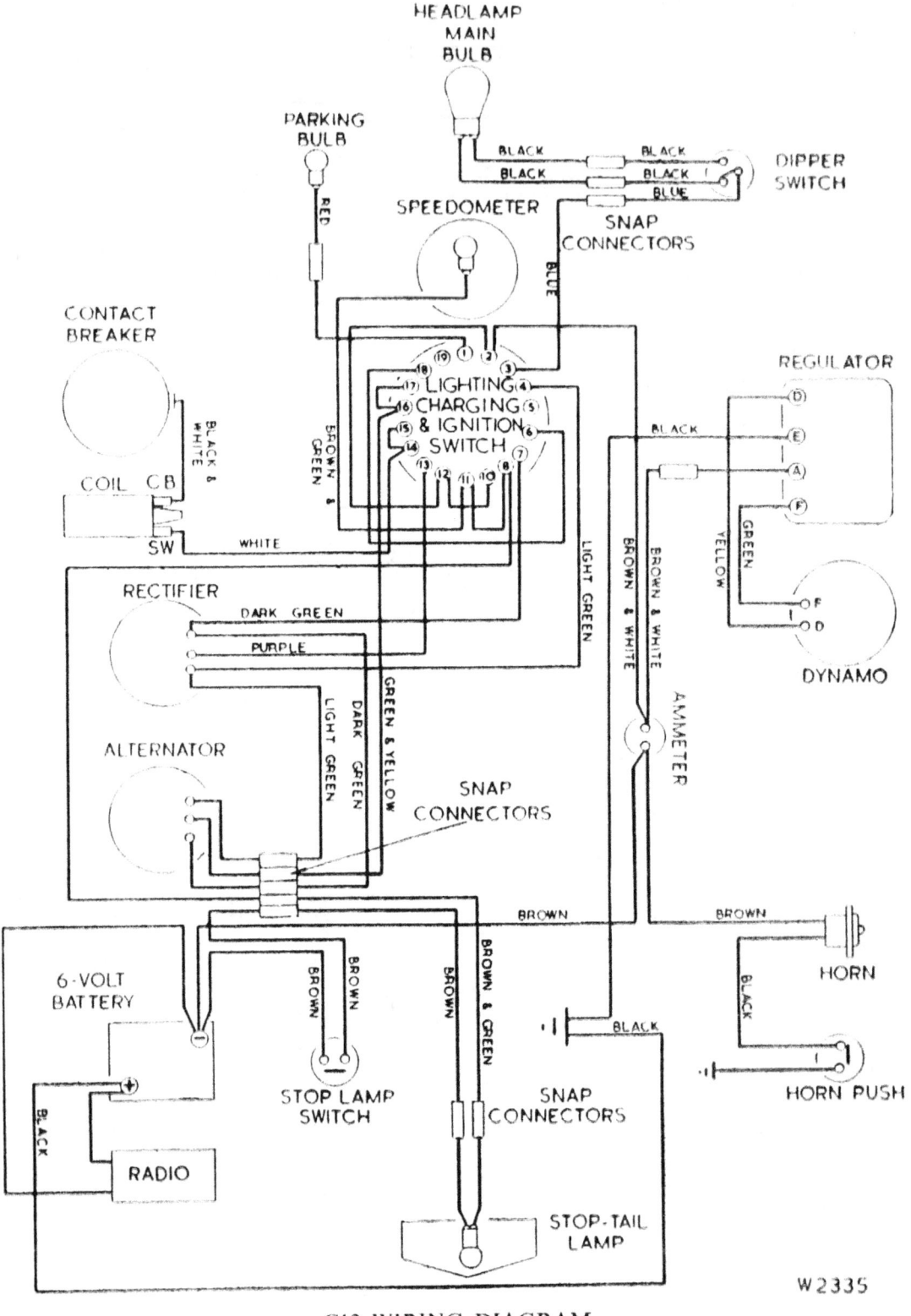

C12 WIRING DIAGRAM

B.S.A. Service Sheet No. 813A—*continued*

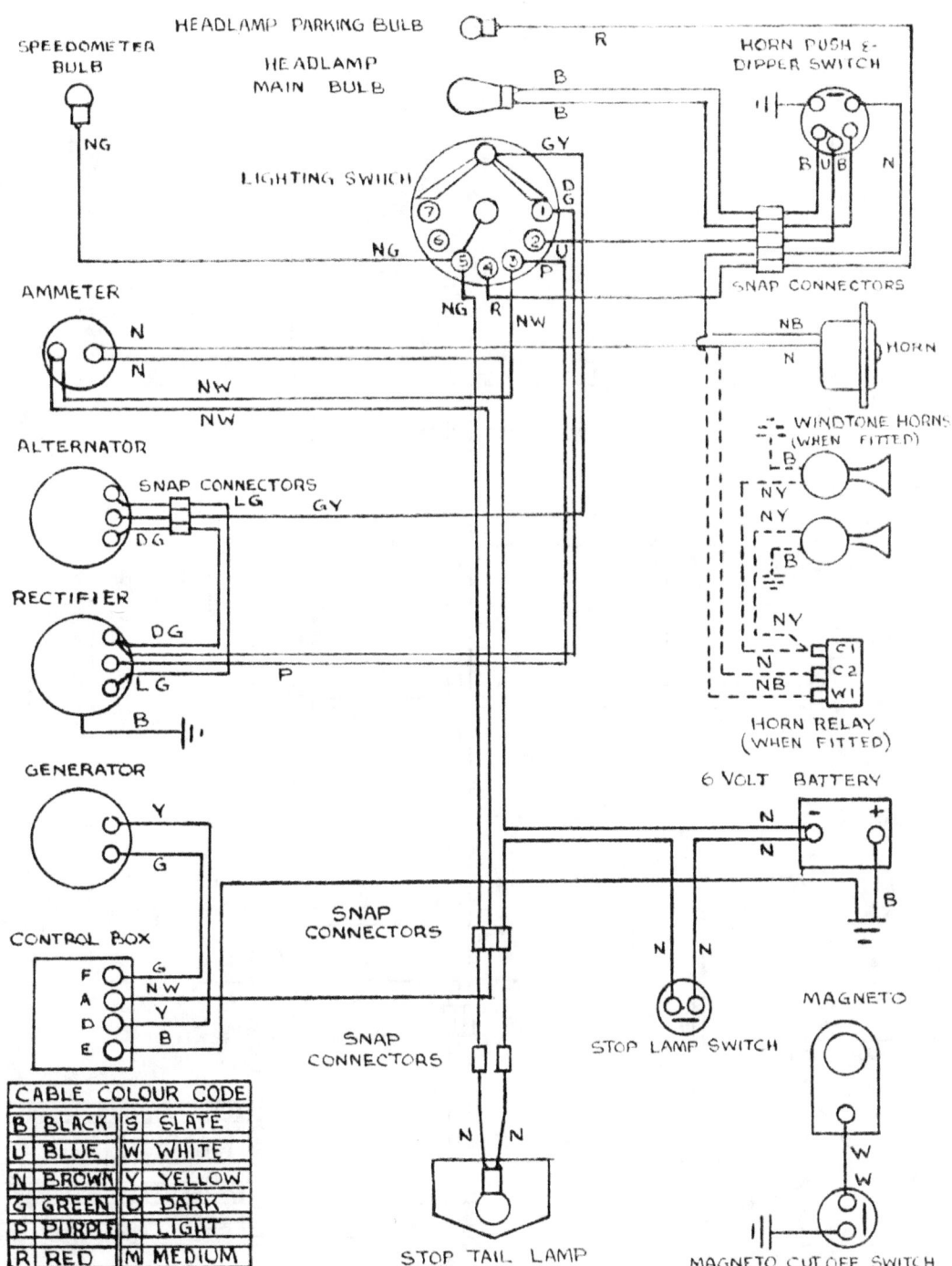

"A" GROUP WIRING DIAGRAM

B.S.A. Service Sheet No. 813A—*continued*

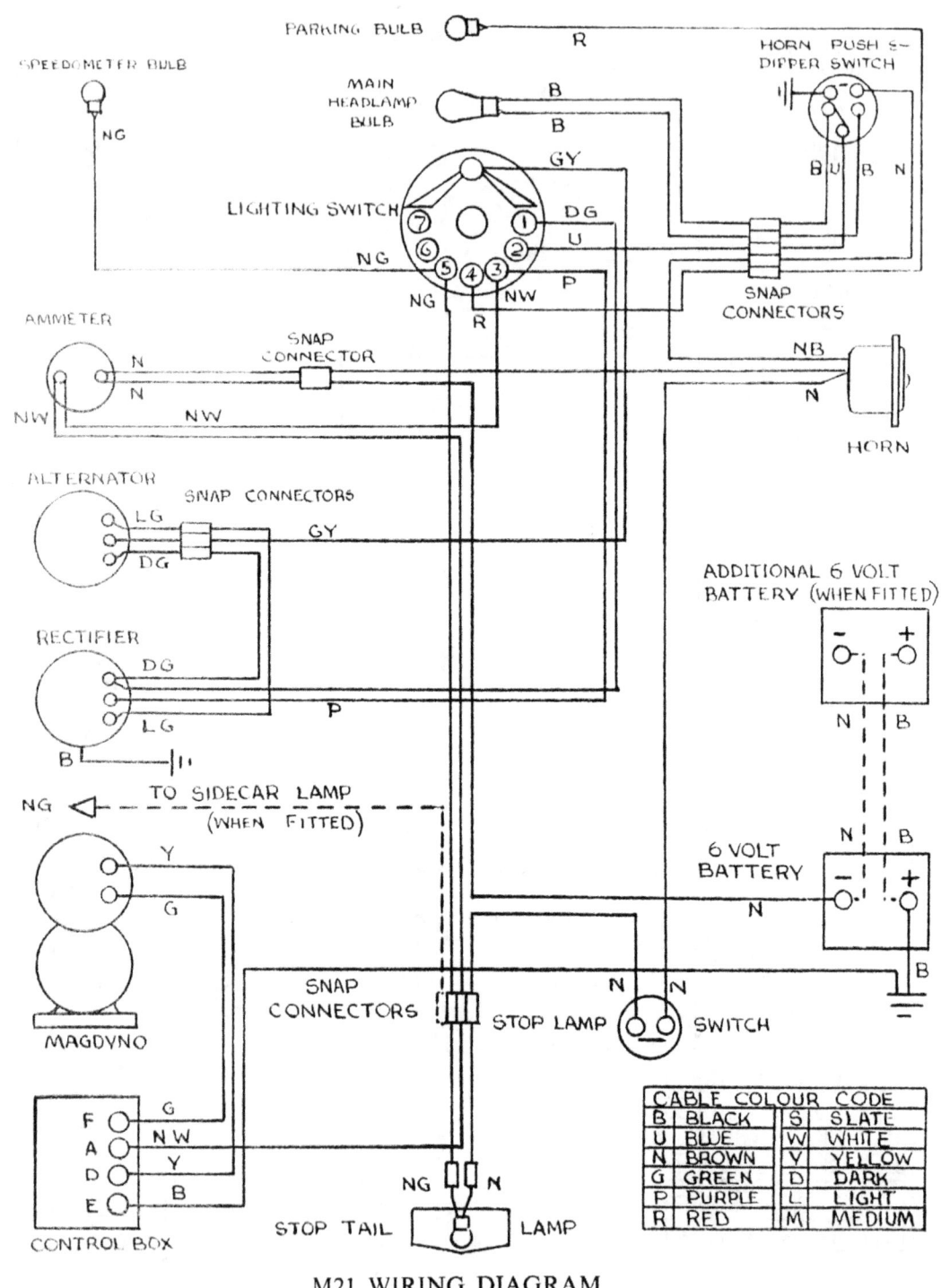

M21 WIRING DIAGRAM

B.S.A. MOTOR CYCLES LTD., Service Department, Armoury Road, Birmingham 11
Printed at The B.S.A. Press

VELOCEPRESS MANUALS - MOTORCYCLE

1930'S BRITISH MOTORCYCLE CARBS & ELEC COMPONENTS (BOOK OF)
1930'S BRITISH MOTORCYCLE ENGINES (OVERHAUL & MAINTENANCE)
1930'S BRITISH MOTORCYCLE GEARBOXES & CLUTCHES (BOOK OF)
AJS 1932-1948 SINGLES & TWINS 250cc THRU 1000cc (BOOK OF)
AJS 1945-1960 SINGLES 350cc & 500cc MODELS 16 & 18 (BOOK OF)
AJS 1955-1965 SINGLES 350cc & 500cc (BOOK OF)
ARIEL UP TO 1932 (BOOK OF)
ARIEL 1932-1939 PREWAR MODELS (BOOK OF)
ARIEL 1933-1951 (WORKSHOP MANUAL)
ARIEL 1939-1960 4 STROKE SINGLES (BOOK OF)
ARIEL 1958-1964 LEADER & ARROW (BOOK OF)
BMW R26 R27 (1956-1967) FACTORY WORKSHOP MANUAL
BMW R50 R50S R60 R69S (1955-1969) FACTORY WORKSHOP MANUAL
BRIDGESTONE 90 SERIES FACTORY WSM & PARTS CATALOGUE
BRIDGESTONE 175 SERIES FACTORY WSM & PARTS CATALOGUE
BRIDGESTONE 350 SERIES FACTORY WSM & PARTS CATALOGUES
BSA BANTAM ALL MODELS FROM 1948 ONWARDS (BOOK OF)
BSA SINGLES & V-TWINS UP TO 1927 (BOOK OF)
BSA SINGLES & V-TWINS UP TO 1930 (BOOK OF)
BSA SINGLES & V-TWINS UP TO 1935 (BOOK OF)
BSA SINGLES & V-TWINS 1936-1939 (BOOK OF)
BSA OHV & SV SINGLES 250-600cc 1945-1959 (BOOK OF)
BSA OHV & SV SINGLES 250cc (ONLY) 1954-1970 (BOOK OF)
BSA OHV SINGLES 350 & 500cc 1955-1967 (BOOK OF)
BSA TWINS A7 & A10 1948-1962 FACTORY SERVICE SHEETS MANUAL
BSA TWINS A7 & A10 1948-1962 (BOOK OF)
BSA TWINS A50 & A65 1962-1969 (SECOND BOOK OF)
CYCLEMOTOR (BOOK OF)
DOUGLAS 1929-1939 PREWAR ALL MODELS (BOOK OF)
DOUGLAS 1948-1957 POSTWAR ALL MODELS FACTORY SHOP MANUAL
DUCATI 160cc, 250cc & 350cc OHC MODELS FACTORY SHOP MANUAL
HONDA 50 ALL MODELS UP TO 1970 INC MONKEY & TRAIL (BOOK OF)
HONDA 90 ALL MODELS UP TO 1966 (BOOK OF)
HONDA 125-150cc TWINS C/CS/CB/CA FACTORY WORKSHOP MANUAL
HONDA 250-305 TWINS C/CS/CB FACTORY WORKSHOP MANUAL
HONDA 450 CB/CL 1965-1974 K0 TO K7 WORKSHOP MANUAL
HONDA C100 SUPER CUB FACTORY WORKSHOP MANUAL
HONDA C110 SPORT CUB 1962-1969 FACTORY WORKSHOP MANUAL
HONDA TWINS & SINGLES 50cc THRU 305cc 1960-1966 (BOOK OF)
HONDA TWINS ALL MODELS 125cc THRU 450cc UP TO 1968 (BOOK OF)
INDIAN PONYBIKE, BOY RACER & PAPOOSE ILL PARTS LIST & SALES LIT
J.A.P. ENGINES 1927-1952 & MOTORCYCLES 1934-1952 (BOOK OF)
LAMBRETTA 1947-1957 ALL 125 & 150cc MODELS (BOOK OF)
LAMBRETTA 1957-1970 LI & TV MODELS (SECOND BOOK OF)
MATCHLESS 1931-1939 ALL MODELS 250cc THRU 990cc (BOOK OF)
MATCHLESS 1945-1956 350 & 500cc SINGLES (BOOK OF)
MATCHLESS 1955-1966 350 & 500cc SINGLES (BOOK OF)
NEW IMPERIAL ALL SV & OHV FROM 1935 ONWARDS (BOOK OF)
NORTON 1932-1939 PREWAR MODELS (BOOK OF)
NORTON 1932-1947 (BOOK OF)
NORTON 1938-1956 (BOOK OF)
NORTON 1955-1963 MODELS 19, 50 & ES2 (BOOK OF)
NORTON 1955-1965 DOMINATOR TWINS (BOOK OF)
NORTON 1960-1970 TWIN CYLINDER FACTORY WORKSHOP MANUAL
NORTON 1970-1975 COMMANDO FACTORY WORKSHOP MANUAL
NORTON 1975-1978 MK 3 COMMANDO FACTORY WORKSHOP MANUAL
NSU PRIMA 1956-1964 ALL MODELS (BOOK OF)
NSU QUICKLY 1953-1963 ALL MODELS (BOOK OF)
PANTHER 1932-1958 LIGHTWEIGHT MODELS 250 & 350cc (BOOK OF)
PANTHER 1938-1966 HEAVYWEIGHT MODELS 600 & 650cc (BOOK OF)
RALEIGH MOPEDS 1960-1969 (BOOK OF)
RALEIGH MOTORCYCLES 1919-1933 (BOOK OF)
ROYAL ENFIELD 1934-1946 SINGLES & V TWINS (BOOK OF)
ROYAL ENFIELD 1937-1953 SINGLES & V TWINS (BOOK OF)
ROYAL ENFIELD 1946-1962 SINGLES (BOOK OF)
ROYAL ENFIELD 1958-1966 250 & 350cc SINGLES (SECOND BOOK OF)
ROYAL ENFIELD 736cc INTERCEPTOR FACTORY WORKSHOP MANUAL
RUDGE 1933-1939 (BOOK OF)
SUNBEAM 1928-1939 (BOOK OF)
SUNBEAM 1946-1957 S7 & S8 (BOOK OF)
SUZUKI 50cc & 80cc UP TO 1966 (BOOK OF)
SUZUKI T10 1963-1967 FACTORY WORKSHOP MANUAL
SUZUKI T20 & T200 1965-1969 FACTORY WORKSHOP MANUAL
SUZUKI TWINS 1962 ONWARDS 125-500cc WORKSHOP MANUAL
TRIUMPH 1935-1939 PREWAR MODELS (BOOK OF)
TRIUMPH 1935-1949 (BOOK OF)
TRIUMPH 1937-1951 (WORKSHOP MANUAL)
TRIUMPH 1945-1955 FACTORY WORKSHOP MANUAL
TRIUMPH 1945-1958 TWINS (BOOK OF)
TRIUMPH 1956-1969 TWINS (BOOK OF)
VELOCETTE 1925-1970 ALL SINGLES & TWINS (BOOK OF)
VESPA 1951-1961 (BOOK OF)
VESPA 1955-1963 125 & 150cc & GS MODELS (SECOND BOOK OF)
VESPA 1955-1968 GS & SS (BOOK OF)
VESPA 1963-1972 90, 125 & 150cc (THIRD BOOK OF)
VILLIERS ENGINE UP TO 1959 INC. 3 WHEELERS (BOOK OF)
VILLIERS ENGINE UP TO 1969 (BOOK OF)
VINCENT 1935-1955 (WORKSHOP MANUAL)
YAMAHA 1961-1967 YA5 & YA6 (WORKSHOP MANUAL & ILL PARTS LIST)
YAMAHA 1971-1972 JT1& JT2 (WORKSHOP MANUAL & ILL PARTS LIST)

VELOCEPRESS TECHNICAL BOOKS – MOTORCYCLE

CATALOG OF BRITISH MOTORCYCLES (1951 MODELS)
LUCAS ELECTRONICS BRITISH M/CYCLES REPAIR & PARTS (1950-1977)
MOTORCYCLE ENGINEERING (P.E. Irving)
MOTORCYCLE ROAD TESTS 1949-1953 (Motor Cycle Magazine UK)
SPEED AND HOW TO OBTAIN IT (Motor Cycle Magazine UK)
TUNING FOR SPEED (P.E. Irving)

VELOCEPRESS MANUALS - THREE WHEELER'S

BSA THREE WHEELER (BOOK OF)
VINTAGE MORGAN THREE WHEELER (BOOK OF)

VELOCEPRESS MANUALS - AUTOMOBILE

ALFA ROMEO GIULIA WORKSHOP MANUAL 1300 TO 2000cc 1962-1975
ALFA ROMEO GIULIA TECH MANUAL CARBURETED CARS FROM 1962
ALFA ROMEO GIULIA TECH MANUAL FUEL INJECTED CARS FROM 1969
ALFA ROMEO GIULIETTA & GIULIA 750 & 101 SERIES 1955-1965 WSM
AUSTIN-HEALEY SPRITE & MG MIDGET WORKSHOP MANUAL 1958-1971
BMW 600 LIMOUSINE FACTORY WORKSHOP MANUAL
BMW 600 LIMOUSINE OWNERS HAND BOOK & SERVICE MANUAL
BMW 2000 & 2002 1966-1976 WORKSHOP MANUAL
BMW ISETTA FACTORY WORKSHOP MANUAL
CORVAIR 1960-1969 WORKSHOP MANUAL
CORVETTE V8 1955-1962 WORKSHOP MANUAL
FIAT 500 FACTORY WORKSHOP MANUAL 1957-1973
FIAT 600, 600D & MULTIPLA FACTORY WORKSHOP MANUAL 1955-1969
JAGUAR E-TYPE 3.8 & 4.2 SERIES 1 & 2 WORKSHOP MANUAL
JAGUAR MK 7, 8, 9 & XK120, 140, 150 WORKSHOP MANUAL 1948-1961
METROPOLITAN FACTORY WORKSHOP MANUAL
MGA & MGB OWNERS HANDBOOK & WORKSHOP MANUAL
MG MIDGET TC, TD, TF & TF1500 WORKSHOP MANUAL
PORSCHE 356 1948-1965 WORKSHOP MANUAL
PORSCHE 911 2.0, 2.2, 2.4 LITRE 1964-1973 WORKSHOP MANUAL
PORSCHE 911 2.7, 3.0, 3.2 LITRE 1973-1989 WORKSHOP MANUAL
PORSCHE 912 WORKSHOP MANUAL
TRIUMPH TR2, TR3, TR4 1953-1965 WORKSHOP MANUAL
VOLKSWAGEN TRANSPORTER, TRUCKS & WAGONS 1950-1979 WSM
VOLVO 1944-1968 ALL MODELS WORKSHOP MANUAL

VELOCEPRESS TECHNICAL BOOKS - AUTOMOBILE

FERRARI 250/GT SERVICE AND MAINTENANCE
FERRARI GUIDE TO PERFORMANCE
FERRARI OWNER'S HANDBOOK
FERRARI TUNING TIPS & MAINTENANCE TECHNIQUES
HOW TO BUILD A FIBERGLASS CAR
HOW TO BUILD A RACING CAR
HOW TO RESTORE THE MODEL 'A' FORD
MASERATI OWNER'S HANDBOOK
OBERT'S FIAT GUIDE
PERFORMANCE TUNING THE SUNBEAM TIGER
SOUPING THE VOLKSWAGEN
SOLEX CARBURETORS (EMPHASIS ON UK & EU AUTOMOBILES)
SU CARBURETORS (EMPHASIS ON UK AUTOMOBILES)
WEBER CARBURETORS (EMPHASIS ON ALFA & FIAT)

VELOCEPRESS BOOKS & GUIDES - AUTOMOBILE

ABARTH BUYERS GUIDE
COMPLETE CATALOG OF JAPANESE MOTOR VEHICLES
FERRARI 308 SERIES BUYER'S AND OWNER'S GUIDE
FERRARI BERLINETTA LUSSO
FERRARI BROCHURES AND SALES LITERATURE 1946-1967
FERRARI BROCHURES AND SALES LITERATURE 1968-1989
FERRARI OPP, MAINTENANCE & SERVICE H/BOOKS 1948-1963
FERRARI SERIAL NUMBERS PART I - ODD NUMBERS TO 21399
FERRARI SERIAL NUMBERS PART II - EVEN NUMBERS TO 1050
FERRARI SPYDER CALIFORNIA
HENRY'S FABULOUS MODEL "A" FORD
MASERATI BROCHURES AND SALES LITERATURE

VELOCEPRESS BOOKS – RACING

CARRERA PANAMERICANA - MEXICAN ROAD RACE (BOOK OF)
DIALED IN - THE JAN OPPERMAN STORY
IF HEMINGWAY HAD WRITTEN A RACING NOVEL
VEDA ORR'S NEW REVISED HOT ROD PICTORIAL

AUTOBOOKS WORKSHOP MANUALS & BROOKLANDS ROAD TEST PORTFOLIOS

FOR A COMPLETE LISTING OF THE AUTOBOOKS & BROOKLANDS TITLES THAT WE CURRENTLY HAVE AVAILABLE, PLEASE VISIT OUR WEBSITE.
www.VelocePress.com

Please check our website:

www.VelocePress.com

for a complete
up-to-date list of
available titles

www.ingramcontent.com/pod-product-compliance
Lightning Source LLC
Chambersburg PA
CBHW080432230426
43662CB00015B/2259